There are Mountains to Climb

An Inspirational Journey

BY

Jean Deeds

To Andy —
Go for it!
Jean Deeds
11/98

Silverwood Press
Indianapolis, Indiana

For information address:
Silverwood Press
1508 East 86th Street, #105
Indianapolis, IN 46240
317-844-1690

Library of Congress Catalog Card No. 96-092085

ISBN: 0-9651487-1-8

Cover design by Jane Gard

Printed on recycled paper

To my dad, with love

Acknowledgments

I want to thank my family, especially Mom, Greg, and Brad, and the many friends who provided the nourishment that carried me along the Appalachian Trail. Without them, I wouldn't have a story to tell. And thanks to the wonderful people I met along the way who call themselves thru-hikers. They are my heroes.

Many people gave the gift of their support and time to help this book become a reality—from those who suggested I write it to those who lent their wise counsel and sharp eyes to the fine-tuning and proofing process. They kept me on track, and I am deeply grateful.

Heartfelt gratitude goes to the following people, whose presence is strong on the pages of my book:

Bill Corbin and his staff at UN Printing, whose input stretched far beyond simply putting ink on paper.

My son Brad, who turned the tables and became my mentor and teacher in the early stages, and whose editing skill showed he was awake and listening during all those writing classes at USC. He's the real writer in the family.

My dear friend and editor Maggie Oman, a.k.a. Blue Pencil, who often understood what I had written and why much better than I did, and who added much more to the process than her editing expertise.

And finally, special thanks to John Shaughnessy, whose columns sparked the public interest that led to my many new roles—including author.

Foreword

She was a parent who had seen her two children grow up and leave home—growing into lives that no longer depended on her.

She was an employee who wondered if there was more to life than waking up, driving to work, immersing herself in her job, returning home, going to bed and starting the cycle again the next day.

She was a person who wondered if the adventure in her life had ended.

Maybe that's why so many people identified with Jean Deeds when she began her remarkable journey—trying to walk the 2,155-mile Appalachian Trail by herself.

She wasn't an incredible athlete or an experienced hiker when she started her six-month trip along the country's longest marked footpath. She was 51, a mother and an office worker. And her two previous trips into the wilderness were group excursions that had lasted a week.

But she had a dream, and she dared to follow it.

Not that she didn't have doubters. When I first wrote about Jean's planned adventure in *The Indianapolis Star*, most people thought she would never last, that she would leave the trail within two weeks.

But Jean kept walking, and the accounts of her adventures kept fascinating readers. When a story noted that she had reached the halfway point of the trail, one reader said, "I never thought she would get this far. Now I hope nothing goes wrong. I'm rooting for her to go the distance."

It was a common theme. Jean's journey had struck something deep in many people—a longing to do something different, a challenge to find our own limits and pass them, a belief that there's something heroic in all of us.

As you accompany Jean on her walk into the wilderness, you'll learn it wasn't just a journey of steps and miles, it was a journey of the heart and soul.

John Shaughnessy, columnist
The Indianapolis Star

The Appalachian Trail

Preface

"Why am I doing this? Why am I here?"

Those questions ran through my mind a thousand times as I made my way north on the Appalachian Trail. Some days there were no answers. Other days new insights propelled me forward with renewed resolve to conquer the physical adversities and mental challenges of spending six months backpacking the length of our nation's most famous wilderness footpath.

I knew when I made my decision to attempt a "thru-hike" of the Appalachian Trail it would be an immense physical challenge, stretching me beyond any limits I'd ever set before. I knew I'd need to find the mental discipline to rise above those hardships. But I didn't realize the trail would become a pathway for spiritual evolution and a remarkable teacher of fundamental truths. Many lessons of the journey through life became clear to me on the Appalachian Trail.

I had little backpacking or camping experience and almost no knowledge of the AT just a year before I took my first step on its southernmost mountain. Now I know its ancestry and personality as if it were a treasured family member.

The man who could be called its father was Benton MacKaye. He was a dreamer, conservationist, and outdoorsman who articulated his vision for a wilderness footpath in the October 1921 issue of the American Institute of Architects' trade journal. Thousands of volunteers responded to his dream, and between 1922 and 1937 the trail was carved through the highest and most rugged mountain ranges of the eastern United States.

The AT is approximately 2,155 miles long, winding northeasterly through 14 states between its southern terminus at Springer Mountain, Georgia, and its northernmost point atop Mt. Katahdin, Maine. The trail runs along mountain ridges and through forests, valleys, and towns in Georgia, North Carolina, Tennessee, Virginia, West Virginia, Maryland, Pennsylvania, New Jersey, New York, Massachusetts, Connecticut, Vermont, New Hampshire, and Maine.

Each year approximately 2,000 people attempt to travel the entire Appalachian Trail. Only 10 to 15 percent succeed. These thru-hikers carry their gear and supplies in backpacks, usually weighing between 35 and 60 pounds. They periodically go off the trail to resupply in nearby towns.

A thru-hiker must be prepared to face temperatures ranging from the 'teens to 100 degrees during the five to six months necessary to traverse the trail's length. Rain, hail, snow, and 60-mile-per-hour winds add their own challenges.

Many people envision the AT as a gravel pathway stretching benignly along fairly level ground. In reality, much of the terrain is rocky and the trail is rarely flat. The principal activity shifts from hiking to mountaineering as hikers attack vertical rock slabs in the White Mountains of New Hampshire and in southern Maine.

I discovered a world completely unknown to me as I gradually made my way north over mountains, cliffs, and rivers; through valleys, forests, and small towns; across bridges, highways, and railroad tracks. There were exhilarating moments and ones filled with despair, times I thought I was seeing the best life has to offer and times I wanted to do nothing so much as to quit and go home.

While on my journey, I received more than 400 letters from family and friends, sent to me in small towns along the way. Those letters formed a powerful network of support that kicked in every time my resolve failed me. My letters back home from the trail form the framework for this book.

The fascinating people I met on the trail—my thru-hiker buddies—were an important part of my adventure. An index at the back of the book gives you information about many of them.

I have shared my story with thousands of people through speeches, letters, and newspaper and magazine articles. It seems to have struck a chord. Now I'd like to share it with you.

1

Have I lost my mind?

Indianapolis, Indiana
March 1994

*W*e each have defining moments in our lives which guide us toward those life lessons we are meant to learn. For me, one such moment came on Sunday, March 21, 1993. I was scanning *The Indianapolis Star* when my attention landed on an article about a young woman who had hiked the Appalachian Trail. I didn't know much about the trail at that time. All I knew was that it was a wilderness footpath running through the mountains in the eastern United States. My mental picture of someone who would try to hike the entire Appalachian Trail was a bearded man with a huge backpack and stick walking in isolation over mountainous terrain and sleeping in a tent. It wasn't a very appealing image to me since I wasn't a hiker, backpacker, or camper—nor a man with a beard.

But here was a young woman who had spent six months traveling through the mountains from Georgia to Maine. She told how exhausting and painful it was, how she wanted to quit almost every day. She told how unlikely it was that she would become one of the small percent of hikers who complete the whole trail in one year.

Surprisingly, in reading about the challenge, adversity, and sheer magnitude of the undertaking, I became captivated by the idea of trying it. I went to the library that very afternoon and checked out several books about the Appalachian Trail. When I began reading about the trail, I realized that attempting to hike its entire length, some 2,155 miles, would be unlike anything I'd ever done or aspired to do. It would mean carrying a hefty backpack up and down mountains, day after day, for up to six months. It would mean sleeping by myself in a tent in the middle of the woods or on a mountaintop. It would mean living for 24 hours a day in the heat, cold, rain, and snow, amid the insects and wildlife of the forests.

Not one of those components was appealing to me, and yet, within a week, I'd decided to do it. My decision made no sense to me. I woke up in the middle of every night that week in a cold sweat, visualizing myself in the pitch-black darkness on a wooded mountaintop in a tent. As I would near consciousness, I'd start thinking, "I don't *want* to sleep in the wilderness all by myself. I'd be scared to death!"

And then I'd snuggle down under my cozy blanket and think, "I don't have to do this; no one's making me. Why would I want to, anyway? It's a crazy idea. I'll just forget it."

Despite my misgivings, by the end of the week, my decision was firm. I had no clear idea why I wanted to hike the trail. It just felt like something I was meant to do.

It certainly wasn't a lifelong dream; I wasn't a backpacking enthusiast with an unfulfilled desire to spend six months in the mountains. I had just turned 50. I'd spent the last 20 years in an Indianapolis suburb, first as a stay-at-home mom with my two sons, and then following a divorce, developing my career as a public relations director.

I wasn't unhappy with my life. My job at the world's largest children's museum was interesting and challenging, I did satisfying volunteer work, and many friends and activities occupied evenings and weekends. But I was beginning to feel that there was a sameness about my routines. I didn't want to wake up every day for the rest of my life doing pretty much what I had done the day before. In the past, I had changed jobs every few years and that always provided a new challenge. But this time I wanted to focus my energies in a different arena. Increasingly, I was thinking, "There is more to life than work."

I tried to identify what the Appalachian Trail's attraction was for me. I'd spent little time in the wilderness. I loved being outside, but in a civilized environment—on the golf course or beach, riding my bike, walking on neighborhood sidewalks. Not out in the woods with bears and bugs and rattlesnakes! I would be putting myself far outside my comfort level, living in circumstances for six months that I wouldn't ordinarily seek out even for a weekend. It would force me to stretch my personal limits, both mentally and physically, and to test my determination. I would meet new types of people and see a part of the country with which I had little familiarity. It would be a major transition, to what I didn't know, but to something new.

Although these thoughts kept running through my mind, they didn't seem sufficient to cause me to quit my job and set out on a six-month journey through the mountains. But something seemed to be pulling me toward the experience, as if this were supposed to be part of my life plan. I decided to trust the instinct and plunge ahead.

On April 1 I thought, "A year from now, I'll start my hike on the Appalachian Trail." As soon as I made the decision, I started mentioning it—to my sons first and then to a couple of close friends. Every time I talked about it, I was locking myself further into doing it. Putting the pressure on. Forcing the action by making a public commitment. For I'm the type of person who doesn't say I'm going to do something and then not follow through. And even if I say it to just one other person, the commitment is made.

"Greg, I think I'm going to hike the Appalachian Trail next year."

"But Mom, that's over 2,000 miles long!"

"I know, dear, but I feel like I'm going to do it."

And I'm locked in.

As I started telling people about my plans, it was a reality check for their knowledge and impressions of the AT. My older son, Greg, reacted exactly as I'd have expected, with his extensive knowledge base. (Most people have no clue how long the Appalachian Trail is.)

My younger son, Brad, had done some backpacking, and he thought it was a great idea. But he didn't think I knew what I was getting myself into. I remember he said, "You know, Mom, it's one thing to look at the catalogues and buy the equipment. That's the fun part. But when you've been out camping for three or four days and you're hot and sticky and haven't had a shower, it can get pretty uncomfortable."

He knew. He'd done it. His mom wasn't the type.

My own mother was very upset and wouldn't even discuss it for at least a month after I told her. She thought it sounded dangerous, lonely and foolhardy. She expected me to leave and never come back.

One lady asked if you had to make an appointment to start. Another wondered what all the hullabaloo was about; she thought the trail was about 60 miles long.

I spent a full year planning for my journey. I joined the Appalachian Trail Conference in Harpers Ferry, West Virginia, talked to their helpful staff, and ordered several books from their catalogue. I went to the local sporting goods store to look at equipment (my main criteria: how much does it weigh?) and discovered two young men working there who had thru-hiked the trail. They became a valuable source of information. I often slipped over to the store during my lunch hour and asked them question after question about every aspect of the experience. I met another man who had backpacked extensively on the Appalachian Trail, and he spent months mentoring me through the planning process.

I knew it would be important to be in excellent physical condition, so I joined the local YMCA and began using the weight machines and free weights to build muscles. I built stamina by loading my new backpack with encyclopedias and finding places to hike where no one would see me. (It's not a common sight to see someone walking through Indianapolis neighborhoods with a fully loaded backpack. To avoid embarrassment, I did that only after dark.) Several times I went to a nearby college and walked up and down the bleachers in the football stadium, over and over for a couple of hours at a time.

I gradually told more people about my plan, gave 10 weeks' notice at my job, rented my house, and found a friend willing to take my Elwood, the world's nastiest cat, for six months.

I planned what kinds of food I would eat and other supplies I would need. I packaged 12 boxes of food and supplies that 12 different people agreed to mail to me in small towns along the way. I anticipated approximately when I would arrive in those towns, then distributed a "mail drop" list to friends and family so they could write to me.

I turned my finances over to Greg, stored my car and personal items, forwarded my mail to a friend, and said goodbye at three wonderful farewell parties. I promised to write.

The last night I spent at home I thought, "Tomorrow I leave. Have I lost my mind?"

2

Too late to turn back

On March 28, my adventure began. I had spent a year planning, and often the idea of hiking the whole Appalachian Trail seemed overwhelming, but finally spring arrived and I just started walking. An old Taoist saying is, "A thousand-mile journey starts with one step." I hoped the Taoists didn't have different advice for starting a 2,155-mile odyssey, because I just put one boot in front of the other and headed up the mountain.

Tornadoes and hail changed the beginning. The day before I left, an afternoon hailstorm signaled the onset of a bizarre weather pattern over Springer Mountain. By evening, tornadoes were touching down in the area. I spent my last night in civilization huddled on the basement floor of the Amicalola Falls Lodge during four tornado alarms.

Each time the alarm went off, all the lodge guests hustled down to the basement where we crowded together on the floor, talking quietly, listening to hollow winds tearing through the trees, until the all-clear was sounded. My floor-mates were members of an organization of llama owners attending their annual convention. It was the first time I'd met people who raised llamas as pets and then traveled across the country to attend conferences with other llama owners. One little girl told me the names of her four pets: Molly, Highstep, Fuzzy, and Panda. I started seeing a new slice of life before even setting foot on the trail.

Several people were killed during the night when a tornado ripped through a town just a few miles from us. It seemed like an ominous beginning to my much-anticipated journey and reminded me that I would be living amid the forces of nature, which were not to be taken lightly. I didn't sleep much that night.

As I prepared to set out on the trail the next morning, it was misty, rainy, and chilly—not a friendly welcome to my new home for the next six months. It was a good test of my rain gear, though. I put my rain cover over my backpack and—as an extra precaution—slipped a giant trash bag over my rainproof jacket. It wasn't much of a fashion statement, but it set the tone for the months to come: It's not how you look, but whether you can stay warm and dry that's important on the trail.

A friend had planned to drive me via an obscure logging road to the top of Springer Mountain, where the AT began. But with flash-flood warnings and storm damage, we decided not to chance it in the car. Instead, I would hike up seven miles from the lodge to the beginning of the AT on a steep approach trail. I had already heard that dozens of people each year who start at the bottom of the mountain with the intention of backpacking all the way to Maine quit before they ever get to the Appalachian Trail. They had no idea it would be so rugged, demanding, and steep. I didn't look forward to this unexpected test on the very first day of my journey. The trail was already demonstrating the importance of being flexible and adapting to the circumstances in which you find yourself.

After an early breakfast, I became extremely nervous and said to my friend, "I've got to get going! If I don't leave right now, I don't think I'll be able to do this." She took the obligatory pictures of me taking my first step on the approach trail, we waved goodbye, and I set off alone. All alone.

I started up a steep incline in the rain. I didn't remember my backpack feeling so heavy when I was taking practice hikes around the neighborhood.

Within 100 yards, I was feeling panicked. I looked around and thought, "What am I doing here? I'm wet, freezing to death, and this backpack weighs a ton. I have no idea where I'll be tonight, tomorrow night, or any night for the next six months except out here in the woods. Was everyone right? Am I crazy to be doing this?"

I took a few deep breaths, wiped away some tears, and told myself, "It's too late to turn back. I've spent a year preparing for this; I can't quit on the approach trail."

I tried to focus on just taking the next step and started repeating what would be my mantra in the months to come: "I'll get through this. I'll be okay. I'll get through this. I'll be okay." I couldn't turn back, but it took all the courage I had to keep going.

Several hours later, I saw a man ahead. He was loaded down with a pack even larger than mine, slowing with every step. Handsome and fit, he looked about 40 years old. As I approached, he stopped to rest. We started talking and immediately realized that we were both headed for Maine. I had found another thru-hiker even before reaching the beginning of the Appalachian Trail! Although Denver Dan was an experienced hiker and had skied all winter, that first mountain was a real test. He was struggling as much as I.

We were both excited to meet a fellow thru-hiker, and we had much to talk about. After getting acquainted, we continued up the mountain together. He seemed knowledgeable about the plant life and stopped occasionally to point out types of vegetation.

When we reached the top, Denver Dan and I took pictures of each other at the southern starting point of the AT. Four hours into my adventure, I had warmed up from the exertion of hiking, but my back, knees, shoulders, and feet already ached as I took my first steps on the official Appalachian Trail. I felt reassured, though, with Denver Dan there. His presence was comforting, and my earlier anxiety dissipated a little.

The second of the trail's insights that day was how important people would be to the journey, providing companionship, energy, and incentive to continue.

Near us was a shelter, where Dan and I stopped for lunch. He fired up his stove and boiled water to eat a dehydrated meal and drink hot coffee. Peanut butter on a cracker and trail mix sufficed for me. I hadn't planned to use my stove until evening, and it was buried in my backpack.

Denver Dan seemed confident and experienced with his stove, and he wasn't concerned about running out of fuel. I, on the other hand, had been nervous every time I lighted mine in the garage at home. And although I hadn't even used my stove on the trail yet, I was already worried about how long my fuel would last. I watched Dan and tried to gain confidence from him.

That first night I shared a shelter with Denver Dan and two other hikers, Swan Song and John. Shelters were three-sided lean-tos, with a roof and wooden floor. They were spaced periodically along the trail, sometimes with up to 15 miles in between. Usually near a water source—a stream, river, or spring, some shelters were a few feet from the trail and others as much as a half-mile. They were built by local hiking clubs, whose members also provided various types of trail maintenance, including cutting weeds and clearing away trees blown down by storms.

The size of the shelters varied, but many were just big enough for five or six people to lie on the floor side by side. Although they provided protection from the rain, one side was completely open to the elements, so the temperature was the same inside and out. Nails in the ceiling with ropes hanging from them allowed hikers to suspend their food, foiling the mice that frequented shelters in hopes of finding an easy meal. If food was left in a backpack, the mice would chew their way through to find it.

I saw immediately that sleeping would be one of the trail's challenges. The floor was hard, the temperature dropped into the 30s, I was sleeping between two people I didn't even know, and mice were scurrying around my head and over my sleeping bag. (The previous spring I had been the one standing on a chair screaming when a mouse invaded a condo where I was vacationing with friends.) I may have nodded off a few times briefly during the night; most of the time I was lying there wondering when the next mouse would scuttle by and hoping I wouldn't wake the others if I bolted out of my sleeping bag when it happened. I thought to myself that this might be the last shelter I'd sleep in.

During the night I decided to scoot around and put my head at the open end of the shelter, praying there wouldn't be as many mice there. I had left my pan sitting on my stove so I could heat water for oatmeal in the morning. As it started to get light, I heard the pan tip over with a crash and looked up to see a skunk dashing away about a foot from my head. Mice or skunks? I opted for mice and turned back around to the other end.

The mountains on the Appalachian Trail were brutal. They were steep and high. I quickly learned that climbing a mountain at 9 a.m. was completely different from ascending one at 2 p.m., when it was the fourth one that day. Standing at the bottom looking up, I often thought, "Pretty soon, I'll be *way* up there at the top," and it was hard to believe it was possible. But somehow I always got there.

My hiking stick was seeing me through, acting as a third leg when descending steep, rocky areas or crossing streams. The uphills were hard on the legs, back, and heart; the downhills hard on the toes and knees.

Thus far, Swan Song was the only other woman I had encountered attempting to thru-hike the AT alone. One of the most physically fit 47-year-olds I'd ever met, she was a super-athlete who thrived on extensive physical undertakings. Swan Song was a marathon runner, and two years before we met she had ridden her bike 4,700 miles across the United States. Nevertheless, her next-door neighbor John came along to hike with her during her first week on the trail. He was an experienced outdoorsman, but he let her set the pace and was just there to support her and make sure that she was comfortable on her own.

I had once ridden half of the Hilly Hundred bicycle race and had run one mile in a Corporate Challenge race. And now I was out on the Appalachian Trail with little backpacking experience, all alone. Somehow I knew that said more about my naiveté than my courage.

Swan Song and I decided to try to camp together at night. So far, she was finding this the most difficult thing she had ever done. That was not reassuring!

Denver Dan crashed and burned the second day. His toes got hammered on the steep declines so he planned to hike just a few miles the next day. We both felt a bond from having started the trail together. I hoped I would see him again.

I'd better tell you about trail names, so you won't think that only people with very strange names hike the Appalachian Trail. Most thru-hikers adopted a nickname, based on some personal characteristic or event. (You probably can figure out how Dirt Eater got his.) It was a nice tradition that helped to build camaraderie and made you feel like part of a fraternity. Plus it was much easier to remember names like Slacker, Rainbow Rocker, and Lonesome Dove than Bob, Bill, and Mike.

Questions and conversations with the other hikers were always the same: "How much does your pack weigh?" "Why are *you* doing this?" "How do you like those boots?" (My boots looked like moon boots and they weren't very common on the trail. My son Brad had done some research and found what he thought were the best hiking boots on the market, and he gave me a pair for Christmas. When I first put them on, they rocked me forward across the living room with each step. I hoped they'd be as good at rocking me up the mountains.)

After that first night spent battling mice and skunks, I slept in my tent. I usually pitched my tent near water, and upon awakening in the morning, I sometimes mistook the sound of a babbling brook for the patter of raindrops. One morning I thought, "Oh no, not rain again!" and I carefully packed up everything inside my tent, preparing to step out into the drizzle. When I opened the flap, it was a beautiful, dry morning! The sounds of the forest take some getting used to.

Spring hadn't begun to show its colors yet, and much of the mountainside was still bleak. Huge rhododendron trees surrounded the trail in many areas, and I could tell it would be magnificent when they finally bloomed. There was a dusting of snow one day at a high elevation and I loved seeing the bushes, trees, and ground covered in soft, powdery white.

In those first days on the trail, I crossed more mountains than I had ever hiked during the first five decades of my life. I had read that the 400 miles at the beginning of the trail were 50 percent up and 50 percent down. I believed it. I hadn't seen any level ground yet.

How would I find my way to Maine? Well, the Appalachian Trail was marked with white blazes, 2 inches wide by 6 inches long. Sometimes they were painted on trees, sometimes on rocks. They might be a few yards apart or several hundred. They were often very visible, but at times you had to really search to find one. The rule of thumb on the AT was that after a quarter-mile without seeing a blaze, you'd better turn around because you were probably off the trail. I was doing the AT version of following the yellow brick road— tracking white blazes from Georgia to Maine.

My *Appalachian Trail Data Book*, updated annually, gave the mileage between shelters, water sources, roads, and other landmarks. *The Thru-Hiker's Handbook* filled in the details with facts about towns and various interesting spots along the trail. Maps were another source of information about elevation, profile and mileage.

Neels Gap was the first benchmark on the trail: 31 miles into the trek, it was a touch of civilization. Approximately twenty percent of the backpackers who started out on a thru-hike quit before they reached Neels Gap, so when I arrived there I already felt like a survivor of sorts.

A state road ran through the gap, where there was a center with hiking supplies and groceries. The proprietors had seen many thru-hikers come by, and they were experts at helping them pare down their weight and send extra gear home. One of the reasons people gave up so early in the trip was because they were carrying too much weight. It was exhausting trekking up mountains all day, especially with 60 to 80 pounds on your back. One of the most important parts of the planning was figuring out how little you could get along with, thereby eliminating every single unnecessary pound from your pack. With my food and water included, I carried between 35 and 45 pounds; it felt like double that by the end of the day.

"And miles to go before I sleep." On day three, I found myself with tears flowing as I thought of the beautiful imagery of Robert Frost's poems. That lovely refrain comforted me as I hiked along the trail, and it created an inviting picture in my mind of a warm, cozy cabin with glowing candlelight just ahead. Unfortunately, that image was not a bit like the cold, dark, three-sided lean-tos I would be staying in during the next few months.

When I was a teenager, my mother had given me two poems that my dad, who died when I was 5 years old, had always carried in his billfold. I liked the idea and wanted to be like him in that small way. So I selected my own two favorites, Frost's "The Road Not Taken" and "Stopping by a Woods on a Snowy Evening," and had carried them all these years, along with my dad's poems, in my billfold. It was a link to a father that I didn't know. In the small town where we lived, long before divorce became commonplace, I felt like the only girl in town without a dad. Sometimes I was embarrassed, often sad. Our family (my mom, brother, and I) seemed so small without a father.

How ironic that suddenly those poems held so much meaning for me. Since I had decided to take the road less traveled, my life had taken on a new tenor. The anticipation and excitement during my year of preparation for my journey had increased each month. By the time I left home, I had experienced such an outpouring of friendship, encouragement, and love from friends and family that I was completely overwhelmed. The decision to follow a new path had made all the difference.

Thus far, my time on the Appalachian Trail had been what I expected: a test of endurance and fortitude, a myriad of new experiences and new people, physical and emotional challenges, and lessons in how to co-exist with forest creatures in their homes in the woods. And my adventures had just begun.

The Appalachian Trail

3

"Deliverance" was filmed here!

Plumorchard Gap Shelter, Georgia
71 miles hiked
April 5, 1994

My criteria for judging what a good day is had changed in the brief time I had been on the trail. Although my journey was just nine days old, it had already included one that seemed like the best day of my life—one that perhaps would have been closer to the other end of my list just a few weeks before, given the rigors involved. It was Day Five: I started hiking with an anxious mind because I was heading out of Neels Gap with seven days' food—my heaviest load yet. I wondered how much difference the additional weight would make since my backpack was burdensome before.

The morning was glorious, with comfortable temperatures and clear skies. It was two full hours before I even looked at my watch. I was relieved that the additional weight I was carrying didn't feel uncomfortable, even though a couple of the climbs were extremely steep. I felt strong and capable, and my confidence soared. I was alone all day, encountering other hikers only occasionally.

I thought about possible trail names all morning, and that provided an opportunity to review some of the best aspects of the journey. I considered Serendipity because I thought the only way to hike the AT was to be open to whatever unexpected incidents came my way and enjoy them to the fullest. That name would serve as a reminder to take each experience as an opportunity. I also thought about the name Skywalker, after Luke Skywalker in *Star Wars*, because it felt as if something very powerful, like "the Force," was with me on the trip. I believed the power to get to Maine was within me, if I could just tap into it. But I didn't settle on a name that felt right. (Wouldn't it be interesting if we could name ourselves as adults, choosing something that fits our self-image? I wonder how many of us would choose the name our parents gave us.)

My lunch stop was unbelievably perfect. I was all by myself on top of a peak with a stunning view of a deep valley surrounded by mountaintops as far as the eye could see. The sun was shining, birds were singing, leaves were rustling in the soft breeze. I took off my boots and sat on a rock in complete comfort, with the best of the natural world laid out before me—as if it were for my eyes only. I wanted to capture the images and feelings and put them in a little pouch to wear around my neck so I could pull them out whenever I forgot what a magnificent world God has created.

In the afternoon I climbed the steepest, most treacherous mountain yet—the kind where it was too scary to look down at the dropoffs and too intimidating to look up and see how far it was to the top. So I just put my head down and took it one step at a time, using my hiking stick for balance and knowing I'd make it because "the Force" was with me. Eventually I started to feel the exhilaration of knowing the summit was near, and I felt the way I do when the dentist says, "Only a few more seconds..." I took my first breath in what seemed like 15 minutes.

I decided I'd much rather be alone on a strenuous climb like that. By myself, I didn't have to worry about whether I could keep up with someone else, or keep hiking if I felt a desperate need to rest, or be brave if I wanted to close my eyes in fear. I could just focus all my energy on getting up that mountain.

What amazed me as I struggled through that arduous terrain was that the feelings of exhaustion and even fear were not negative feelings. Since they were an expected part of the experience, they didn't gain control of me. Hiking the trail would be the most difficult thing I'd ever done. But I knew that going in. I could accept the hardships, because learning how to deal with them was part of the growing experience of being out there. The journey on the trail—and through life—is difficult. It's very empowering simply to accept that.

That night I tented near Swan Song and John in Low Gap, near a stream. We sat on the ground by some logs and ate our dinners together, and I enjoyed the companionship of my new friends. Then Swan Song helped me learn a few tricks of operating my stove while John wandered off to do some birdwatching. We spent an idyllic, peaceful evening in the woods before I slipped into my tent, the sound of nearby water lulling me to sleep.

What made that day so special? The simplicity of activity, the purity of the environment, the serenity of spending time alone, and the comfort of gaining a deeper understanding of myself and my world. Those may not always have been the elements I'd choose to create a perfect day, but right then they were.

Also that day I really believed for the first time that I could hike the entire Appalachian Trail. Barring illness or injury, I knew I could complete it if I wanted to. (Come mosquito season, maybe I wouldn't want to!) I wasn't sure until then, but for that day at least, I believed in my heart that I could endure the physical part.

Why did I think I could do it when those much younger and stronger were already dropping out all around me? Because I was 51 years old and I knew that the pain wouldn't last. Because I had trained myself physically; I built the right muscles and increased my stamina practicing with a backpack. Because I read the books, talked to the experts, and chose the right equipment. Because I planned, prepared myself mentally, and knew what to expect. It seemed like a pretty good formula for making one's way along the Appalachian Trail—or through life.

Does it diminish other significant events in my life to say that day was the best? No, I don't think so, because that day I brought with me the memories of all the other wonderful things I had experienced. Spending most of that day alone in the wilderness, I had time to enjoy those memories as they swirled around in my mind, and savoring them was part of what made that day so special.

That kind of euphoria seldom lasts. Mine lasted just one day, for the next day was a rude jolt of reality. Brad and I had talked recently about that: Often when something goes particularly well, it's followed with a real letdown. It almost makes you not want to experience the best—but not quite.

And now I'll tell you about Day Six.

After hiking for a few hours in the morning, feeling good, I sat down to rest and experienced a strange shortness of breath and general feeling of dizziness. As I sat there feeling weaker and weaker, with labored breathing, Swan Song and John appeared. They knew immediately something was wrong.

While we were pooling our medical knowledge, I told John and Swan Song that I'd had an episode working out at home about a month before leaving for the trail. My heart started palpitating wildly and felt like it was leaping out of my chest. Since I'd never experienced anything like that before, I thought perhaps I was having a heart attack. A trip to the emergency room and various tests showed that my heart was healthy, but because I would be in the wilderness undergoing strenuous physical activity, my doctor prescribed a drug called Lanoxin.

Although I had filled the prescription and carried the medication with me, I had decided not to take it. I felt certain the "heart episode" was an isolated incident. Now, however, I immediately took a pill. John and Swan Song were very concerned about my weakness, dizziness, and slow speech and they thought I needed medical assistance.

John hurried on to seek help at a road that crossed the trail about five miles ahead. Swan Song stayed with me. She started looking for a level area where I could lie down, since we were stopped on a rather steep incline. After finding one a few hundred yards ahead, she carried my pack and supported me while we moved on together. It was rough going. Every few steps I had to stop and rest; I felt like I was in such a complete state of exhaustion that I could barely move. It took a long time to hike that short distance but we made it; then I started to feel nauseated.

The nausea concerned Swan Song even more, and she was prepared to leave her backpack with me and run out to get help if necessary. She said, "This body is made for running! I can get out and back in a hurry if I need to." She was certified in CPR and I admitted to her that I'd meant to take a refresher course before leaving but had neglected to get that done. She said, "You mean I can save your life, but you can't save mine? Thanks a lot!"

After a short nap, I felt better, and a couple of hours after the episode began, I felt good enough to go on. Swan Song took part of my pack weight and we slowly hiked toward a shelter about two miles away.

As we were making our way along the trail, suddenly John appeared, hurrying toward us carrying an oxygen tank. He had made it to the road crossing and hitched a ride to the nearest phone where he called 911. An ambulance soon arrived at the trailhead and the crew started up the mountain to "rescue" me.

Once John saw that I was all right, he admitted, "Well, I'm a little disappointed with this emergency team. I thought they'd be a bunch of crack hikers who could really move up a mountain, but I think it may take them 'til sundown to get here!"

John had left his backpack at the ambulance and moved ahead with the oxygen to administer it until the medical crew arrived. This was about three hours after I'd initially had my spell, so I was glad it wasn't a real emergency. But then you shouldn't expect to get immediate help when you're on top of a mountain.

Eventually two Emergency Medical Technicians came struggling along, carrying their equipment and having a rough time negotiating the steep mountain trail. When they saw I didn't need them, they radioed that message to the volunteer firemen who were also on their way up the mountain with a stretcher, but farther back. We talked for a while and they told me to take my medication and to see a doctor when I had a chance, but not to worry. Everything checked out fine. I offered to pay for their emergency response, but the EMTs said it was free, provided by the local county. What a pleasant surprise!

We gave one of the EMTs a Power Bar so he'd have enough energy to make it back to the ambulance, about three miles away, and they headed down the mountain. They were a very nice pair, and I appreciated the free emergency care out in a remote area like this part of the trail. I just hoped none of us needed help in a hurry.

We laughed later about the sight of those EMTs struggling up the mountain. Backpacks to carry their equipment for mountain rescues, instead of the suitcase-type kits they had, would have made a big difference, but I think a few trips to the local gym would also have helped.

I was emotionally shaken that evening. Unexpected breathing difficulties, extreme exhaustion, and heart palpitations were scary. I hoped I didn't have a health problem that would knock me off the trail. The ambulance crew hadn't seemed unduly concerned, but I did decide to stop in a town at the next opportunity and see a doctor.

The next day I hiked just eight miles. I wanted to take it easy. Although there were no apparent aftereffects of my episode, I felt somewhat nervous all day. That night was cold and rainy. Eight thru-hikers shared a shelter that would have held five comfortably— Swan Song and me with six men. Since no one wanted to tent in the rain, we all lay shoulder-to-shoulder on the wooden floor, with sleeping pads touching. Everyone joked and laughed after dark, before we went to sleep. We decided we were so close together that if one of us rolled over, it would create a domino effect and we'd all end up rolling over. It was kind of like the slumber parties of my youth, only with people I'd never met—mainly a bunch of 20-something guys.

The following morning Swan Song decided she wanted to pick up her pace. Since I was still feeling a little anxious about my health, I didn't want to push myself too hard. By now, she could hike faster and farther than I could in a day, and she was eager to start putting in more miles. When we parted, we hugged and cried (gee, I'd just met the lady seven days before!) because we both knew that perhaps we wouldn't cross paths again. We had gained courage from each other in our week together and now we were comfortable going on alone. We could already tell that we were going to be among the few solo female hikers, and even though we were very different in almost every way, that one bond was strong.

Getting to a hiker hostel called the Blueberry Patch provided another first for me: my first hitchhike. I wouldn't say it was much of a success, but I figured I would get better at it. The Blueberry Patch was 3.5 miles from the trail via Route 76, and I decided to spend the night there so that I could go into a nearby town and find a doctor. My two options for traveling those miles were to hitchhike or walk. The choice seemed pretty clear to me.

I walked with my thumb out most of the way, but had no luck in getting a ride. A man jogged by and we exchanged greetings. When I came to his house, he was still outside and I asked him how far it was to the Blueberry Patch. He responded, "It's about a mile more up the road. You want a lift there?" I don't know if it counts as hitchhiking when your benefactor offers you a lift from his front yard, but I was sure grateful for the ride.

As the man dropped me off, Tortoise and Hare, two young thru-hikers from California, were trying to hitch into Hiawassee, a little town about 10 miles farther up the road. The driver said he'd take them. He hadn't even planned a trip into town, so he certainly earned his good neighbor points that day.

I could tell immediately upon arriving at the Blueberry Patch that I'd made the right decision in going there. I was greeted by several other backpackers—Strider, Slacker, Peanut, and Cashew—and by Lennie, the lady of the house. She was a beautiful, wholesome-looking young woman married to Gary, a '91 thru-hiker.

After his journey on the Appalachian Trail, Gary wanted the trail to continue to be part of his life. Lennie was agreeable, so they looked for a home to buy near the AT. They purchased an organic farm, named it the Blueberry Patch, and started welcoming thru-hikers to their home. They built bunks in the garage and covered them with straw mattresses. They stocked the space with tables, a hot plate, and extra fuel for hikers. They even built a small structure out back to house a toilet and shower—an unbelievable treat for a backpacker. Lennie did our laundry for us. We put all our dirty clothes in a basket; she picked it up and returned everything smelling fresh and clean! The best part of all: They cooked a *huge* breakfast and invited the thru-hikers into their kitchen to eat it.

Gary and Lennie never knew how many backpackers would be there; some rolled in as late as suppertime and there was no way to let them know from the trail that we were coming. So for about three months each year, their whole lives were devoted to thru-hikers. I had the feeling they really cared about each one of us.

When I arrived at The Blueberry Patch and told Lennie I needed to see a doctor, she gave me the name of a general practitioner in Hiawassee who accommodated hikers. I called at 4:30 p.m. and was told I could come in the following morning at 9. I doubt there are many doctors who take a non-emergency *new* patient first thing in the morning.

The next day, Lennie drove me to town and I went into the clinic to wait my turn for the doctor. It wasn't long before I was called in. The nurse was fascinated by my journey and talked with me for quite awhile about it. Then the doctor came in, and he also was very interested and asked a lot of questions. He said I was in no danger from the exhaustion episode, recommended a smaller dosage of the Lanoxin I had started taking, and said I should try Benadryl for my swollen eyes. After a full half-hour with me, he sent me on my way with a bill of just $30. It was as if the calendar had turned back a quarter-century.

After leaving the clinic, I meandered through town, stopped by the drugstore and grocery store, and had lunch at a restaurant where the waitress also wanted to discuss my thru-hike. Then I called Lennie to come pick me up. It all seemed like something out of a dream: Wandering around a small town in Georgia, population 2,000, going to the doctor, chatting with the local folks, sleeping on a straw mattress. I felt like I had just stepped onto a movie set or into a Norman Rockwell painting. Another slice of life. . .

By the way, when I told people I was going to hike the trail, the most common response was, "What's wrong with you? Don't you remember the film *Deliverance?*" Parts of it were filmed not far from Hiawassee. Word has it the actor who played the albino boy in the dueling banjos scene still lives in the area. But that was just a movie.

We asked Lennie and Gary what they did for entertainment: not much. There was a bowling alley and movie theater in a larger town about 20 miles away, but usually they just passed the time at home. They had discovered the simple life, and it fit them like a custom-made backpack.

That afternoon, Gary loaded six of us into his pickup truck and took us back to the trail where we continued north. He and Lennie were planning to go to a thru-hiker gathering called Trail Days in Damascus, Virginia, in May, so I hoped to see them again there.

A few hours later I was sleeping in the nicest shelter I had seen to date—Plumorchard Gap Shelter, built just two years before. Since it was raining, I had decided to stay inside instead of tenting. Even with 10 people there, it was not too crowded. Although the weather was drizzly and chilly, it actually seemed rather cozy. And there were no mice!

It had been a good day. The doctor said my health was fine, I had a hamburger and milkshake, I hiked only 4.5 miles, and I was in my sleeping bag on a wooden floor with a roof to protect me from the drizzle (but no wall to protect against the 40 degree temperatures). Everything's relative in life. A month before, I would have felt like I was roughing it; that night, I was in the lap of luxury because I had a roof over my head.

4

A scary-looking dude

Rainbow Springs Campground, North Carolina
104 miles hiked
April 9, 1994

*T*he last three days had included three significant firsts: my first state line, my first night pitching my tent in the pouring rain, and my first night completely alone. I had crossed from Georgia into North Carolina: One state down, 13 to go! The border was marked by a magnificent gnarled, misshapen oak tree that was Mother Nature at her most creative. I stopped briefly to enjoy the significance of the moment and take a picture of the tree. My excitement was short-lived, however, because the trail immediately climbed up two very steep rises. It was hot and muggy, and gnats started swarming around my sweaty face. I kept thinking that if I could just hike faster, I would outrun them, but that was impossible. I waved my bandanna in front of my face and sometimes draped it over my head to keep the gnats out of my eyes, and I plodded on. It was not a very pleasant entry into North Carolina.

That afternoon a spring storm set in and I could tell it wouldn't let up soon. I trudged along completely soaked, hearing a squishing sound inside my boots with every step and hoping I wouldn't get blisters from hiking in wet socks. I stopped once and sat down on a rock by the trail to take my boots off, pour the water out, and wring out my socks. It was a waste of time. Within minutes they were squishing again. With the trees still leafless in the early spring, there was no refuge from the rain and no alternative but to hike on.

By late afternoon I considered pitching my tent, but the thought of spending hours sitting in that tiny space in the rain wasn't appealing so I decided to press on to a shelter a couple of miles ahead. It would be a little easier to get dry under a roof where I could at least stand up; my tent had enough head room to sit, but not stand. Since the temperature was dropping, I didn't even mind the thought of being crowded. There would be more body heat to draw on. But when I reached Standing Indian Shelter, it was stuffed with people who gave me glazed stares that said, "It's all full. Get here earlier next time."

A trail adage is, "A shelter is never full until the last person is in." I learned another quick lesson: That wasn't always realistic and you had to be prepared to sleep in the rain. One of the causes of the overcrowding that night was a group of youths—Boy Scouts, I think. I searched around for a fairly level spot and put up my tent in the downpour. It was something I'd not done before, but after floundering around a bit, I ended up inside with all my equipment and not *too* much water. I changed into dry clothes and cooked dinner on my little stove under the front flap. My tent was just big enough to sit up at one end, but then it sloped sharply down. There was enough room for me to lie down and put my backpack right beside me, but no place to spread things out. I had heard that one way to get your clothes dry is to "wear them dry." You leave them on and sleep in them: the moisture's gone by morning. I thought I'd wait until it was warmer to try that option.

Let me count the ways to spend an evening in a tiny tent in the rain: 1. Read or write by candlelight. 2. Try to sleep.

As I lay there listening to the drumming of the raindrops, scrunched down into my sleeping bag on the hard ground, with damp equipment and clothes all around me, I couldn't help but envision my warm bed at home, comfortable, cozy, and dry. One more time I asked myself: "Now why am I doing this?"

The following morning was the coldest yet, in the 20s, and everything was frozen, even the shock cords in my tent poles. Getting out of a warm tent into the early morning chill was incentive to start moving so I could warm up while hiking.

I heard that day that one of the boys in the youth group had started getting hypothermic during the night and the others helped him warm up, so those in the shelter didn't get much sleep. Hypothermia was one of the real dangers hikers faced on the trail. Wetness, chilling, fatigue, and hunger could drain the body's heat to dangerously low levels, even when it was above freezing. Most former thru-hikers had a story to tell about someone who had a close call.

The next night was an opposite experience—a really splendid evening. The rain had stopped, temperatures warmed up, and I had a good day hiking. I traveled about 11.5 miles until I came to Betty

Creek Gap, where I followed a narrow, rutted path off the trail to a lovely little clearing.

I was all alone. It was the first night that no one else was anywhere near. After pitching my tent and spreading things out to dry in the tree branches, I slipped through the woods to Betty Creek, where I sponged off and secured water for dinner. It was nice to be by myself. I treasured the solitude, listening to the stillness of the forest and knowing I could be self-sufficient in an environment that recently had been so foreign to me.

Even though I was often overwhelmed with the beauty of nature, especially as spring started to unfold all around me, the real highlight for me so far had been the people, both on and off the trail. A reason I had sought this adventure was to experience a different way of life, and sometimes I felt like I was living on a movie set. The cast of characters was fascinating.

While the rest of us were just bit players in this drama of life on the trail, Freight Train was worthy of a starring role. He wasn't your typical thru-hiker. He hopped a freight train in Dallas to get to the AT, hence his trail name. He was a scruffy, scary-looking dude with long dark hair, an earring and stud in his nose (he said that backs people off), Harley T-shirt and black jeans, baseball cap worn backwards, one black front tooth, and sores all over his hands— from a liver disease, he said. He found his backpack in a dumpster; everything he had was grimy; he rolled his own cigarettes.

When I first met him, he was sick, lying in a shelter looking very grungy. I didn't want to go anywhere near him. But I have to tell you, I'm proud to say that Freight Train and I became buddies. When I got beyond the cover of this one, I discovered he had extensive literary knowledge (he read every day on the trail), knew a lot about nature and almost any topic, *always* had an opinion, and was gentle, witty, and resourceful. He came along while I was having my exhaustion episode, and he stayed with Swan Song and me until I was able to lie down. He was very supportive and caring.

Last time I saw him: "Jean! Got me some hiker pants. I look more like a hiker now!" (He'd found some long johns and shorts: real trail fashion. None of the thru-hikers wore jeans because they were too heavy and didn't keep you warm.) A standing joke when someone saw a piece of clothing cast aside on the trail was, "Next time we see that, Freight Train will be wearing it!" He had become part of the trail lore of '94 and everyone had Freight Train stories.

Strider, who was 31, owned a used bookstore near a college campus in Pennsylvania and was also widely read. One morning over breakfast, he started reciting Arlo Guthrie's "Alice's Restaurant" in perfect cadence and made it through the whole song without missing a beat. (It was about 20 minutes long.) I loved it; I didn't know how I had missed it when it came out in the late '60s. I made him repeat it about a week later, and he said he would make a tape for me when he got home from the trail. Strider was a gentle soul, obviously on a tight budget, so he made do with minimal equipment. He had been in the Army, as had many of the men on the trail, and had led a number of outdoor expeditions with kids at church camps, so he was a solid hiker and a good source of information.

Peanut and Cashew were high-school seniors (girls) on a month-long trek from Springer Mountain through the Smokies for school credit. They planned their trip very carefully, from hiking strategy and equipment to food purchases, and then came out to the AT to implement their plan. I was impressed that their school allowed such innovative ways to earn credit while gaining life experience. They were attractive, friendly, and at home in the wilderness. They each carried about 50 pounds, and I never once heard them complain. They ate like horses. If one got ahead of the other, they left notes along the trail for each other. At their age, I was wondering if I'd have a date for the prom. I admired them—and their parents for letting them do this.

Denver Dan had reappeared. I was sitting by a picnic table at Rainbow Springs Campground, wearing nothing but underwear and my waterproof jacket, with *everything* else in the washing machine. A car pulled up and I heard "Jean!" Out jumped Denver Dan—big hug—I hadn't seen him since the morning of Day Three. His toes were better and he'd caught up to me. He hitched a ride into the campground with a woman, and during that one-mile ride he asked if she'd have dinner with him. I don't know too many men who could pull that off, but Dan's a charmer. He shaved and put on his clean pair of shorts before she picked him up to head into town to a restaurant. (He said when he returned that she was a very nice person and the first 35-year-old virgin he'd ever met. Came up in the dinner conversation, I guess.)

While I was at that same picnic table, another car arrived and let out a backpacker, a man in his 50s. He came over and asked, "Are you Jean Deeds?" It was beginning to feel like a small world.

It turned out he was a thru-hiker named Larry from a small town in Indiana. He had read a column in *The Indianapolis Star* about my planned thru-hike, published three weeks before I left home. Larry said, "I've been chasing you since Springer Mountain so I could give you a copy of that article!" And he pulled out the clipping he'd been carefully guarding to keep it clean. He had started his thru-hike on April 1, and as the article reported, I began March 28. He'd made up four days on me in less than two weeks. He moved quickly, arising at dawn and hiking straight through until dusk. The hardest part for him on the trail was not being able to take a shower.

I asked Larry how he knew who I was when he saw me. He said he'd passed a Boy Scout troop on the trail earlier in the day and talked with them, as I had. They mentioned that a lady from Indianapolis was about two hours ahead of him. That was one of the ways news traveled on the trail. It was just a coincidence that he and I both went to the campground.

Those "off trail" experiences were as interesting a part of the journey as being on the trail. It seemed incredible to me that while I was at a little campground in North Carolina, two people with whom I had a connection arrived.

I stayed at Rainbow Springs the next day and didn't hike. My body was screaming that it needed a rest, so on Day 13, I rested. All day. My first day in almost two weeks not to backpack at all. Hallelujah!

On the trail, you needed to pay attention to your body's messages. I had already met many people who pushed too hard and ended up hurting their knees or feet, or getting blisters. They wound up losing more time than if they'd taken it a little easier. One of my goals was to cut myself a little slack, out on the trail and perhaps when I got back to civilization. Most thru-hikers planned on taking five to six months to hike the trail; there was no need to kill ourselves the first two weeks.

I doubt many people would try to hike for 180 straight days without a break to rest now and then. I intended to take a day off about every two weeks to rest my body and get my equipment cleaned up, but I felt a little guilty the first time doing it. And that led to my wondering:

What was my goal? To see how fast I could get to Maine? (For some it was, and that was okay; they had their own agenda and a very different plan for their thru-hike than I. Some would make it all the way.)

Was it to stop at every vista, to enjoy every single view? (For some it was, and that was okay too; they proceeded very slowly and sometimes hiked far into the evening. Some of them would get to Maine.)

Was it just to have fun? (For some it was. One thru-hiker told me he would stay on the trail only as long as he was having fun. If that were my criteria, I would have gone home the first night.)

Was it to test myself, to challenge myself, to see what I'm made of? (For some it was. And it was certainly a worthy challenge. That's probably closest to where I fit, and for me, how quickly I got to Maine wasn't important, but getting there was.)

Taking time to relax and enjoy the serendipitous experiences didn't come naturally to me. (Perhaps it's a good thing I didn't choose that as a trail name, since it was a goal, not a characteristic.) Even when spending all day every day out in the woods, there was still the pressure of getting to Maine, so I reminded myself I would need to keep a healthy balance of moving north and stopping to gaze at the rhododendron. At Mt. Katahdin, in northeastern Maine, winter started settling in by mid-October. Its trails were closed from October 15 to May 15, and no thru-hiker wanted to get all the way to the base of that final mountain and be told, "Sorry, the mountain's closed. You'll have to come back next summer to do the last five miles of the Appalachian Trail." So we did have a deadline to meet: Katahdin by the ides of October.

Many friends told me before I left that just making the commitment to undertake this huge journey was a significant accomplishment and that no one would think any less of me if I decided to quit along the way.

I appreciated that sentiment and knew it was meant to reassure me that I didn't have to prove anything or be embarrassed if I didn't make it to Mt. Katahdin. But it never occurred to me to just see how far I could get, or to hike until I stopped enjoying it, or to stay just long enough to be able to say, "Well, I gave it my best shot." I had come out to hike the Appalachian Trail all the way from Georgia to Maine, and that's what I intended to do. And I was on my way: 100 miles down, 2,055 left to go!

5

No favors asked, none granted

Nantahala Outdoor Center, North Carolina
134 miles hiked
April 14, 1994

I had been following the ridge of the Nantahala Mountains, going over summits that were at least 5,000 feet high and descending into gaps between 3,500 and 4,000 feet. As I started down the steep decline toward the Nantahala River, I could feel it getting cooler and see the vegetation become more lush. Fingers of mist seemed to rise up from the valley and drift among the trees in front of me. I began to hear the water from the rapids which were still far below. At 1,723 feet, the river seemed a long way down, and I could feel my knees protesting with every step during the 30 minutes it took to reach the gorge. I never knew how fascinating—and how painful—it could be to change elevation by a few thousand feet.

Not having backpacked before, I didn't realize that descents would be much more stressful for my knees and toes than the ascents. Carrying a heavy backpack puts an unnatural pressure on your knees when you are hiking at a sharp angle downhill or climbing down rocky sections. And your toes can get pushed forward against the front of your boots. I would much rather go up, even though that's hard on the lungs, heart and back. I prefer exhaustion to pain.

The Nantahala Outdoor Center (NOC) was a small, very rustic resort on the Nantahala River. Although it was primarily known for its white-water rafting opportunities, thru-hikers were an important source of income in the spring. However, a cabin with bunks for hikers had slid down the side of the mountain in a rainstorm a few weeks before I arrived, so there were fewer beds available than usual.

When I reached NOC, all the rooms were full. I had looked forward for days to sleeping in a motel room. This would be my first time in a real bed since starting on the trail. I cursed myself for not getting an earlier start in the morning. The clerk told me I could hike up a very steep hill to a little wooded knoll overlooking the railroad tracks and pitch my tent there. It seemed to be my only option. Two other hikers were already up there, young men I didn't know. The climb was so steep that one of them grabbed onto my hiking stick to pull me up the last few yards. I pitched my tent and spread everything around to air out in the breeze.

I went back down to NOC's center of activity—the store. Soon the check-in clerk from the motel found me to report that several other hikers had offered to let me stay with them. A few minutes later, Scrap Iron came by and offered the floor of his room. There were three beds, and he already had two other roommates, Colby and CC.

Scrap Iron was a marathon runner, about my age, with a metal plate in his leg. After arriving at NOC, he went for a five-mile run, "just to keep in shape." I had met him only a couple of times, but he was a very congenial hiker whose fiancé would be joining him soon for a few days on the trail. Colby was a quiet young man in his 20s from a small town not far from the Nantahala River. CC was from Canada; his trail name stood for Canadian Club. He was traveling with Joey, a large black dog with bright blue eyes who also had a trail name: Mule. CC signed the trail registers "CC and the Mule."

Sleeping on the floor with the dog sounded better than in my tent, especially since the room had a bathroom with a shower. So I climbed back up the hill, repacked all my gear, and brought it down to the motel. Sharing a small motel room with three guys and a dog was another new experience.

Denver Dan and I met up in the laundry room and decided to have dinner together in the resort restaurant. Thank goodness it was warm enough to wear my shorts and T-shirt, since my cool-weather clothing option was to add long underwear. That worked on the trail, but might have appeared a little strange in a restaurant.

Several other hikers joined us and together we put away a huge quantity of food. It was a good thing the restaurant prices were reasonable, because we all had vulturous appetites. I had read that thru-hikers burn as many as 4,000 to 6,000 calories a day. We ate hearty whenever the opportunity presented itself. Dan ordered three desserts.

In that restaurant, I felt like a regular person in a real place: sitting at a table and chair, not on the ground; eating fresh food, not something that had been stuffed into a backpack for days; drinking water that came from a faucet, not out of a stream; seeing women with purses, not hikers with backpacks. Not like being out in the woods for days at a time, which seemed like another world. I would be heading back out to that world within hours.

The highlight of that stop, though, was getting my mail from my first mail drop, the only one not at a post office. People could send mail to hikers at the NOC and it was all thrown together in a box in the store. I sorted through everyone's mail and found my own. It was kind of like being at camp. I received 23 letters—about half of all the letters in the box! When I took them downstairs to read, the other hikers couldn't believe it. Everyone else received just one or two letters, if any. Someone wanted to give me the trail name Mail Lady because they had seen all the letters addressed to me. It didn't seem like a very good name, though. Somehow the idea of introducing myself as "Mail Lady" and having someone mistake that for "Male Lady" seemed rather risky.

The letters were wonderful, supportive and encouraging. The other hikers got a big kick out of Paulette's, written on toilet paper so I could "reuse" it, and the one Janet and Maggie wrote on a napkin for the same reason. My friends thought of everything! I needed and treasured every one of those letters. I found a quiet place to sit and pore over them where no one would see me crying. They made me so homesick. But I knew the love and support from family and dear friends would be in my heart as I trudged along the trail each day, and that's what would carry me to Maine.

That same day, while waiting for my laundry, I met four young men who were thru-hiking the trail together. They had been friends in high school and were at various stages in their college careers. We called them the Goatherders because they planned to carry a plastic inflatable goat with them all the way to Maine. They offered me some beer, and I shared my chocolate chip cookies that Mom sent.

The Goatherders didn't necessarily hike together all day, but tried to end up at the same place each night because they were sharing equipment. It was difficult to hike at the same pace as another person. As with every other endeavor in the world, we all had our own natural pace. It could be very wearing to hike more slowly or quickly than felt comfortable. I really respected those young men for undertaking a challenge of this magnitude and for doing it as a team, with all the compromises that entailed.

I never considered trying to find someone to hike the trail with me. Several of my friends and family worried about my safety, since I would be traveling alone. But frankly, I couldn't imagine finding someone with whom I'd be compatible in the distance to hike each day, when and how often to take days off, and how fast to hike. It would involve many compromises, and I felt I would need to focus all my energy on just getting *me* to Maine, not on trying to adjust my style or pace to someone else's.

There were advantages to having a hiking partner: the companionship and moral support, and carrying less weight since you could share a stove, water filter, and tent. Nevertheless, I liked being on my own. There were enough other people on the trail that I didn't think I'd be lonely. There would be fewer thru-hikers as we proceeded north, though, with the ranks thinning every day.

Since the second week of my trek, I had been waking up most mornings with very swollen eyes, and they remained puffy all day. I looked like some sort of balloon-faced Cabbage Patch doll. Although I had prepared for the natural look on the trail, with no makeup, not worrying about what my hair looked like, wearing the same shorts and T-shirt for days at a time, there was a limit to my lack of vanity. The grotesque eyelids pushed me over that limit. I wanted to find a cause and solution.

At Rainbow Springs, I had met thru-hiker Del Doc, a retired research physician from Delaware who was very willing to give advice or opinions about backpackers' medical ailments. I asked him about possible causes and cures. (The doctor in Hiawassee had told me to try an antihistamine, but it didn't help at all.) In true research fashion, Del Doc started asking questions. He loved playing the sleuth and finally concluded that I was allergic to my down-filled sleeping bag. It made sense. It was still very cold most nights and by morning I was snuggled down inside my sleeping bag and breathing in "down dust." I'd always suffered from general allergies so this seemed logical.

I bought a new sleeping bag with synthetic filler at NOC and sent my other one home. I hoped that would solve the problem.

Del Doc was an interesting character: 69 years old, very physically fit, a marathon runner who had thru-hiked the trail two years before. Now he was doing it again. I think his wife was more supportive the last time but at this point would prefer that they were traveling in Europe.

As medical editor of the Appalachian Trail Conference newsletter, Del Doc was doing research about various topics and making himself available to answer hikers' medical questions. And we had many. At Rainbow Springs, it seemed almost everyone had some problem: a rash, blisters, sore knees, numb toes, a boil where the backpack rubbed, aching muscles. I think mine were the only swollen eyes. He wrote a column for each issue of the ATC newsletter based on what he heard from hikers.

However, just to show we don't always listen to our own good advice: Del Doc's wife was picking him up at Rainbow Springs so he could go home to see his podiatrist. He had developed a foot problem after doing 13-mile days from the beginning of the trail rather than breaking in his feet gradually. He'd probably be at home a week or so and then come back. He knew better. The trail didn't allow lazy thinking or tolerate overconfidence.

Perhaps that's why many of the young, fit men who seemed so capable of meeting any physical challenge dropped out within the first few weeks: They tried to macho-hike rather than using prudence and settling in for the long haul.

A recommendation most hikers heeded was to not keep food in their tents at night, since it might attract animals. Hanging my food in a tree was just one more trail challenge. Here's how it worked: I looked for a horizontal branch about 10 feet up in the air, tied a piece of rope around a carabiner (a metal ring often used in rope climbing), and tried to throw it up over the branch without getting it tangled in all the other branches. Sometimes I stood there for 10 minutes tossing that carabiner up before I ever got it over the branch! When it finally came down on the other side, I tied my food bag to the end of the rope and raised it up into the air, away from the trunk of the tree. Then I tied the other end of the rope around the trunk. Unfortunately, I hadn't honed my throwing skills in preparation for hiking the trail. I always felt a flush of success, though, when that carabiner went over the branch. I think it was right up there with sinking a long putt on the eighteenth green.

Denver Dan, Strider, and I were camping together one evening near Wine Spring and in a moment of generosity, Denver Dan offered to throw Strider's carabiner and rope over the tree branch. The carabiner got stuck up in the tree, and that's when we discovered that although Strider had several carabiners with him, he was sentimentally attached to that particular one from his Army days.

(It seemed to me that was the same as being sentimentally attached to a pair of pliers or a nail.) But Dan seemed to understand this concept, perhaps because he's a former Navy man—or perhaps just because he's a man. There appeared to be no question in either mind that they would do whatever it took to get that carabiner out of the tree. First Dan put on his long pants to protect his legs from the bark, then he climbed up onto Strider's shoulders, hoisted himself into the tree, and then picked his way up 15 feet through the branches to retrieve it.

All of this was happening at dusk while it was misting and starting to rain. Denver Dan needed to pitch his tent, filter his water, and cook his dinner before the deluge began. Instead he was up a tree. I was rolling on the ground laughing and taking pictures of the whole incident. You find your fun where you can on the trail.

6

It's the mountains, not the miles

Fontana Dam, North Carolina
164 miles hiked
April 18, 1994

After three weeks on the trail, the days seemed to all run together in my mind. I usually had no idea what day of the week or date it was. Since I wore a watch, I did keep track of the time; perhaps I would just learn to live by the sun.

My insight after 22 days on the Appalachian Trail: It was the mountains, not the miles; it was the weight, not the walking. Give me a flat path and a fanny pack and I think I could have walked forever, but these mountains were fierce and my backpack a burden.

The section between Nantahala and Fontana Dam was grueling. For the first time, I found myself angry at the people who carved out the trail. Several times it went straight up the mountain at an angle so sharp I didn't think my ankles would bend that far, especially in hiking boots. I kept thinking that if they really wanted people to use the trail, they shouldn't have made it so difficult. God, why did you make those mountains so steep?

The variety of thru-hikers on the trail continued to fascinate me. I recently had met Suds, age 62; his wife Canjo, 60, and Poet, 72. (Suds was retired from Stroh's Brewery, Canjo was carrying a small homemade "banjo" made of a tin can and stick with a couple of strings, and Poet often wrote poems in the trail registers.) Canjo, a former school-bus driver, sometimes led singing at shelters in the evenings, in true campfire fashion. When she temporarily left the trail with a knee problem, Suds and Poet began traveling together. They were excellent backpackers: wiry bodies, steady gait, at ease in the woods. Although they were 10 to 20 years older, I couldn't keep up with them.

They had all backpacked before. At age 17, Poet and a friend hiked across Ohio with homemade packs because they'd not been able to buy what they needed. Equipment was scarce in 1940. Suds and Canjo went hiking on their very first date and had logged thousands of miles since. For them, thru-hiking the Appalachian Trail was a lifetime dream. I often felt that I was on the trail because I had to be, because something was compelling me to be there. They were there because they loved it, and that amazed me.

Trail registers provided a unique communication system on the AT. Each shelter had a register—a notebook for people to write in if they wished. It was left there by one of the trail maintainers from a local hiking club or by a thru-hiker. They always put their name and address in the front of the notebook with the request that someone mail it to them when it was full. Return postage and a "reward" were offered as an incentive. Many thru-hikers carried a blank notebook with them, hoping they would reach a shelter when the current notebook was full, so they could leave theirs. Having your own trail register was a much-coveted memento of a thru-hike. (I wasn't carrying any extra weight, not even a notebook.)

Some hikers didn't write in the registers at all; others never missed a one. Some wrote something very simple, like "4/10. Passing through. Rainbow Rocker." Others waxed philosophical, wrote poetry, poured out their emotions, told about their days, or mentioned something they were looking forward to. We could leave messages for those behind us, but that communication was a one-way path. Most hikers read the registers even if they didn't write in them, because it was fun to see who had recently been through. You could find out lots about who was ahead of you, but nothing about who was behind.

Though it was an interesting mix of people on the trail, I found I was way outside the norm. I had seen only one other female thru-hiker traveling alone—Swan Song. The other women, such as Canjo, were part of a couple and there weren't many of those; almost none were middle-aged. Once I didn't see another woman for three days. At Rainbow Springs I slept in a 12-bunk hostel (four triple-deckers), and I was the only female. Just 11 guys and me.

I wondered where all the women were. Was I really so far out of synch with the other females in the world? I never thought so before. No one on the trail seemed to notice, or at least to mind. No favors asked, none granted. The guys were my buddies and the camaraderie was wonderful, but when I was the last one in, I pitched my tent or slept on the floor with the dog.

My trail friends had decided to call me Indiana Jean. It was perfect, because a couple of hikers from Indiana who knew I was on the trail were trying to connect with me: "Have you seen Jean from Indiana?" or "Did you meet a lady from Indianapolis?" So the name was an identifier. However, some people must have thought my trail name was a reference to the film character Indiana Jones, because they asked me where I was from. I liked that concept. Indiana Jones was a mild college professor in his "real" life, and then he took on the persona of a grand adventurer who lived on the edge, overcame hardships, and met new challenges daily. My experiences hadn't lived up to his wild escapades, but then I wasn't using a stunt man either.

At Fontana Village I slept in a real bed with sheets, blankets, and a pillow for the first time since my journey began. It was a touch of paradise. I'm not a good sleeper in the best of circumstances and I hadn't adjusted yet to sleeping on the trail. Since I still didn't feel comfortable sharing my sleeping space with mice, I preferred my tent to the shelters. It was my little home away from home, where I could have all my "stuff" around me, take my sponge bath, and even read by the light of a candle. The bad part was putting a wet tent into my backpack in the morning if it had been raining— which it usually had—and carrying the extra weight of the water.

I treated myself to a night alone in a little cabin instead of staying in the hiker hostel at Fontana. There I'd have shared the space with up to 16 other backpackers, on a bunk with no mattress, just a slab of wood. In the cabin I could spread out my gear, wash my water bottles and spoon in the sink, and repackage my food and supplies from my mail drop. I received 12 more letters! After reading each and trying to commit as much as possible to memory, I put them all in a large envelope and mailed them home for my scrapbook. I would be able to enjoy them again when I finished my journey and found them all waiting for me at home.

I saw both Denver Dan and Strider at Fontana; they were staying in a shelter on the trail a couple of miles away and had hitched a ride to the village to do laundry and buy groceries. I even saw Lonesome Dove driving a car; his girlfriend had come to visit him. How strange to see a thru-hiker driving! Did these people I was meeting really have normal lives off the trail, with cars, houses, regular clothes, families, and significant others?

I called several friends and family members, and it felt good to make contact with the people I missed. Although I felt lonely after talking to them, it was worth it to hear their voices.

At home, we take water for granted. We turn the faucet, and out it comes. I had always appreciated the beauty of water in its natural state—in oceans, lakes, waterfalls, and rivers—and its calming quality, as well as its fury and power. But I'm not sure I ever before had sufficient appreciation for its control over our lives. In the wilderness the most basic elements took on the importance they deserved, and it was easier to see what the balance of nature was all about.

Water determined how far I hiked each day and where I spent each night. I could find water late in the afternoon and carry it with me to a campsite, but adding that extra weight was not a desirable option so I looked for a place to tent near a water source. Shelters and campsites were usually positioned near springs, streams, or rivers. Most of us started out in the morning with one or two quarts of water, enough to last until evening, so we wouldn't have to stop during the day to find and filter it.

Most thru-hikers carried a water filter; we pumped the water through it so that we wouldn't get a disease called giardia from drinking untreated open water. Giardia, a microscopic organism, could contaminate surface water, even though the water looked, smelled, and tasted good. It was risky to take a chance because giardia caused symptoms much like the stomach flu, only it didn't go away in a few days. It required prescription medication and could linger for weeks. Each year a few aspiring thru-hikers were knocked off the trail by it.

Boiling water was also effective in killing the organisms. Some hikers used chlorine or iodine tablets, but reaction from the medical community to those types of purification was mixed. A few hikers never treated their water and swore they were immune or the danger was overstated. Most didn't want to take a chance. I was one of the cautious ones.

The number-one topic of conversation among thru-hikers was blisters and other painful body parts. We were all still dealing with the shock our bodies were going through during the conditioning period. I was grateful for the physical training I had done at home because it got me through the first few days. But early in the journey, my body had started asking, "Is this really what you expect of me during my 51st year?" Given the affirmative, I had been engaged in a kind of mind/body struggle ever since. I realized it would take the full six to eight weeks I'd been told to expect for my body to adjust to the rigors of the trail. Most days, no matter how many miles I'd traveled, the last hour was an endurance test, with various parts of my body fighting for attention to send their message, "I'm ready to quit for the day!"

Elastic bandages and lots of ibuprofen helped the knees, but some nights I ached for several hours before going to sleep. Virtually everyone on the trail agreed this was the toughest thing they'd ever done, and these were physically fit people. Thru-hikers were dropping out each week, many with knee and foot problems, so I was trying to pace myself and not push too hard for distance. My longest stretch so far had been 13.5 miles, and I paid for that one with aching knees and feet that kept me awake far into the night. I was still more comfortable at 10 to 12 miles per day, but eventually I would be able to increase that.

The beauty of the Appalachian Trail was everything I thought it would be. The trail went over peaks, along ridges, and through gaps. As far as I could see in every direction were more crests and valleys, all shimmering with the budding greenery of April. I couldn't imagine ever tiring of the sights. Every view was different, every tree, plant, flower, and rock had its own shape and color and position on the forest floor. Each one caught or cast a different shadow. Every vista offered its own rewards.

Each mountain seemed like an untouchable monument when seen from afar, but up close one discovered a myriad of life forms clinging to its landscapes. Under the canopy of the trees, invisible from an airplane or an adjoining mountaintop, there was a world of living creatures, each busily trying to ensure its own survival.

Singing birds in the springtime and new plants popping out of the earth had always reminded me of my favorite book as a child, *The Secret Garden*. I still read it every few years, and it never failed to evoke a longing to be among the creatures and plants of the earth as they began their annual life cycles. I was in the secret garden. Everywhere I looked, every minute of the day, it was spring.

The Appalachian Trail

7

The middle of nowhere

Mountain Moma's [sic], North Carolina
235 miles hiked
April 25, 1994

I had spent the last week crossing through the Great Smoky Mountains National Park. The AT entered the park at Fontana Dam, climbed to the crest line, and followed it for about 70 miles to Davenport Gap. Hikers were required to register when entering the Smokies and keep the permit displayed, but I never saw a ranger or anyone checking for permits.

Clingman's Dome in the park was the highest point on the whole Appalachian Trail. The day I traversed the summit (6,643 feet above sea level) was also my longest hiking day to date: 14 miles. It wasn't a particularly tiring day. Perhaps I was gradually becoming trail-hardened without realizing it.

Park rules required that hikers stay in the shelters instead of their tents. And those shelters were the reason I was thrilled to be beyond the park: They were crowded and dirty, and the mice were incorrigible. Those little critters didn't even wait until dark to come out and start rummaging through backpacks looking for food. And they ran around all night long. I woke up often to see mice zipping by no more than a couple of inches from my head. I swear they were grinning, with crumbs dangling from their whiskers, as they scurried by. The shelters had two sleeping levels, with as many as 16 people, thru-hikers and weekenders, packed in like sardines and sleeping side by side in a small space on a wooden floor, with backpacks scattered everywhere.

The shelters were called bear cages, which was a misnomer because the people were on the inside looking out and the bears were on the outside looking in. These bear cages were the same three-sided structures as other shelters, but the open side was covered with chain-link fencing. At night, we latched the door with a chain.

There were reports the year before that bears were very aggressive in late spring and early summer, after thru-hikers had gone north. Some had learned to "bluff-charge" backpackers, causing them to leave their food and run away. Goal accomplished. The bears weren't people-eaters, but by feeding them, thoughtless individuals had taught the bears to expect food when they encountered people. Once again, humans caused their own problems.

My first two days in the Smokies wore me down, mainly because my pack was heavier than usual with seven days of food. The second day was extremely hot and sunny. Mid-afternoon I stopped and collapsed in the middle of the trail, too tired even to move a few feet off the path. I have to admit I sat there staring at an M&M that someone had dropped and trying to decide whether to pick it up and eat it. I must have been succumbing to the thru-hiker stereotype: If it was food or resembled food in any way, we would eat it.

Thank goodness I didn't have to find out what my decision would have been, because right then Earth Frog, a young ex-Navy SEAL, came along and distracted me. I was getting sunburned and Earth Frog shared his sunblock with me before we hiked on. I had been told to expect snow in the Smokies so wasn't prepared for the opposite. You should never count on the weather.

I had planned to hike 11.5 miles to Derrick Knob Shelter that day, not a long distance at this point in my journey. But the data book *must* have had the mileage mismarked, because the last two miles seemed like four. (That was always my conclusion when the miles seemed inordinately long: The data book was wrong.) By late afternoon, I became convinced I had missed the shelter. The next one was five miles farther on and I knew I couldn't make that distance by sundown. With regulations in the Smokies requiring us to stay in shelters, I was very nervous at the thought of tenting in bear country.

I sat down on a tree stump and tried to control my exhaustion and rising anxiety. What would I do? The terrain was so uneven that there was no place in sight to pitch a tent, even if I were brave enough to do that. Every time I had started up another steep incline in the last hour, I thought the shelter would be there when I reached the top, but it hadn't been. I rested, tried to calm down, and ate a snack to pour a little energy into my body. I was finding I could think much more clearly when I wasn't exhausted and hungry. Soon I decided there was nothing to do but keep going as long as I could or until darkness fell. Within a half-hour, I came upon the long-anticipated shelter and, with a huge sigh of relief, knew I would be safe that night.

The day included an ironic ending: I wound up tenting after all! Earth Frog had arrived about a half-hour before I did. The shelter was so crowded that we both decided to pitch our tents, despite the warnings of possible repercussions from park rangers. Upon appraising the number of hikers stuffed inside the shelter, suddenly bears and fines didn't seem so bad compared to being squashed between snoring men on a wooden floor with mice running over my sleeping bag. In fact, when others saw that Earth Frog and I were going to tent, they offered to let us have their space in the shelter so they would be justified in sleeping out. No way.

Soon Denver Dan rolled in and decided to sleep out under the stars without even pitching his tent. Earth Frog and I thought that was a great idea. If a bear came, it would go for Denver Dan first, since he would be an easier target. We would have time to seek safety in the shelter while Dan wrestled with the bear. We thanked him for acting as bait. However, the next day we weren't so cocky when we heard that, in fact, a bear had spent most of that night at a shelter about six miles back. He kept sticking his paw through the wire caging trying to swipe food.

Usually the bears were more frightened of people than we were of them. I'd been told that it was rare to even capture a bear on film, because they headed the other direction when they spotted a person. All day every day in the Smokies, I kept my camera hanging around my neck hoping to see a bear, but I never spotted one. I was disappointed, but bears inhabit the Appalachian Trail as far north as New England, so I figured I had lots of time to see one.

With spring arriving daily, I had begun to take pictures of each new variety of budding flowers. I loved following the spring north and being where I could see the plants sprouting their new growth under my daily scrutiny. The woods were turning from dull brown into a variety of greens, sprinkled with yellows, whites, soft purples, and light blue.

I saw my first snake, another species that was right at the top of my list of animals I'd rather not share my personal space with. He was about 12 feet long (well, maybe three) and black. I knew he wasn't poisonous and wasn't really afraid of him. I did realize, when I thought about it rationally, that I could move faster than the snakes.

If I were alert enough not to step on them, they wouldn't bother me. Since I'm sounding so casual about snakes, I must admit that I've always been very frightened of them. But for some reason, they didn't seem so scary in this environment. I had come into their home. I kept remembering that I was the unwelcome guest and they were the unwilling hosts.

When I passed by Newfound Gap, I discovered what it was like to be a celebrity—or perhaps a curiosity. The gap was a tourist spot situated on the Tennessee-North Carolina border with splendid views of the mountains. After slinking through the wilderness for days, the trail suddenly burst out of the woods onto a road and a parking lot filled with cars, campers, and tourists. I didn't even get across the highway before people started approaching, quizzing me and offering me food. "Are you a thru-hiker? Would you like an apple? How about something to drink? Where are you from? Why are you doing this?"

I attracted quite a crowd as I sat on the grass massaging my feet and eating trail mix. Some even took my picture. I had the feeling that when they whipped out their vacation photos, right there among the bears, deer, and other wild things would be this grimy, sweating lady and they would tell their friends about the thru-hiker sighting. I guess we were a pretty rare breed, and we even had our own season—about six weeks long, as we were migrating north.

What made me so recognizable as a thru-hiker, or at least as someone who was journeying a long, long way? I guess it was the combination of the heavy backpack, the elastic bandages on the knees, the hiking stick, the hard-core boots, and the bandanna. Or maybe it was the distinctive odor thru-hikers acquired after days of sweating, wearing the same clothes, with no deodorant. "How far you going?" "Maine." It seemed simple to me, inconceivable to them.

I had been enjoying my many encounters with people on the trail. I knew I added to their experience, and they were certainly adding to mine. I met three fellow backpackers who were so inspiring that it made me proud to be in the same fraternity with them. Methuselah was 75 years old; Moses, 65; and Choo Choo, in his 50s. Choo Choo told the story this way: The previous winter he had received a phone call from Methuselah, a retired English Literature professor. Methuselah had heard that Choo Choo thru-hiked the trail several years before. He wanted to attempt a thru-hike himself and was looking for an experienced backpacker to go along with him. "You see," Methuselah said to him, "I'm 75 years old...and I'm legally blind." Since this sounded like a formidable challenge for both of them, they day-hiked together in the Smokies to see how it would work. Choo Choo wanted some time to decide whether he would take on the responsibility for leading this man who couldn't see the ground in front of him all the way to Maine.

In the meantime, Methuselah contacted Moses through the "hiking partners wanted" section of the ATC newsletter, and they decided to start out together on March 24. Choo Choo joined them a few days later and the three continued north together. Methuselah followed about six feet behind Choo Choo, who warned him of rocks, roots, and step-ups or -downs. Choo Choo said it was inspiring to walk the trail with Moses and Methuselah: They quoted poetry and Bible verses as they hiked, and had the most positive attitudes of anyone on the AT.

When I first met them, as they came into a shelter in the Smokies, they were laughing and talking like all the other hikers. I didn't even realize Methuselah was blind until he said, "Now Indiana Jean, if I don't recognize you the next time we meet, it's not that I don't remember you, it's just because I can't see. So tell me your name again and I'll know who you are." No big deal, I just can't see...

Methuselah had a wonderfully self-deprecating sense of humor about his handicap. One morning after struggling for a while to get his gear into his backpack, he said, "Well, I just learned another lesson: It doesn't work very well to try to stuff your sleeping bag into your underwear!"

Methuselah gave the rest of us inspiration, courage, and faith that you can do anything at all in this life if you just set your mind to it.

One night I arrived at a shelter to find two men from Indianapolis who had driven out to the Smokies for a weekend of backpacking. It was a wonderful connection with home and made me feel like I wasn't so far removed from the real world after all. We spent the evening sitting by their fire, talking. They had built a huge campfire and were cooking steaks while we thru-hikers cooked our pitifully bland noodles over our little stoves. At least they had the foresight to build their fire away from the shelter so the tantalizing aroma of the steaks wouldn't cause a riot or a sneak attack by the hikers. They had even brought a small saw so they could cut firewood. You can really go first-class with this camping if you're only out for a weekend and don't have to carry your equipment for 2,000 miles.

It was interesting to listen to our conversation through their ears. We sounded like a bunch of truckers with CB handles. "Has Model-T come through yet?" "Hi Slacker." "Hear about the big feed Rat Patrol's puttin' on?" "Hey Cloud Walker, haven't seen you since Fontana." "Anybody seen Shelter Boy recently?" Once again I realized what a strong bond is formed among people who share a common experience. I felt like I was straddling a fence between this strange new wilderness life I was leading and the world of Steve and Paul, guys with real names who live real lives in a real place called home.

I spent one night at Mountain Moma's Kuntry Store and Bunkhouse. It could be another movie setting. Stopping at places like that and meeting the people who lived there was a fascinating part of my journey. My experience would have been just as interesting, in a very different way, if I had walked from Georgia to Maine along rural roads instead of over the mountains. I'm fortunate that both were part of my adventure.

After leaving the Smokies, Mountain Moma's was the first opportunity to resupply. It was 2.5 miles from the trail on a hilly, gravel road. It would have been a long walk, but I was lucky. After walking about half a mile, I stuck out my thumb as a pickup truck went by and rode the rest of the way in the back. Pickups were excellent for hitching rides. I just jumped in and didn't even have to take off my pack.

Eventually we reached a large, dilapidated old former schoolhouse, out in the middle of nowhere—*really* in the middle of nowhere. There didn't seem to be any paved roads nearby. A huge truck trailer sat out front and various vehicles and large objects were everywhere. Inside the schoolhouse was a restaurant/grocery store with a massive tobacco section. I had noticed the stores in the South were half-filled with tobacco products, and more generic cigarette brands than I knew existed.

The food was delicious; very large portions were cooked on a grill behind the cash register. A sign in the restroom exclaimed, "Hey, your moma [*sic*] don't live here, so flush the toilet yourself!" Various other signs were equally folksy. Checks and credit cards weren't taken. It was cash only, although traveler's checks would do.

Out back were two small wooden buildings, about 8-feet-by-8-

feet, built as cabins for thru-hikers. Six bunks were crammed into each structure, and hikers paid a nominal fee to sleep in them. A bathroom with shower stall was at the back of the building, with a line of hikers waiting to bathe. More signs there about taking care of yourself since "your moma ain't with you."

When I asked about laundry facilities, Mountain Moma said, "There's a washer out back under a tarp and clothespins on the line." Sure enough, scattered about in the yard behind the building were four large objects under tarps. One turned out to be a washing machine. Another was a large circular saw; I couldn't tell what the others were, just big old machines. It seemed like a natural part of the ambiance to be using a washing machine in the middle of the yard, about 20 feet from a river, and a clothesline running between two trees. But it wouldn't be easy to do your laundry on a rainy day.

The river was magnificent, with rapids spilling around large rocks which emerged from the water's surface. In the late afternoon I sat on a boulder in the middle of the stream, immersing my weary feet in the cold water as it rushed by. I soaked up the sun and rested.

I asked if there were a phone. "Yep, there's one 'bout a half-mile down the road, after two crossroads. Keep goin' by the river, and you'll come to a ranger station with a pay phone." I walked there (walking a half-mile after a shower and without a backpack was almost like flying) and waited for a couple of other thru-hikers to finish using the phone before calling my sons.

That night, I came up with a plan to rescue our country from the crime problem. Those who commit crimes should be given a choice of going to jail or spending six months in the wilderness, backpacking 2,000 miles. I'm sure many would choose the latter option, thinking they were taking the easier route to freedom. But I am equally certain the recidivism rate among the backpackers would be dramatically lower than among those who had spent their time in jail. I think they would develop some very strong values and respect for what life on this earth is all about. They would end up with a sense of accomplishment and pride that would serve them well for the rest of their lives. And they wouldn't risk having to go back and do it all over again. The trail is a masterful teacher.

The Appalachian Trail

8

A little room in my bed. . .

Hot Springs, North Carolina
270 miles hiked
April 29, 1994

*W*hen arriving in Hot Springs, one of the first things I did was stop by the post office to get my mail. There was a sign on the door: "The post office will be closed tomorrow for Richard Nixon's funeral." I didn't even know he'd died. What a shock to realize how isolated and out of touch I was. News didn't reach the mountaintops.

Hot Springs was a true trail town: The Appalachian Trail ran right down the main street, and everything was within easy walking distance (population 678: every person counts!). Therapeutic mineral springs with a spa built around them gave the town its name. Everywhere I looked were thru-hikers taking a little time off, doing laundry, getting groceries, buying fuel at the hardware store, repairing equipment, eating in a restaurant, resting up. AT travelers added dollars to the local economy, so I could understand why the people in trail towns liked backpackers.

My time in towns such as Hot Springs was minimal; the vast majority was spent just putting in miles, day after day after day, on the trail. But the towns provided a very welcome respite and a distinctive way to do a little sightseeing in the small communities of Appalachia. I gained a unique perspective traveling through on foot.

I stayed at The Inn at Hot Springs, run by a former AT thru-hiker. (It was my second bed in a month.) The Inn was a large white Victorian house filled with antiques. Its bedrooms had quilt-covered four-poster beds, and bathrooms featured antiquated fixtures. Guests signed up for breakfast and dinner on a chalkboard so Elmer, the innkeeper, would know how much to cook. You could find him in the kitchen during the afternoon baking pies or cooking up some gourmet vegetarian specialty. A hiker box on the back porch provided an exchange system where hikers shared things they didn't want with others.

Elmer served the meals family-style. At dinner, with 10 of us around the table, he led the conversation by having us each introduce ourselves and tell what vegetable we'd like to be. That initiated some lively discussion. My broccoli choice was interpreted as a political statement; I guess since George Bush declared his broccoli-aversion, every self-avowed broccoli lover is thought to be a Democrat.

My room had a double bed with dressers, a desk and chair, and a small day bed in an alcove by the windows. I told Elmer that if anyone else needed a place to stay, they could use the day bed in my room. So he said if a female came looking for a room, he'd place her there.

When I saw Sunday (a new thru-hiker friend) and several other backpackers on my way to the grocery store, we stopped to chat. I thought the rooms at Elmer's were all full, but I told Sunday he could stay with me because, I explained, "I've got a little room in my bed." As everyone looked at me rather strangely, I realized I'd meant to say, "I've got a little bed in my room." Oops. We all laughed at my slip of the tongue. Sunday did, in fact, sleep in the little bed. Somehow it didn't seem a bit unusual or uncomfortable to share a room with a man, even one I barely knew, after sleeping next to him in a shelter, no more than a foot apart. I guess it was just part of the thru-hiker code.

I had planned to hike out 24 hours after I arrived in Hot Springs. But about 2 p.m., as I was stuffing everything into my pack, a thunderstorm swept in, complete with lightning and high winds. Flare and I were at Elmer's trying to decide whether to head for the mountains in the storm or wait it out in town. Choo Choo told us his philosophy: There were times when he had to hike in the rain, but he didn't *start out* in a downpour.

By mid-afternoon, with the rain continuing and Elmer's inn full for the night, Flare and I hiked over to a Jesuit hostel in town, available to backpackers for a donation. It had bunk rooms with the usual hiker fare: You put your sleeping bag on a bare mattress and slept 10 to a room.

Several other thru-hikers were there, including Freight Train. I was happy to see him again after nearly three weeks. He had actually shaved, although he looked about the same as with a three-week stubble, and he was playing chess with Hurricane. As I've said, he was an enigma. I needed to learn how to clean my stove so Freight Train sat me down at the picnic table and proceeded to show me all the mysteries of my camp stove. (There really aren't many mysteries, unless—like me—you're mechanically challenged.)

He walked me through the procedure and demonstrated each step. I wondered how to clean my hands, which grew black and sooty during the process. That wasn't a problem for Freight Train; he just wiped them on his pants. (Gee, why didn't I think of that?)

I noticed that Choo Choo was taking pictures of the stove-cleaning session, and it occurred to me that it must have looked like the perfect description of life on the AT: Two people from completely different worlds who probably never would have connected in any part of the rest of their lives, but here were engrossed in a project together. He was teaching. I was learning. We were having fun.

I should tell you about Flare, because she was one of the first female thru-hikers I'd seen since Swan Song. Flare was 24 years old, from Cincinnati, and had a fiancé at home. She came to hike the AT alone, but was not really comfortable being by herself at night, so she tried to connect with other hikers and camp with them. She had spent a week on the trail the year before, in kind of a trial run to see if she could do it. Flare called her fiancé and mother at every opportunity. I found it incredible that she had the courage to hike the trail, with her basic discomfort about being alone.

Flare carried a huge backpack, which included Mace and an emergency flare, the source of her trail name. One of the other hikers tried to help her pare down her equipment in Hot Springs so she could shed some of the weight in her backpack. She was loathe to give any of it up. There must have been a solid core of emotional strength in this young lady that was not readily discernible. What an interesting study it would be to determine where that underlying strength came from in the diverse group of thru-hikers. The young ones amazed me. How did they develop the necessary qualities so early in their lives? It took all of my 51 years to prepare me to undertake a challenge of this magnitude.

For the fourth year, a former thru-hiker, Rat Patrol, and his family provided a "feed" for backpackers. (Doesn't that make us sound like a bunch of animals?) They brought a camper full of provisions to the trail, set up their tents and grills, put the food out, and for three days they cooked hamburgers and hot dogs for anyone who came hiking down the Appalachian Trail. They fed almost 60 backpackers! Word had spread that they would be at Brown Gap on April 23, 24, and 25. Many hikers either speeded up or slowed down in order to arrive during that time period. Eating was a very high priority on the trail, especially when the food was free.

Rat Patrol's wife was due to have a baby so she didn't come with the group. I heard later that she gave birth while he was out in the woods feeding all of us, and I wondered if she resented the decision he made about where to be that weekend. I think thru-hikers have their own set of priorities and they must find mates who either share or put up with them.

How many people would take three days of their time to go sit in the woods cooking food for people they'd never met before and would probably never see again? The people who lived near the AT made me feel very humble. What did I do for others that compared?

The Rat Patrol feed provided another treat: one of my nicest nights camping in the woods so far. Sunday was at the feed, and when I arrived, he said, "Come on, I'll show you a great place I found to tent near a stream."

Soon Flare, White Rabbit, Jabberwocky, Sally and Charlie (no trail names) decided to camp with us so we had quite a community of hikers, all with our tents nestled among the trees surrounding a fire ring. Sunday had built a blazing fire and we stoked it in the evening while we talked and listened to the eerie sound of owls hooting in the nearby trees. Eventually we crawled into our tents, long after dark. Camping with others provided an enticing combination of aloneness and togetherness. I had the privacy of being inside my own tent, the sound and feel of the forest, and the security and warmth of knowing others were nearby. It seemed like the best of everything.

I've never been a creative cook, and that was more obvious on the trail than at home, where I could add variety to my diet at a restaurant or deli. On the AT, I was on my own. Even many of the young men seemed to eat more interesting meals than I. In the mornings, many hikers boiled water for instant oatmeal, coffee, tea, or hot chocolate. Those who didn't want to fire up their stoves ate toaster pastries, breakfast bars, granola, or something else cold. I discovered one easy breakfast. Just put granola and powdered milk in a plastic bag, add water, and presto: cereal with milk. No dishes either. Eating out of a plastic bag would probably offend Miss

Manners, but etiquette was pretty lax on the trail.

Some backpackers waited until they'd hiked one or two hours before eating breakfast. One man put two packets of instant oatmeal in his pocket and when he had hiked an hour or so, he stopped and added cold water, ate the cereal right out of the packet, and moved on. He swore it tasted good with the cold water, but it sounded disgusting to me.

At first I cooked hot cereal in the morning. Later I didn't want to go to the trouble of boiling water so I usually ate two cold Pop Tarts for breakfast. I liked to put my stove away after dinner in the evening and not use it in the morning. Otherwise it seemed to take forever to get everything packed up.

For lunch I usually ate peanut butter on crackers, pita, or English muffins; cheese and crackers; and candy bars or trail mix. (I didn't realize cheese could be kept unrefrigerated, but it was fine, even after being stuffed inside my backpack for a few days.) Lots of snacking on energy bars, candy, nuts, and dried fruits helped add calories—the more calories the better.

Dinner was something boiled with water: pasta or rice dinners, dehydrated food, or macaroni and cheese. Hikers often brought summer sausages, spices, and various other goodies to add variety and make their meals more interesting. I saw some pretty strange combinations go into a pot, but amazingly, it usually smelled really tasty! I stuck to the basics.

I didn't eat many fruits and vegetables on the trail, nor much meat (except for jerky that a friend sent me), but when I reached a town and hit the grocery store or restaurant, I tried to make up for it. We thru-hikers had huge appetites because we burned so many calories, and I ate lots of junk food without guilt. Many hikers carried a container of squeeze margarine and poured it liberally on almost everything they ate to add fat to their diets. Powdered sports drinks and energy bars added extra pep. Vitamin pills eased my conscience. I knew this diet was terribly lacking in some of the basic food groups, but for the few months I was on the trail, the weight/calorie ratio took precedence over everything else.

On the trail I recognized more clearly than ever before that the function of food is to fuel the body. I think the role of food in our society has gotten inflated way out of proportion to its basic purpose. Much of what we eat and when we eat and why we eat has nothing to do with our body's needs. But once again, the trail took us right to the bottom line: Food is the body's energy source. You wanna hike, you gotta eat.

I had become aware of a problem that could arise when traveling with others. Poet, Suds, and I had connected in the late afternoon one day and were hiking near one another. We stopped for water and some conversation and then they moved on ahead. None of us knew where we would spend the night. We were just looking for a place to pitch a tent.

After walking farther than I wanted to without finding a place to stop, I happened to see a clearing through a stand of rhododendron. It was tucked away off the trail, a cozy little space near a waterfall with water flowing by on both sides. I slipped through the trees and pitched my tent, fetched water, took a sponge bath, hung my food, and cooked my dinner. I loved being by myself in a snug spot just big enough for one tent, especially when there was water nearby. I could sponge off and change clothes at the water's edge without worrying about being seen, and I had a satisfying sense of self-competency, knowing I had the right equipment and sufficient knowledge to take care of myself in the forest. I felt peaceful and content as I fell asleep that night to the soft sound of the nearby waterfall.

After 15 minutes of hiking the following morning, I encountered Poet and Suds starting off from where they'd spent the night at a camping spot up ahead. It was off the trail a short distance, and Sally and Charlie had camped there also. Under the assumption I was not far behind them the evening before, Poet had stayed out by the trail to wait for me so I wouldn't miss the turnoff to the campsite. Pretty soon, Charlie relieved him and he waited for me by the trail. Eventually, they all went back to their campsite after forming an arrow on the path with some little white stones so I wouldn't miss the turnoff. Here I was camped about a quarter-mile back, not even knowing they were expecting me to arrive. When I found out they'd gone to all that trouble, I felt very bad. On the trail as in life, it's important to communicate carefully so you're not off doing your own thing when someone has different expectations for you.

For the next five days, I would try to average about fourteen miles a day to reach Erwin, Tennessee. From there I would find a way to the airport in Johnson City and fly to Los Angeles for my son Brad's graduation from the University of Southern California. I couldn't miss this big event in his life, so had made all the arrangements for the trip before leaving home. The timing was working out perfectly; after hiking 340 miles, I would arrive in Erwin exactly when I thought I would. Going out into the woods with a schedule to meet seemed like a strange juxtaposition of my "real" life and this new existence, but it was necessary for the first leg of the journey.

As the date for the graduation trip drew near, I was more and more eager to see my family and spend a few days away from the trail. During the times when my whole body was aching and exhausted, or I was dripping with sweat or huddled up against the cold, or I was going up a long incline or down a steep decline, I held onto the thought that I would have a respite soon. And I would think, "I can hold out until then."

The Appalachian Trail

9

My scary night was over

Erwin, Tennessee
338 miles hiked
May 3, 1994

*S*ome of the hikers who had left Hot Springs during the thunderstorm instead of waiting until the next day, as Flare and I had, faced a treacherous time hiking through the mountains with lightning flashing very close all around them. There were a few scary incidents, with tree limbs falling and near-misses, although no one was actually struck. It made me aware that I needed to be careful in storms. Trees, mountains, and lightning were a dangerous combination.

On a sad note, Methuselah left the trail in Hot Springs to have arthroscopic surgery on his knee. He was such a kind and gentle soul that I would miss knowing he was on the trail. But Methuselah had left an impression on my heart that would be with me as I continued north toward Maine. When I came to a particularly difficult part of the trail, all I had to do was remember that 75-year-old blind man who hiked 270 miles of very rugged terrain through the mountains, and the trail kind of smoothed out ahead of me.

Friends often worried that I would encounter threatening people or animals on the Appalachian Trail. I had no frightening incidents, though, until one night when I was tenting all alone near the top of a mountain in a small clearing, surrounded by forest. Suddenly in the middle of the night I was awakened by the sound of animals outside my tent. I could tell they were close, they were moving around, and from the sound of their heavy breathing, they were large. I was terrified. My heart began pumping so loudly, it filled my whole chest cavity and resonated in my ears. I lay completely still, not wanting to make a sound, praying they wouldn't know I was there if they couldn't hear me. My mind went over the list of possible animals that size. I figured it had to be bears or wild boars, but they sounded too big to be boars. It had to be bears.

I had hung my food in a tree about 50 yards from my tent and it sounded like they were headed in that direction. I was relieved that I had followed the advice of other hikers and had gone to the trouble of hanging my food instead of keeping it inside my tent. If they snagged my food, the next morning I'd have to go back to a road I had passed about a mile earlier and hitch into a town to resupply. Just as I started to relax slightly, thinking worse things could happen, I realized they were coming back. They seemed to surround my tent. One posted itself just a few feet away from my head and stayed there, breathing loudly. My earlier terror increased.

I had two thoughts in my mind: "Oh no, I forgot about the two Fig Newtons in my waist pack!" And, "Dear God, I don't want to die being mauled by bears." Soundlessly, I pulled my little Swiss Army knife out of my waist pack and opened it. My only plan was that if they came in one side of the tent, I'd try to slice open the other end and get out. I lay there without moving a muscle, eyes wide open, staring, listening, praying.

They stayed for at least an hour, one near my tent, the others moving about, snapping tree branches and twigs. What were they doing? Why were they staying such a long time? When were they going to make their attack? And what was I doing all by myself in the middle of a woods inside a tiny tent with no protection?

Suddenly, it began to thunder, lightning, and pour. I had never in my life been so glad to have a thunderstorm arrive. I figured the storm would drive the animals away and, sure enough, I was no longer able to hear them. An hour of absolute terror had exhausted me, and I soon fell asleep.

At 6:30 the next morning, I awoke feeling instant relief that my scary night was over. But within moments I realized I could *still* hear the heavy breathing outside my tent! I'd heard of people being trapped in shelters—or even in a privy—in the Smokies all day by bears, and I reluctantly contemplated the thought of spending the day in my tent until someone came along to help.

I was a little braver in the daylight, however, so I carefully unzipped a small section of my tent, peered out from under my rain fly, and saw a huge cow calmly staring at me, chewing her cud! She didn't look the least bit threatening. I just lay there shaking my head at my own idiocy. And then I fell back asleep for an hour. When I awoke again, she was gone, but there was a fresh cow pie near my tent.

I saw four more cows nearby when I began hiking and immediately started crying, perhaps as a release from the bottled-up terror of the night before. I had no idea the trail on the top of that mountain was near a pasture with a broken-down fence in between. Does it seem as if our worst fears often turn out to be groundless? That day I intended to travel as far as possible so I'd have a short day going into Erwin. But after hiking 11 miles, I came in the late afternoon to a camping area on the bank of a river with rapids and mini-waterfalls. There were good trees for hanging food and level areas to tent, right at the water's edge.

Sunday was there, with his tent set up and a clothesline strung between two trees. I was so happy to see him! He'd spent the day resting, reading, and writing, which he does every Sunday (get it?). Tortoise and Hare had stopped to cook their dinner and were planning to hike a few more miles before putting up for the night. I prepared dinner and intended to do the same, but after my encounter with the terrorist cows, I was nervous about being by myself that night. (I guess even though you find your fears ungrounded, sometimes a residue of anxiety lingers on.)

I wasn't eager to hike on, but felt I should. Why did I always push myself, sometimes for no discernible reason? Eventually, though, I let Sunday, Tortoise, and Hare convince me to give myself a break and stay there for the night.

I'm so glad I did. It was a marvelous evening. I had time to relax and calm down from my night of panic, and I enjoyed being with Sunday. He built a fire and we talked into the evening as darkness fell and the blazing flames and sparks turned into red, glowing embers. Sunday boiled water and we each drank a cup of tea. The night was clear and still, the silence broken only by the quiet crackling of the fire and our low voices. The stream, just a few feet away, added its gentle, lapping sound. When we put out the fire and said good night, I crawled into my tent feeling as if the evening had massaged all the tension out of my body and mind.

Sunday was in his 40s, retired from the Army, with a wife and children at home. He seemed like such an outdoor expert, with all the skills needed to hike the trail. He was comfortable with his equipment, could repair anything that broke or rig some sort of replacement, could build a fire better than anyone else, and made backpacking seem easy. He got an early start in the morning and seemed to be taking his time but covered many miles in a day. He was the kind of person who made me wonder how I ever thought I could hike the Appalachian Trail by myself. He knew how to backpack; I was just out there floundering around, trusting that my desire would carry me through. Since I was taking several days off to attend Brad's graduation, I knew I probably wouldn't see Sunday again, but he seemed like a thru-hiker who would make it all the way to Maine. I planned to watch for his entries in the trail registers.

Since leaving the Great Smoky Mountains National Park more than a week before, I was so relieved to be out of those crowded shelters that I had tented every night. Most evenings I camped by myself, and that provided a type of serenity that was hard to create at home. It was a very different kind of "aloneness" in a forest, high on a mountainside, near a waterfall. I remembered my nights of waking up in a cold sweat at home when making the decision to hike the AT, visualizing exactly the nights I was now experiencing: tenting completely alone in the pitch-black of the night with the sounds of the woods right outside my safe little cocoon. It had seemed scary in my dreams; in reality it was peaceful and serene. It was a restoring and recuperating time, a time to rebuild my confidence, which was often flagging as I trudged those last few miles of the day through a fog of weariness, throbbing toes, and aching knees. It was a time of satisfaction that I had made it through another 24 hours and optimism that tomorrow the terrain would be more level. (It never was, but the optimism remained.) Yes, the ground was hard, it was sometimes cold, and there were the occasional animals scurrying about, but the nights weren't scary. That giant nature preserve in the mountains bestowed the best of God's creation, not the worst.

The long, steep descent into Erwin convinced me I would have to buy a larger pair of boots. My feet had expanded, and my toes were being constantly crushed against the front of my boots, causing numbness and almost constant pain. I hoped I could find an outfitters' store in Los Angeles.

In Erwin I stayed at Haven Farm, a hiker hostel run by former thru-hiker Mookie. I had met Mookie in Indianapolis, where he was working at a sporting goods store. He was one of my sources of information about equipment for my journey. After thru-hiking in 1992, Mookie wanted to keep the trail in his life. So he had recently moved to Erwin where he and a friend turned their home near the trail into a stopover for backpackers. There was a communal feel: They didn't charge a fee, but asked hikers to help with the daily chores, such as gardening or building a privy. For meals, everyone pitched in either money or food, and someone always volunteered to cook. When I was there, thru-hiker traffic was at its height and people were sleeping everywhere: in the barn, in tents, on the living-room floor. Mookie never knew how many hikers would arrive each day or how long they would stay, but somehow it always worked out.

Places along the trail like Haven Farm were often a test of resolve for the younger thru-hikers. Some of them "got stuck" and stayed for several days, partying and relaxing. They found it hard to move back to the task of the trail. It was not a temptation for me, but I could remember back to my college days facing a similar decision: whether to hit the books or hang out with friends. For some, it required the same willpower and commitment to decide to hit the trail again instead of chilling out with hiker buddies.

Johnson City, Tennessee, was a metropolis compared to the small towns near the AT. I shared a room at a motel with Flare and Camp Pro, a young man from Kansas. White Rabbit and Jabberwocky, a married couple in their late 20s, were next door. It was a far cry from my life in the woods for the previous five weeks, and the beginning of my transition to the culture shock that awaited me when I reached LA.

Getting there was another of those "I can't believe I'm doing this" experiences. Since Flare, Camp Pro, White Rabbit, Jabberwocky, and I all wanted to go to Johnson City, about 20 miles from Erwin, we decided to see if we could find a shuttle service. White Rabbit made a few calls from Haven Farm and came up with someone who said he would take us for a very reasonable fee.

White Rabbit told the driver how to find us at Haven Farm (it was several miles out of town, on a rather obscure mountain road), and we waited for him to arrive. We expected to see a van pull up, but soon we saw a very old, decrepit, full-sized school bus, painted blue, bouncing down the gravel road toward us. The trouble was, the road to the farm was very narrow and it eventually just ended with no place to turn around. So we had a fat bus trying to turn around on a thin road with a stream on one side and a fence on the other. It took about 20 minutes and four people shouting instructions, but eventually the bus was headed in the right direction. The driver was unflappable, even when the front end of the bus hung way out over the water midway through the ordeal.

We all piled in and set off down the road. Just the five of us and our backpacks, riding down the highway with a driver wearing a reggae tam, with hair down to the middle of his back, and his dog. He planned to put a hot tub in the back of the bus and rent it out for parties. Somehow it seemed par for the course to arrive in the city by exiting a big blue bus carrying a backpack and hiking stick into the parking lot of a Ryan's Family Restaurant.

We headed next door to the motel, where we drew numbers for who would take the first shower. Then we went to the restaurant, where we took full advantage of its all-you-can-eat buffet. I had never been at a table with five people who ate so much food for lunch. The franchise would go broke if all the customers ate like thru-hikers.

I wanted to do my laundry, and the waitress told me the city bus stopped outside the restaurant every half-hour. So I crammed my little six-month supply of clothes into my sleeping bag stuff sack and hopped onto a city bus. The bus route took me right by a laundromat, where I got off, washed my clothes, and took the return bus, back at the motel in about an hour and a half. It was an interesting challenge doing chores in a strange city with no means of transportation.

The next task was finding a place to leave my backpack, hiking stick, and boots while I was in California. (I rented a locker in the airport.) I had mailed clothes to Mookie for the graduation trip, and I would mail them back home when I returned. The logistics of this little side trip made me glad I was an organizer.

I was eager to see my family in Los Angeles and share in the thrill of Brad's graduation. It would give me a break from the trail and a chance to rest my body after five weeks of pushing my physical limits almost daily. The timing seemed perfect. I remembered hearing that when you take a new job, it's a good idea to schedule a few days off after the first five or six weeks to step outside the experience and bring it all together in your mind. That timing was falling into place for me, and I expected the days away from the trail would serve that same purpose.

10

A painful but important week

Damascus, Virginia
452 miles hiked
May 15, 1994

I sat in the local Dairy King in Damascus listening to country music on the jukebox and reading letters from my family and friends. Upon arriving at the post office and telling them my name, they had said, "Thank goodness you've arrived! Your mail is taking up a lot of space!" I received 40 letters plus several packages and it was wonderful to read them. I wanted to respond personally to each person who took the time to write, but there was no way I could do that. I did compose letters in my mind and wished there were a way to shoot them out over the airwaves. Wouldn't mental telepathy be a time-saver?

An unexpected bonus of my odyssey was all that I was learning about my friends and relatives from their letters: who their favorite poets were, what scholars inspired them, where they spent their honeymoon, their dreams and aspirations—things I might have never discovered in years of conversation! They added so much to my journey, and I was humbled by their interest, support, and sharing.

Brad's graduation at USC was impressive, as George Lucas and Steven Spielberg received honorary doctorates and headlined the speakers. It was Greg's first trip to California, so we did the obligatory touring of Rodeo Drive, Beverly Hills, and other well-known sites. (What a shock it was after being out in the wilderness for five weeks to find myself mired in long lines of traffic every time we got into the car.) Sharing the time with my mother and my former husband Dave made it very special. On the important occasions in our sons' lives, I am always grateful that Dave and I have "the world's friendliest divorce," as our friends say.

My knees were so painful all weekend that the guys had to help me out of the car. My feet were so swollen I couldn't wear the shoes

I had brought. I couldn't get out of a chair without using my arms to push myself up. I walked slowly and painfully, but could only sit for short periods before my legs started to cramp. I was grateful not to be carrying 40 pounds up mountains, but my body seemed to be protesting the return to more normal activities. The guys, expecting me to be in the best physical shape of my life, asked, "How can you hike up those mountains when you can hardly walk up the stairs?" I had no answer. And I knew that five more months of physical abuse awaited me on the AT.

Taking those steps onto the plane at the LA airport to return to the Appalachian Trail was more difficult than ascending the steepest mountain I had encountered so far. I clung to my family members as if I'd never see them again. I knew the rest of them would return to their normal lives, while I was going back to face five months in the wilderness. Why? Didn't it make more sense to just stay in civilization, my natural habitat? But I'd set myself a challenge and I couldn't fold up my tent and go home. If I could just get through that first wave of loneliness, I knew I'd feel better.

Reentry to the trail was difficult. My first three days back I was as lonely and empty as I had ever been in my life, and I wanted to be back in the warm embrace of my family. I saw no other thru-hikers for the first two days and I felt like the last person on the trail. I cried often while hiking and kept trying to answer that ever-present question that nagged at me constantly: "Why am I doing this?" My week of introspection provided some new answers which seemed to be anchoring this quest of mine.

Brad's graduation felt like the official end of an era in my life, my "mom" years. Perhaps the timing of this odyssey was my way of proving to myself that there is life after the parenting years, but that I needed to broaden my own horizons and seek experiences that I could do by myself. I knew the boys (young men) couldn't remain the focus of my life; they had flown out of my nest and were now building their own.

One of the most painful passages for parents is that time when, gradually, the kids are moving out and becoming independent. Our role is to prepare them for that and then let them go, but oh, it sure hurts when it happens! And it seems like the only healthy way to deal with it is to look around and ask, "Well, now what am I going to do with the rest of my life?" If this was my way of addressing that question, I thought I could have found an easier answer! No, I didn't imagine I would spend the rest of my life hiking on wilderness trails, but I did realize there would be many grand and glorious adventures awaiting, if I would just go seek them out.

In exploring reasons for hiking the AT, I recognized that my motivations were very different from those of most of my fellow thru-hikers. I often realized that I was the true visitor in the woods. For many others, this was the culmination of a lifelong interest in backpacking or an extension of their interest. They were in their comfort zone.

Many of the men had military careers or were involved in scouting and thus were comfortable with all the equipment and the spartan lifestyle. For them, taking a sabbatical in the woods was a life's dream. Even the young people in their 20s had spent time backpacking and seemed at home in the wilderness. As one of them said to me, "I'm doing this just because I love to hike!"

Then there was me. Except for a couple of brief experiences, I had never done any of this before. (Never wanted to.) I sought the adventure because it was a complete contrast to my suburban lifestyle. One of my greatest satisfactions was discovering I could take care of myself in a foreign environment. But since I was so far outside the norm, I realized that my perceptions were probably very different from those of my peers, who seemed so at ease on the trail. Was it as hard for them? It didn't appear to be, but perhaps my anxieties and discomfort weren't apparent to them, either.

Later that week I was coaxed out of my funk by the stunning sight of a vast field covered with tiny white flowers, coddled in their green leaf-hands, luminous and lovely in the late afternoon sunlight. I could feel my loneliness and depression lifting. How could I be sad when surrounded by such beauty? I tried to give myself over to the visual stimulation of the trees, plants, flowers, and patches of sky or cloud that could be seen at each glance in every direction.

The scenery gradually worked its magic on me. I crossed several balds (round, grassy mountaintops devoid of trees) where the view was unobstructed for miles. If I crossed a bald on a gorgeous day, the hike was smooth and fluid and the commanding vantage point made me feel like I had leverage on all my problems, indeed on all the world.

If it was pouring, with gale-force winds and a mist that allowed just 30 feet of visibility, I could barely stand up. It became a pitched battle against the wind. Just when I was leaning into the blast with all my strength to stay upright, it would suddenly let up and I would almost fall over. During the worst gusts, I just planted my stick, braced myself, and hung on. I felt like a warrior fighting the wrath of a mighty adversary. I don't know which was greater—the exhilaration or the relief—when I finally reached a protected area and paused briefly to breathe in big gulps of air, realizing I had survived another of the trail's challenges before moving on to face the next.

One day I encountered a group of fourth-graders on Watauga Dam near Hampton, Tennessee. Several classes of students, along with their teachers and chaperones, approached me as I was crossing the dam. They could tell I wasn't just out for a day's hike, so the children gathered around and started quizzing me about where I'd been and how far I was going. When I told them, they clustered closer and started firing questions furiously, so we had a geography, history, wilderness, and fitness lesson right there on the dam. Most of them knew little about the AT.

I hiked with them for a short distance while the trail followed the road, feeling like the Pied Piper, and then I ducked back into the woods as it went up the side of the mountain. They waved and shouted goodbye, and I gained a sense of how exciting it must have been for them to meet someone who was traveling by foot from Georgia to Maine. I hoped perhaps a few of the children were inspired to plan an eventual adventure of their own.

At the annual Trail Days celebration in Damascus, I was in a parade! With a population of 1,200, Damascus was "the friendliest town on the trail," according to *The Thru-hiker's Handbook*. Each year they planned a five-day festival during May when most thru-hikers are in the area.

Many hikers hitched forward or back from the trail to be in Damascus during Trail Days. There were tents everywhere. The Saturday parade featured local floats and a large contingency of thru-hikers. It was a real reunion and an opportunity to see hikers I hadn't seen for weeks. I was surprised at how many people I knew. It was hard to decide who to cheer for in the Twinkie-eating contest because I knew three of the four contestants and wanted to support them all. The three young men in their early 20s were beaten by a quiet thru-hiker about 40 years old, who sat there and calmly ate 23 Twinkies in an even, rhythmic manner while the young men blustered, boasted, and competed with each other. They provided the entertainment; he got the job done.

Remember the Goatherders (Pigeon, Ox, Frenchy, and Phishstick) with their plastic inflatable goat? Well, somebody kidnapped their goat back in Tennessee. At the shelters along the trail, the kidnappers left ransom notes: "If you don't do such and such, the next time you see your goat, he'll be goat jerky. . ." The Herders appointed Ox as the sheriff, and he had been leaving notes back telling the kidnappers what would happen to *them* if they didn't return the goat.

The kidnappers' plan was to have the goat reappear in the Trail Days duck race, a charity event in which little plastic ducks with numbers float down the river. They wanted to put a number on the goat and have him float down with the ducks.

But the Herders were too sharp for them. They recaptured their goat several days before the big event, but pretended they still didn't know where it was. They kept expressing more and more frustration at wanting their goat back. Then, during the parade, in the middle of the route, Frenchy quietly sneaked the goat into the procession. Pigeon suddenly hoisted it aloft as all the hikers in the parade cheered its triumphant return: "The goat is back! The goat is back!"

It was really quite a moment. One of the highlights of the journey, I'd have to say. (Sometime later that night, after several hours of partying, the goatnappers were put on trial and sentenced to various punishments which will remain undocumented here.)

Although many of the young men on the trail liked to party and have a good time, they were serious about thru-hiking and didn't take the experience for granted. They treated the wilderness and each other with respect. I don't know what careers they will pursue, but I feel certain they will be environmentalists and achievers. I am happy knowing they are among the leaders of the future.

It had been a painful but important week for me as I readjusted to life on the AT. Trail Days in Damascus came along at just the right time so I could reconnect briefly with friends and enjoy the companionship that was becoming an important part of my journey.

I was in my fourth state, heading north with a full backpack and a positive mindset. My new, larger pair of boots couldn't prevent the aching caused by mile upon mile of hiking, but they gave my toes more room and took away that source of pain. I felt good about the trail, and I knew that the best and the worst were yet to come.

During the rough times following my trip to Los Angeles, I

found myself often talking to the spirit of my dad. I could feel him whispering words of encouragement into my ear. I knew there would be time ahead for daily conversations with him to ask all those unanswerable questions. Perhaps he would find a way to answer some of them.

11

Pepperoni up ahead

Atkins, Virginia,
528 miles hiked
May 21, 1994

*T*he devastation from Hurricane Hugo was still evident south of Atkins: hundreds of trees twisted, broken, or ripped up by the roots. Going through an area like that was a graphic reminder of the time it takes for a forest to restore itself after a natural disaster. But it also pointed out how many trees there are in the mountains. In spite of the hundreds felled by the storm, there were thousands upon thousands more.

Immediately north of the hurricane devastation, another area had been decimated by two recent ice storms. Volunteers from local hiking clubs had spent untold hours clearing the "blow downs" from the path. I talked with a couple of the maintainers. They said the AT was impassable in many places after the storms.

They hadn't finished clearing the trees yet, which meant I had to climb over, under, and around huge trunks and branches that blocked the path. That was no easy task with a backpack, especially where the mountain went straight up on one side of the trail and straight down on the other. Clambering over huge trees every few yards also sapped energy and inflicted scrapes and bruises. Each week that went by, though, the volunteers got more limbs cut and cleared. The earlier thru-hikers had a harder time going through the storm section.

We were all grateful to those volunteers who spent their weekends maintaining the AT. On a regular basis, they also did upkeep on the blazes, signs, and shelters. This didn't give the trail a manicured look, though. In fact, there were restrictions on what they could do in certain areas. Sometimes they couldn't even use power tools or put up new signs. In the most remote sections, it still seemed as if no man or woman had ever set foot in that part of the wilderness.

As I was trudging along the trail one day, intent on getting to a scenic spot I knew was just ahead, I happened to notice a chain of black insects winding their way across the trail. There were at least 20 of them all linked together, somehow making slow forward progress as a unit. I stopped to watch them for a few seconds and then went on.

Later that day, I mentioned the phenomenon to a couple of other hikers and they had also noticed it. We all agreed that we wished we had taken the time to just sit down right there on the trail and watch those insects to see where they were going and examine how they were able to move, all hooked together like that. Many of us felt so driven by the time pressure to reach Mt. Katahdin by mid-October that we passed up opportunities to just sit in the woods and enjoy nature's oddities.

I spent my coldest night to date on the trail in a shelter near Mt. Rogers, at 5,729 feet the highest mountain in Virginia. I'd been advised not to send home my winter gear until after Mt. Rogers. I'm glad I didn't. The shelter had an upper level, where I slept along with about eight other hikers, including trail maintainers who were out for a few days. Even wearing my heavy pants, jacket, hat, and gloves inside my sleeping bag, and with people on both sides of me, I was freezing. I would have been warmer in my tent, but the ground wasn't level and the wind was blowing so hard that I wasn't sure I could set it up.

The next morning as I hiked on, I came to a level area protected by a grove of trees partway down the mountain, and I knew I would have been much warmer there in my tent. But when you don't know what lies ahead, you can't always make the right decisions. If I were to go back and hike the trail again, I could make better choices. The same could be said of life, I guess.

One area in which I think I made good choices was in selecting gear and equipment for my thru-hike. As I've mentioned, keeping weight to a minimum was essential, and everything I carried reflected that. Sleeping equipment included my tent, ground cover, sleeping pad, and sleeping bag, all together weighing close to nine pounds. Water supplies were a water bag, filter, two plastic bottles, and some iodine tablets. My kitchen comprised a stove and fuel bottle, pan, cup, plastic bowl, spoon, matches, and bag for my food. My "medicine chest" included a few ointments, pills, bandaids, and moleskin. Also, a toothbrush, toothpaste, all-purpose environmentally friendly soap, rubbing alcohol, baby powder, lotion, toilet paper, tissues, and a small comb. An emergency kit included duct tape, safety pins, needle and thread, extra batteries, and a compass. In the clothing category, I carried three T-shirts and shorts, underwear, and several bandannas, as well as three pairs of thick socks and liners for hiking, and one pair for evening and town wear. A pair of sandals sufficed for evenings, towns and wading through rivers. For warmth, I had a waterproof jacket and pants, long underwear, fleece jacket, hat, and gloves. Miscellaneous equipment included a rain cover for my backpack, extra plastic bags, rope, candle, flashlight, netting for bug protection, pens, paper for writing letters and for journaling, a few stamps, postcards, and envelopes.

In my small waist pack, I carried my camera, reading glasses and sunglasses, maps, data book, handbook, snacks, ibuprofen, Swiss Army knife, money, credit card, calling card, address book, identification, and insect repellent. All laid out together it probably seemed like a pitifully small cache, but the weight added up and I had everything I needed. Waiting for me at each mail drop was a box with extra supplies and food.

A weight dilemma for me was always how much food to carry. More than four or five days of food made for a heavy backpack, but taking less food meant going off the trail more often to resupply. If I couldn't get a ride, it was more miles to walk. Some of the roads were not heavily traveled, so the opportunities for hitchhiking were few.

For instance, I left Damascus with just four days worth of food instead of six, which would have lasted until Atkins. When that ran out, I had to go into Troutdale, a town 2.5 miles from the trail, to a grocery store. No one picked me up and I walked all the way along a hot, blacktop road. By the time I arrived in the town, I had made up my mind I wouldn't leave until I found a ride back to the trailhead.

Troutdale had one grocery store and a restaurant. After buying food, I ate a quick lunch and found a truck driver in the restaurant who agreed to give me a ride back to the trail. He was on his way to pick up a load of manure. Thank goodness I found him on the way *to* his pickup! That little side trip took nearly three hours and added 2.5 road-miles to my feet that day. Weight vs. miles—the hikers' dilemma.

Another note about the Troutdale area: I saw Steady Eddy and the Yeti, two really nice men in their early 20s, the next day. They had also tried unsuccessfully to hitch into town. Steady Eddy said some of the drivers even made obscene gestures at him. He discovered in a discussion at the grocery store that there was a proposal to put a major highway near Troutdale. Area residents favored the plan because it would bring dollars into the local economy. But the Appalachian Trail Conference evidently wanted more research completed to determine the possible negative effect on the trail and surrounding environment. Some of the locals didn't like hikers because they assumed we were all supporting the ATC stance. I had discovered that even on the trail, you couldn't get away from politics.

I lost my carabiner. I figured it would happen. One night, when I was tenting all alone, I tied my rope around my carabiner as usual and tossed it up over a branch. That time when it went up, it didn't come back down. It had gotten stuck in a crevice between two branches and no amount of tugging or jostling the rope would get it unstuck. Perhaps Strider or Denver Dan could have figured out a way to climb up into that tree, but not me. I had to leave it there and cut my rope as far up as I could reach. So now I had a shorter rope and no carabiner. In the future I would have to use a rock. Another trail challenge: learning to tie my rope around a rock so it wouldn't come off when I threw it up in the air.

A few days later, I had just crossed a road at the top of Grayson Highlands and was headed out across a bald when a car with two men inside pulled up and stopped. One of them leaned out the window and yelled at me, "How far you going?" When I replied I was headed for Maine, both men jumped out of the car and rushed over to talk. They were from a nearby town, Abingdon. One was a minister and the other was one of his parishioners. They asked a number of questions about my journey, and then the minister asked if he could take my picture with the parishioner before they let me go on my way. I couldn't imagine what they were going to do with it, but I realized that a number of people in states along the AT were going to have pictures of a grimy Indiana Jean in their albums. And once again I realized that thru-hikers were considered an oddity and provided a tale to be told with great relish at the dinner table.

I discovered that Domino's delivers, even in the mountains! I had stayed in a shelter with several other hikers one night, and in the morning they talked about stopping 12 miles up the trail at the Mt. Rogers National Recreation Area Headquarters. The trail went right by the headquarters, and our handbook reported there was a pay phone where you could order pizza. That sounded pretty good to everyone and really spurred us on. It's amazing how much more quickly you can hike when you know there's pepperoni up ahead.

Mid-morning, I was sitting by the trail resting and eating a snack when Wood Rat came by. He wouldn't have any money until his next mail drop, so he wasn't planning to stop for pizza. I offered to split one with him and pick up the tab. He continued with renewed energy and a smile on his face, anticipating a full stomach by bedtime that night.

The headquarters had a recently remodeled visitor center with a gift shop and a room with chairs and padded stools for relaxing and reading. Additional amenities were a restroom and pop machine, and thru-hikers were usually allowed to stay overnight on the cement porch under an overhang.

I decided to pitch my tent nearby instead, since it would be softer sleeping on the grass. Feather, a tiny thru-hiker in her 20s, had recently confided that it had become uncomfortable to sleep in the shelters, because she had gotten so thin she didn't have any padding left on her bones. I knew what she meant. I never thought the ground would seem soft, but compared to wood floors or cement, it did.

We had a great time at the headquarters. Several hikers were already there when I arrived and more kept coming throughout the late afternoon and evening: Hulagan, CC and the Mule, Del Doc, Brrr, Feather, A Harmony of Spheres, Wood Rat, the Goatherders, Babbles, Porta Can Dan, Moses, Steady Eddy, Tired Dogs and more. Domino's made at least six deliveries. About the time a delivery car would arrive with pizza, someone else would be placing another order.

Everyone decided to stay overnight instead of hiking on, so about 16 of us slept there. Tents were scattered everywhere and a number of hikers slept side by side on the cement. The staff was very nice; they were used to thru-hikers and we purchased a few snacks and supplies in addition to the pizza, so perhaps the income offset the hassle.

People have asked me whether I ever got discouraged and wanted to quit hiking the trail. Oh yes! Sometimes I wanted to quit seven days a week. Although I had settled back into the trail routine since returning from California, the life of a thru-hiker hadn't gotten any easier. It seemed amazing to me that, no matter how far I decided to hike in a day, the last mile always seemed like one mile farther than I wanted to go. By late afternoon when my knees were hurting incessantly and I was plodding up seemingly endless mountains, only to see another grind still to come, I often wondered why I was putting myself through this. But no matter how uncomfortable I was or how discouraged I felt, I couldn't go home. I wasn't finished yet. I still had 10 more states to cross.

12

Angels of mercy

Pearisburg, Virginia
614 miles hiked
May 28, 1994

I had been on the Appalachian Trail for two months. It was a long time to backpack almost every day, all day. I was beginning to reach a comfort level, both physically and mentally, that pleased me.

If I were to reach Mt. Katahdin in the six months I had planned, then one-third of my time in the wilderness was gone. I hadn't hiked a third of the 2,155 miles yet, but that was to be expected. Thru-hikers usually averaged more miles daily from northern Virginia to New Hampshire because the terrain wasn't as steep and rugged. So far there hadn't been much level ground, so I was looking forward to some of that. However, even that was relative. I would still be in the mountains.

For the past several days, I had averaged 14 miles, with my longest day 16. I found that my feet got very tired taking so many steps. I hoped they would become accustomed to it. I massaged them every night with rubbing alcohol and then sprinkled them with baby powder. I wasn't sure why; somebody told me to do it and it felt good, so I did. I had read that a typical thru-hiker takes five million steps getting from Springer Mountain to Mt. Katahdin. I wondered how many years it took most people to put five million steps on the soles of their feet.

I was beginning to feel more at one with the woods, to enjoy each moment more instead of wondering how far it was to the next landmark or anticipating the next town stop. I thought how exhilarating it was to be spending every day in the middle of nature, with spring at its height. One day I made up a little song as I hiked along: "Life is. . .making the best of it; life is. . .making the most of it. Life is. . .loving every minute of the day." (It loses a lot without the tune). I sang it over and over, because I was feeling exuberant and enjoying every single moment. And because, with my backpack on, I couldn't skip. Usually I skip when I'm happy.

Still, I needed to pretend sometimes that I was just out for a day hike instead of feeling the burden of the whole journey so I wouldn't forget to feel the wonder and joy of the natural world. I should have stopped several times each day, just to breathe deeply and let the fresh mountain air seep into my pores and settle over my eyelids. I didn't always do it, but I should have.

Some updates: I had met many more women on the trail, but I could still count the solo female hikers on two hands. Most females were traveling with another woman or were part of a couple, and the overall number was still disproportionately small. I had heard that about 20 percent of thru-hikers were female and that matched what I had seen. Whenever I thought it odd that I was the only woman around, I'd remember, "Well, if there are four men and me, I'm the 20 percent!"

I last saw Freight Train in Hot Springs. He and Hurricane were planning to hop a train into Asheville where Freight Train would try to get some food stamps. Hurricane had never hopped a train, but I knew Freight Train was a good teacher. I hoped I would see him again.

Strider and I reconnected in Damascus and spent time together there. Then he left the trail for a week to counsel at a church camp. He hiked faster than I, so I figured he would probably catch up and pass me by again.

When last seen, Denver Dan was riding a horse out of the Smokies to Mountain Moma's and the horse's owner was carrying his backpack. (Dan can charm a person right off his horse!) He was having a serious knee problem and I heard he went to a clinic in Asheville for medical attention. He sent a message to me with Wrong Way that he would continue on the trail if at all possible.

The trail was showing its many faces and the variety provided new surprises each day. I had walked through rolling meadows with soft grasses and wildflowers in the valleys of Virginia. I often crossed gated pastures with herds of cattle where I found myself face to face with a cow. If it didn't move aside, I did. I had to watch where I stepped, though. The trail crossed the barbed wire fences surrounding the pastures over stiles—triangular wooden structures with steps. Some days I climbed over 10 or more stiles. The cows gazed at me with complete lack of concern and weren't the least bit threatening. However, CC said that he and the Mule had two scary incidents in pastures when a bull started chasing the Mule and ended up chasing CC too. He made it to a fence with little time to spare. Evidently bulls don't like dogs crossing their territories.

The trail crossed water frequently, sometimes several times a day. When we were lucky, bridges took us across the rivers; often we hopped across creeks or streams on the rocks. My hiking stick helped me keep my balance so I didn't fall in.

One day I walked next to a stream with rapids and waterfalls nearly all day long. The trail crossed back and forth over it. In places there were sheer cliffs shooting up from the water's edge. Elsewhere a gradual, sandy entry to the water allowed me to wet my bandanna in the cool stream and sponge off my neck and arms. It was one of the most refreshing days I had spent on the trail. Water has rejuvenating powers whether you're drinking it, immersed in it, or simply gazing at its ever-changing patterns, moods, and colors.

The views offered faraway glimpses of life in the small towns tucked away in the foothills. An opening called Angels Rest on a mountain 3,800 ft. above Pearisburg did, indeed, make me feel angelic as I sat on a jutted rock overlooking the whole valley. Brrr and Harmony, two thru-hikers in their early 20s, joined me and we all took photographs while we watched the yellow buses far, far below carrying the children home from school. There were four hawks soaring on the breezes below me; I was perched above the birds that day. I saw how we all live our lives, absorbed in our daily routines, with little opportunity to wing our way to the mountaintop and observe those customs from afar, just to put them into perspective now and again.

Recently I had walked for miles down a path surrounded by brilliant rhododendron in full bloom. The rhododendron rose eight feet into the air along the trail and connected to form a canopy overhead. Often it was so dense that I couldn't see beyond the mantle of magenta. The blaze of color was intense, drawing my eye to it so continuously that I ran the risk of stumbling from not watching for roots and rocks on the trail.

A new problem with summer setting in was finding enough water each day. One afternoon it was in the 80s and very humid. I came to a spot where there was supposed to be a water source—a spring or small stream. I searched for quite awhile and couldn't find it, so I continued on as my water supply got lower. Soon I was hiking on an exposed, rocky ridge in the hot sun with my bottle almost empty. I was becoming very dehydrated and nursed a little bit of water for hours. Every so often I would take a few sips, just enough to wet my mouth. The next water source listed in the data book was miles away and I was already thirsty, exhausted, and miserable.

Now and then I would reach a shaded spot on the mountaintop where a light, feathery breeze would cool me off for a moment. I'd stop and let the soft air blow across my face, allowing it to restore my energy. Before moving on, I would look heavenward to say, "Thanks, Dad." For I believed he was helping to provide what I needed on the trail, and sometimes what I needed more than anything in the world was just a cool breeze on my face.

About 4 o'clock, I approached a gravel road crossing the trail. As I came down the mountain, I could see an Amish family with a horse, buggy, and six children gathered at the side of the road. Moses was there, drinking from a plastic cup. I asked, "Oh, do you have some water?" And the Amish father replied, "No, but we have something better: Kool-Aid!" I was so relieved to have something to drink that I almost burst into tears. The last hour I had been growing more concerned. It was the first time I had run out of water on the trail. It was a scary feeling knowing I had several more miles to hike in the heat when I was already dehydrated. Moses could see me struggling, and he carried on a lively conversation with the family while I was regaining my composure.

The four young Amish boys, who looked about a year apart in age, were all dressed just like their father, in long dark pants, long-sleeved shirts, suspenders, and vests. The little girl was the image of her mom; both wore dresses covering their entire bodies and tucked their hair away underneath bonnets. A baby was in the stroller, another little girl. All the children were very shy, but extremely polite. Their father worked as a wood carver in the valley nearby; he gave Moses and me one of his business cards. I found it odd to be receiving a business card out in the woods, especially from an Amish gentleman, but if I ever get back out that way, it would be wonderful to look them up and remind them of the time they provided desperately needed refreshment for a thru-hiker on a hot afternoon.

After a pleasant visit and two glasses of Kool-Aid, I felt refreshed enough to continue. The family had come up to the mountains for a walk in the woods, and they set off in the opposite direction, carrying the baby and riding herd on their troop of children. I wasn't sure I would ever encounter any trail magic more welcome than that family with their Kool-Aid. They truly seemed like angels of mercy. (In AT jargon, trail magic is that happy coincidence when someone comes along at just the right time to provide something you need.)

I realized I would have to be more careful about drinking as much as I could when water was available and making sure I was carrying sufficient liquid for the upcoming hot days. Since water was so heavy, I had tried not to carry very much, but I would have to take on the extra weight in the summer. I had heard former thru-hikers talk about "cameling up"—drinking a quart or more of water to hydrate one's body before hitting the trail in the morning. I knew I had better start doing it.

That same evening at the campsite where I stayed, the water source was as bad as any I had encountered. Thank goodness other hikers were there, too, and had found the water, because I would never have found it by myself. We had to bushwhack more than a hundred yards across the side of a mountain through weeds and brambles until we came to a very small spring with a tiny trickle of water and gnats swarming all around. It took at least 10 minutes for enough water to dribble into my water bag. I had to keep reminding myself that the woods weren't created to accommodate people.

The campsite was in a clearing high on the side of the mountain, with a view of the whole valley laid out before us. It was perfectly situated, facing west so we could have the added pleasure of watching the setting sun spread its colors all across the sky. Mother Nature once again dug into her bag of tricks to soothe the weary brows of her children before tucking us in for the night.

Although I was meeting new backpackers all the time, the ranks of thru-hikers were thinning, with more dropping out each week. The frequent rain convinced me to stay in the shelters at night. We built fires in the evenings to chase away the bugs and cut the nighttime chill. Since fire building was not a skill of mine, I always offered to gather wood if someone else would build one. I was constantly learning from the others and inspired by them. They were all helping me reach my own comfort level in the woods by their example.

I was surprised at how little I missed my daily shower and

shampoo. The days ran together and I didn't notice how long it had been. Each morning I arose with the sun, ate breakfast, filled my water bottles, gathered all my belongings into my backpack, and set off for a day of hiking up and down mountains. As the day wore on, I stopped a few times for rest, food, or water. Sometimes I paused to enjoy a view or to drink in the sunlight as it filtered through the trees. By late afternoon, I started to anticipate arriving at a spot where I could spend the night. After that last grueling hour of the hiking day, I would finally find a campsite or shelter, where I pitched my tent or claimed my space on the wooden floor, sponged off and filled my water bag at a nearby stream, changed clothes, cooked dinner, enjoyed my solitude if I was alone or passed the evening chatting with other backpackers, and crawled into my sleeping bag with the setting sun. Each day was the same, each day was different.

The hikers' prayer: "If you'll pick 'em up, Lord, I'll put 'em down." It's interesting to dissect the simple act of walking into those two parts when it's really all just one flowing motion, but there were times I wasn't sure I had the energy to complete the entire action. It was comforting to turn half the process over to a Higher Power.

13

My first rattlesnake!

Cloverdale, Virginia
705 miles hiked
June 4, 1994

*S*ometimes I thought my body still hadn't decided whether to accept this challenge I'd set before it. But then I had to admit that this was by far the most rigorous extended experience of my 51 years, so I guessed a little protest now and then was to be expected.

I had another exhaustion episode coming out of Pearisburg. I had hiked about five miles on a very hot morning, and as I was making my way up a mountain, my energy started to completely drain out of me. I became dizzy and disoriented, and it seemed as if I were walking. . .in. . .slow. . .motion. I stopped to rest. As I was taking off my backpack, my small waist pack fell to the ground and rolled back down the path about 50 feet. I was too exhausted to go down and get it. So I just sat and tried to regain enough energy and equilibrium to continue.

Soon Drifter appeared, bringing my waist pack up to me. When I told him I wasn't feeling well, he became very concerned. He had heard about my previous episode from another hiker just a few days earlier. Evidently I was extremely pale and breathing erratically, and he thought perhaps I was having a heart attack.

Drifter stayed with me until I recovered, then took part of my weight and hiked with me until we reached a campsite about a mile up the trail. He pitched my tent, fetched me some water and suggested I try to sleep. I did, for about two hours, in the middle of the afternoon. Even though he had intended to hike much farther that day, Drifter stayed until the next morning before moving on. We had just met a few days earlier and other thru-hikers who arrived at the campsite knew me better than he did, but Drifter wouldn't leave until he was sure I was all right. I was very touched by his concern. I was finding that thru-hikers were an extremely caring group of people.

I didn't want to be a burden to other hikers, and I wouldn't have stayed on the trail if I believed I had a medical problem. But I thought the intense heat plus a sugar reaction to doughnuts I had eaten that morning probably combined to knock me off my feet temporarily. Since I had no medical training, I realized that could have been a completely erroneous assumption. I'll admit it was frightening to feel a helplessness and overpowering fatigue, but once I regained my energy, my apprehension lessened considerably. I felt nowhere near as debilitated as during the previous episode. And one of the thru-hikers who arrived at the campsite was an emergency room physician, so if I had needed medical attention, it was there for me. As I've noted, the trail had a way of taking care of its flock. I felt better by evening and fine the next day.

The emergency room physician went by the trail name White Rabbit. He would start his practice in New York in the fall. White Rabbit had been thru-hiking the trail with his wife, Jabberwocky, until she began to experience discomfort and nausea the week before Trail Days. While they were in Damascus, they went to the emergency room and returned with the news that they were going to be parents! She ended her thru-hike attempt and went home to await the birth of their baby. White Rabbit hooked up with Camp Pro to continue his journey.

One morning, White Rabbit and I left a shelter together to start hiking at 7:30 a.m. By 8:30, I was dripping wet with the work of getting up a mountain. It had been hot and humid recently and we were all feeling the effects, but I was even more fatigued than usual. I asked White Rabbit about the medication I was taking for my heart.

He didn't like the possible side effects of the drug and didn't think I needed to be taking it. He said, "If your heart can take this kind of exertion day after day, it's plenty strong and you don't need to be taking that drug." I was really glad to have his opinion, because I could now stop taking the medication without worrying. (I know it sounds bizarre to be taking medical advice from someone called White Rabbit during a trailside consultation, but somehow that felt perfectly normal on the AT. Passing into the world of thru-hiking seemed somewhat akin to stepping through Alice's Looking Glass.)

White Rabbit had traveled and studied abroad, and with a father who was a doctor at a Methodist mission hospital in Zimbabwe as a role model, he had a strong sense of purpose in life. I expect he will end up using his medical degree to pursue his humanitarian beliefs.

That afternoon I reached a shelter about 3:30 after hiking almost 12 miles. I'd already decided I would rest there and then hike on to find a campsite. The data book said there would be a stream in two miles, and there was often a place to camp near water. Otter's advice was, "Don't just go by the data book to find places to camp. You can always find a place to throw down your tent." Otter was braver and more experienced than I. I had tried his style with varying success: that day, with none.

I headed out with confidence, but the stream turned out to be dry with no level ground anywhere. No water, no place to tent. By 6 o'clock I was trudging up yet another steep mountain, dripping wet again, flies and gnats swarming all around, with a bandanna draped over my face to keep the gnats out of my eyes. Still no level ground. By then I wished I'd stayed at the last shelter. I knew there was a shelter ahead, six miles from the last, but I'd never hiked 18 miles in a day and didn't think I could go that far. I kept looking for a place to pitch my tent.

At 7:15 p.m. I finally found a spot level enough to tent, but there was no water. By then, I'd gotten a second wind. Aren't the recuperative powers of the body—and the mind—remarkable? I decided that by now the next shelter was probably only a mile or so away and I'd go for it. I soon regretted that decision as I started down a steep decline with knees grinding and I remembered that the last mile of the day was always much longer than the rest. (There must be scientific documentation somewhere of this little-known fact.)

By the time I approached the shelter an hour later, darkness was descending and I was once again fighting back tears of exhaustion and pain. All I cared about was pitching my tent and heating up water to take a sponge bath. I didn't even care if I ate dinner. It had been my longest day to date, 18 miles, and not one I wanted to repeat.

But the best part of the day awaited me. For the last several hundred yards, I'd been hearing voices, a sound so inviting and reassuring that my tears started to dry. A group of thru-hikers sitting around a fire in the semi-darkness greeted me with astonishment: "Indiana Jean! Whoa. . .way to go!" Their smiles and friendly greetings redeemed the day. I'd seen many of them the night before and they didn't think I'd make it that far. And they knew I didn't hike that late into the evening. It's amazing how a ring of friendly faces can lift your spirits. I thought again, as I had so often, that the people on the trail helped carry me along just by their presence.

An interesting aside: Soon after I arrived at the shelter following my 13-hour day, Camp Pro arrived. He had stayed at the same shelter I had the night before and had hiked the same 18 miles. However, he had slept that morning until 10 o'clock before setting out and had covered the same distance in almost three hours less time. Once again, I became aware that I wasn't in the same hiking league as these young men and aware that their version of life on the trail was much different than mine.

A highlight that same week was my first encounter with a rattlesnake! I didn't see him as he lay sleeping by the side of the trail until my hiking stick inadvertently nudged him as I walked by. He immediately coiled and started rattling and an instant shot of adrenaline propelled me up onto a rock. That was probably the fastest I had ever moved with a backpack on. Even though I'd never heard a rattlesnake before, the sound was unmistakable. Surprisingly, once I was out of his reach, I wasn't frightened. Remembering that this environment was his home and that I was the intruder somehow took away my fear. I did decide, though, to watch more carefully where I stepped and sat.

I took a picture of him and then moved on within a few minutes because I was upsetting him. That didn't seem fair. He kept rattling until I was out of earshot, way down the trail. My first one-on-one with a rattler!

When I reached a shelter later that day, Otter was there. In his mid-30s, he was one of the men who seemed completely at ease on the trail. But he also had seen a rattler that afternoon, and it had really spooked him. His snake was about a mile from mine. When Drifter arrived and we told him about our encounters, he became very uneasy. He obviously didn't like poisonous snakes. When I saw him the next evening, he said he had hiked slowly all day because he spent most of his time looking down to make sure he wouldn't step on a snake.

I often thought we needed two sets of eyes to hike the trail: one to see the beauty around us and the other to watch the ground. In addition to snakes, there were rocks, roots and branches to trip us up and most of us had taken a spill (or several), even when being careful. The rocks and roots were extremely slippery when wet. There were two basic ways to fall, I had discovered—backward and forward. If my feet went flying out from under me, usually from slipping on wet rocks or roots, I would land with a thump on my pack, which usually protected me from injury. However, I discovered what a turtle must feel like when balancing on its shell, arms and legs flailing about. I had to either take off my backpack or somehow roll over so I could get up. If, instead, I sprawled headfirst onto the ground, my backpack pinned me down, and that was an even bigger challenge. It felt a lot like having Hulk Hogan sitting on my back while I was down for the count.

Backpacks were the most basic life-support system on the trail, carrying everything a hiker needed for survival. Some of the men said their packs seemed almost like an extension of their bodies and they didn't mind the extra weight. Mine felt more like a tormenter, making every activity more difficult, even the simple act of getting up after a fall.

The past week had included two days with the most spectacular views yet. One was the day I hiked up to Dragon's Tooth, a huge rock outcropping on top of a very high ridge. The way up was difficult and after a three-hour hike/climb/struggle, it was disconcerting to see a sign indicating the parking lot to the left. Those tourists! They got to see those beautiful sights without paying the price. Oh, I thought, to be a tourist for a day. . .

From the top of Dragon's Tooth I could see the valleys and peaks for miles in every direction. The day was clear and warm and the visibility unrestricted. Several trail buddies were already there when I arrived. We took pictures of each other climbing around on the rocks, acting like kids. Some of them scaled the side of the nearly vertical "tooth" and sat on top of the world looking back down at us. I wasn't as brave but enjoyed scrambling up the less intimidating rock climbs. It was a time of frolicking and forgetting the sore knees and burdensome backpack.

The descent from Dragon's Tooth was treacherous and brought me to tears within minutes. The ever-present knee pain intensified when I was climbing down steep rocks, and I always felt as if my backpack would tip me off balance and I'd go hurtling down the cliffs. Drifter was just ahead and he kept reassuring me and offering to lend a hand if necessary. I was glad when he went on ahead, though, so he wouldn't see me struggling with my fears. The highs and lows came so quickly on the trail.

The next day gave us McAfee's Knob. It was another magnificent rock formation farther along the ridge, with Roanoke visible on one side of the mountain and several small communities on the other. I could see the ridges I'd just hiked, as well as those ahead. It was quite a lift psychologically to behold such an expansive overview after days of hiking in the woods where all I saw was trees, trees, trees.

There was more picture-taking at McAfee's Knob and scrambling around in the caves and between the crevices of the boulders. McAfee's Knob offered one of the most photographed places on the whole Appalachian Trail, where hikers could stand on the tip of a large rock jutting out into space, with an expansive view far below. Some hikers spent hours at these unique spots, enjoying the rock formations and breathtaking views.

From the Knob, I could see Tinker Cliffs, five miles up the ridge, and I decided to forge ahead and try to reach them by sundown. Since I'd already put in 10 miles, it would be another long day. My horrendous 13-hour experience had been just three days earlier, so I hadn't learned much about striking out mid-afternoon for another major stretch. But this time I didn't regret my decision.

The night on Tinker Cliffs will be emblazoned in my mind forever. Otter and I pitched our tents and cooked dinner high on top of the cliffs. Our backdrop was the brilliant sky, painted orange by the setting sun, far away on the other side of the valley. The changing colors lasted almost an hour, and the only sound to penetrate the evening's stillness was the mooing of the cows far below. Hawks soared so close to me that I could see the individual feathers in their wings.

As darkness fell, lights started to twinkle in the farms and small communities throughout the valley. I felt as if we were up in heaven looking down upon the lives of the inhabitants, and I wondered how many of them had been up there to see this incredible overview of their existence.

I wondered if that's how spirits up in heaven feel as they look down upon our lives. If so, they must ponder why we spend so much of our time in trauma, chaos, anger, and angst. From that perspective high above, I could see how simple life should be. Could this feeling last when I returned to civilization?

The towns along the Appalachian Trail always presented an emotional dilemma for me. I looked forward to them and enjoyed my time there, but as the moment drew near to head back out to the trail, my anxiety gradually increased. I knew that it would feel, once again, like going from a familiar, comfortable environment into a huge abyss of hardship and discomfort. Often on the day I was hiking into a town I anticipated it so eagerly that I lost my appreciation for the wilderness. This was particularly true as I approached Cloverdale.

After spending that perfect evening atop Tinker Cliffs, I knew that Cloverdale, with its comfortable motel, was just 10.5 miles away. I recently had been averaging 15 miles a day, so I thought that would be just a short jaunt and I'd be there in no time. Big mistake. Whenever I underestimated the time, effort, or terrain ahead, I paid in many ways.

Every time I hiked up a rugged ascent, I thought, "Now *this* has to be the last rise, and then I'll be heading down into town." It never was. I knew there was beauty all around me, but I was seeing none of it. I just wanted to get to that motel! Finally, I came to a magnificent overlook with a river snaking through the valley far off in the distance. It was too breathtaking to ignore. And I thought, "Okay, okay, I guess there *are* things to see around here. Another incredible view. I wish I were in the mood to appreciate it."

A few minutes later, I came to a tree with splinters of sunlight streaming through its branches and a soft bed of leaves at its base. It seemed to be inviting me to come inside its space, so I took off my pack and sat down, leaning quietly against the trunk. My eyes closed and my body began to shrug off my impatience. I settled into the tree.

As the atmosphere of the forest gradually penetrated my pores, I realized, "The towns allow me to do my laundry, take a shower, and get the supplies I need so that I can come back out here to the wilderness. Towns are the means, not the end. What am I doing wishing away the woods so I can get to a motel? Why does it matter whether I get to a town at 2 o'clock or at 3:30? I'll still have plenty of time to get my errands done, take a shower, and sleep in a bed. I don't need that extra hour in town. From now on, I'll try to remember that *this* is where I want to be. My journey is on the trail, not in the towns."

A peace and acceptance settled over me as I sat there for a long, long time under the tree, and I had an exquisite experience before moving on. I was looking up into the sky as I often did, trying to feel a little closer to my dad, and I thought, "Dad, if you're up there and you can hear me, I wish you'd send me a signal of some kind." And just at that moment, as I gazed skyward through a round opening in the leaves of the trees above, a single bird soaring high in the sky flew across the opening.

14

A more leisurely pace

Cow Camp Shelter, Virginia
783 miles hiked
June 11, 1994

t had been a rainy, buggy week. We were finding that if the gnats were bad in the evenings, the smoke from a fire usually cleared them out. I had been tenting near the shelters, because there was often a fire ring there. One night we built a huge fire at Punchbowl Shelter, which was rumored to be haunted by a ghost. (It didn't come around that night.) Bohemian, Flare, Howdy, and I gathered wood for a blaze with enough warmth to cut the chill of the recent drizzle and to bake a little dampness out of our boots and socks. Howdy stayed up long after dark tending the fire and then doused it completely before crawling into his sleeping bag. He got angry when people left the embers and coals of a fire burning through the night. His scouting background taught him the dangers of that.

A pond nearby with many resident bullfrogs provided the amphitheater for the chorus that serenaded us that evening. Even with the hard wooden floor as my bed, I enjoyed lying awake, listening to the sounds of a crackling fire and croaking bullfrogs. I felt warm and cozy and content, gazing into the fire, with the natural sounds of the forest lulling me to sleep. I slept very well that night.

Another night I tented near a shelter occupied by a troop of Boy Scouts, a nice group, but rather rowdy. They were earning various badges with their activities and they seemed to be tolerating the rain and bugs without complaint. They were learning to use their water filters in the stream nearby. I appreciated their offer to let me sleep in the shelter with them, but I would have been jammed into a very small space with lots of teenage boys who were up far later than I wanted to be. It rained hard during the night, however, so I carried a wet tent the next day. As I left in the morning, after getting all packed up and eating breakfast, the boys and their leaders were still sound asleep.

When it rained, it was very difficult to get my clothes dried out. It had been so humid that when I ended the day wet and hung my shorts and T-shirt in a shelter or on a clothesline, they were just as wet the next morning. In the evening I tried to anticipate whether it would rain during the night. If my clothes were damp when I hung them in a tree and then it rained, they would be really soaked when I woke up.

I didn't have many choices of what to wear—just two T-shirts and shorts that I hiked in, and one that I slept in. I usually wore one set for three or four days and then switched to the other. Now and then I rinsed them out in a stream or tried to find a laundromat as I passed through a town.

Waking up knowing I had to struggle into wet clothes made it difficult to pull myself out of my comfortable sleeping bag. If I wore dry clothes and stuffed the wet ones into my backpack, naturally they wouldn't dry, so sometimes I hung them on the outside. On those days, I must have looked like the trail version of a bag lady, with socks, T-shirts, and shorts dangling everywhere off the back of my pack. I was learning to live wet. It wasn't my favorite part of the experience.

My dear friend Zelma, who had moved to Virginia with her husband recently, came to meet me and we spent a day together. It was wonderful to reenter the real world briefly, and I was reassured to find it was possible to set up a rendezvous from the trail.

We had agreed by phone that I'd be waiting on the road at 5 p.m. on Friday, where the trail crossed Route 60 east of Buena Vista, Virginia. When Zelma finished teaching school, she drove over from Petersburg. It had been raining for the past three days, and everything on my body and in my pack was soaked and filthy. I waited for her at a picnic table by the side of the road. As I sat there in the mist and rain, I tried to write a postcard, which became soggier with every word. When a thick fog started rolling in, I was afraid I wouldn't even be able to see her as she drove by. But suddenly there she was, stopping by the road in her familiar car. All of my discomfort just melted away when I saw that beloved face appear out of the mist.

Zelma has been my best friend for years, and no one makes me feel more comfortable with who I am than she does. She supports me and loves me, shares in my joys and commiserates in my sorrows.

It seemed so appropriate that she would be here to share in this grand life adventure of mine.

She had brought me some bubble bath in my favorite fragrance—Lily of the Valley. We checked into a motel and I slipped into the tub for a long soak, while she took all my dirty clothes to the laundromat. Now that's a friend!

In the evening, we drove over to Lexington, a picturesque college community nearby, for a late dinner. It felt unbelievably out-of-context: Here I was eating in a quaint restaurant with Zelma, sipping a glass of wine, on a lovely summer evening. It was just the sort of thing she and I would do together. But it was so removed from how I had lived for the past 10 weeks that I realized how far outside my normal life I had leapt. The only difference was that I ate more than usual—lots more.

We spent the next day in the car wandering through the mountain roads while Zelma took pictures of wildflowers. I was thrilled to be riding instead of walking. In the afternoon we stopped at the grocery store so I could stock up on food and headed back to the trail less than 24 hours after I left it.

As Zelma dropped me off at the trailhead, Gophermagne and Frenchy were there, trying to hitch a ride into town. I had been dreading the moment when she would drive away, knowing I would feel an unbearable loneliness again as I headed into the woods. I was pleased to see the two young men, because their presence drew me back into my trail environment. I said to them, "I'm so glad you're here, because now I won't cry when Zelma leaves!" They assured me it was okay to cry, but somehow I didn't need to anymore.

Zelma took Gopher and Frenchy to the store as she started out for home, and I headed up the mountain to a shelter four miles away to spend the night. My time with my dear friend had left me refreshed and reinvigorated, and I felt good. I knew the Goatherders were just a few miles behind me and would probably catch up the next day. Someone always came along on the trail just when you needed them.

That night I became aware again that family members and acquaintances link us to so many people in the world. Four "weekenders" from Washington, D.C., were at the shelter when I arrived. They were young men who had come to the woods for the weekend to relieve the stress of their fast-paced lives in the capital. After they pitched their tents and built a huge fire, we sat around talking and laughing for a couple of hours. When I told them my trail name, one mentioned he had graduated from Indiana University. Since he was the same age as my son Brad, I started mentioning names of kids I knew who had attended IU. We discovered he was a fraternity brother of Jason, one of Brad's closest friends in high school. In fact, I sold my car to Jason several years ago, and this young man had ridden in it many times in college. "The beer wagon!" he exclaimed. He'd even broken one of the windows during a keg run. I couldn't believe it. What were the odds of meeting someone out in the middle of the Appalachian Mountains who broke the window of my car at a fraternity party in Indiana?

Howdy was one of the few thru-hikers I'd met who was my age. He said the only employers he'd had were the Navy and the FBI. Recently retired from the FBI, Howdy was hiking the AT before deciding what the next step in his life would be. He was probably one of the most experienced and best-prepared people on the trail, and he was amazed that I was out there with no prior backpacking experience. He figured I'd crack and go home any day.

Howdy announced one day that he had made up a song that should be our theme. The tune was familiar, perhaps remembered from camp or riding on the bus to football games. It went as follows:

"We are thru-hikers, MIGHTY thru-hikers.

Everywhere we go-o, people want to kno-ow

Who we a-are, so we tell 'em,

We are thru-hikers, MIGHTY thru-hikers.

Everywhere we go-o. . ."

Flare and I chuckled when he sang it for us and she asked, "Did it take you a whole day to think that up?" And Howdy solemnly replied, "No, actually, it took me two or three days." Well, then we really laughed because it was such a simple, mindless song, but I have to admit that I sang it almost every day as I trudged along the path. It always made me smile.

I tried to practice my new promise to myself to stop and enjoy the serendipitous experiences on the trail instead of succumbing to the pressure of cranking out more miles each day. If there had been a drill sergeant at my side, singing "Sound Off" with each step, he would probably have thought he'd found a worthy recruit. So I was trying to stop more often, to take more time at each viewpoint, to embrace each ray of sunlight that filtered through the trees, and to tell that sergeant to let me set a more leisurely pace.

I often felt the same self-imposed pressure on the trail that I did in my job and other activities, so maybe that's a life lesson I was supposed to learn on the AT. If I hiked 12 miles instead of 15, spent two hours watching the fish, frogs, and butterflies, and my legs and feet didn't ache that night, it would be a good day. Mt. Katahdin wasn't going anywhere.

One day I stopped to rest and settled on a rock in the middle of a stream. A little frog sat in a shallow spot nearby with his head above water until I startled him. He immediately dove beneath the water and put his head under a little stick. The rest of him was clearly visible right under the surface, but his head was tucked away out of sight. He reminded me of the proverbial ostrich who sticks his head in the sand, and I wondered how many other animals think that if they hide their heads, no one can see the rest of them. I've seen babies do the same thing. I wonder where on the evolutionary scale of intelligence or life experience you realize that the rest of you is attached to your head.

I stayed on my rock for about an hour watching all the activity under the clear water. I had bought some strawberries in Cloverdale and taken them with me to eat for lunch. As I ate the strawberries, I tossed the tops into the creek.

A huge school of minnows was swimming about, and when they discovered one of the strawberry tops, the whole group attacked it with a frenzy. They were fighting and grabbing it and trying to gobble it up. Then one of them would discover another of the strawberry tops and they'd all go off and attack that one as a group. Instead of spreading out among all the strawberry tops and each getting their share, they had a real gang mentality, and I'm sure many went away frustrated. No signs of independence among those minnows, no striking out on their own to see what other goodies the stream was providing for them that day.

Those of us on the AT were striking out on our own and experiencing life's opportunities without worrying about what the gang did. However, even out there, it was easy sometimes to get sucked into a group, wanting to be where the other hikers were, taking a day off if others did to stay close to them. And that was okay, as long as we didn't let others pull us off course. But in the end, we each had to set our own agenda if we wanted to make it to Maine.

Life hands some of us circumstances conducive to building self-reliance; others need to seek out their opportunities. Fifteen years of being a single parent had certainly schooled me in doing things by and for myself, and not depending on others. Either way you learn it, that feels like a very important characteristic to develop— one that allows us to set off in new directions without worrying whether someone will be there to hold our hand, or beat us to the strawberry tops.

15

His face is all around me

Now it was getting hard. One knee was in almost constant pain and the deadly heat, humidity, and bug bites were taking their toll. Most days I was sweating by 8 a.m., still sweating at 7 p.m., and the insects hadn't left me alone all day. I hadn't been able to figure out if there was one fly that staked me out as his property and stuck with me all day, or if he radioed ahead to a compatriot with the message, "Here comes a hot one. You take her at the maple tree; I'll go back and wait for the next," and then they worked their own territories all day. I had not yet found a repellent that kept the bugs away, but I was trying new ones. Itching kept me awake at night.

When contemplating this journey, the aspect of hiking for six months through the mountains that worried me most was being at the mercy of biting insects for 24 hours a day. And, indeed, I was finding those attacks one of the toughest things to deal with. I wasn't the only one: I had recently heard Gophermagne mutter to himself as he swatted gnats away, "I *hate* these bugs!" The thought of returning home with the explanation that I just couldn't take the insects any more wasn't how I envisioned the end of my quest, but it seemed like a possibility.

The heat and humidity were brutal, with many days topping 95 degrees. I was becoming concerned about the summer. It was only the middle of June and already pushing 100. We all adjusted our pace and mileage expectations so we wouldn't make ourselves sick. This was when that daily shower was sorely missed!

I recently had met another fascinating off-trail character: A man named Rusty lived in the woods near the Appalachian Trail a few miles from Waynesboro. For more than a decade he had welcomed thru-hikers to his home. Rusty was a kind, generous man who epitomized Appalachian Mountain hospitality. His home had no telephone, no electricity, and no running water. A large porch on the front of his house had couches for hanging out, and another on the back offered bunks for sleeping. An outhouse perched not far from the front door. A wood-burning stove was used for cooking, and two more heated the house.

Laundry? You threw your clothes into a bucket of cold water, moved 'em around with a plunger, ran 'em through a wringer, and hung 'em on a clothesline.

Bathing? You took a (cold) shower by standing in a little stall and pulling a chain to release a small stream of rainwater from the vat above. On a sunny day in the afternoon, perhaps the water was warm; when I took a shower in the evening, it was so cold I just sprinkled a little water on and called myself clean.

Refrigeration? You used the cold water of the groundspring inside a shed.

Overnight accommodations? You threw your sleeping bag on a mattress in the bunkhouse, or on the porch, or in the barn. Up to 35 hikers at a time could stay. I shared sleeping space with about 15 others, and once again, I was the only female thru-hiker. I never knew whether that changed the activity or the language.

Rusty took a Polaroid picture of each hiker, and the photos—thousands of them—covered the ceilings of the porches. Signs with cryptic or clever sayings lined the walls. Cans of cold soda or beer floating in the spring water offered refreshment on a hot day. When your can was empty, you put it on a post and used a baseball bat to hit it into the driveway (kind of like T-ball). The driveway was paved with all those smashed cans, and Rusty drove right over them with his truck.

Rusty cooked at least 100 toasted cheese sandwiches for dinner and the same number of blueberry/raspberry pancakes for breakfast. Thru-hikers made donations for the food and chipped in gas money for trips to town. Rusty's truck could hold about 10 hikers, and he made daily trips to resupply. I hoped the hikers were making generous donations, because many were drinking beer and eating food with abandon.

Some thru-hikers stayed for several days at Rusty's Hard Time Hollow before moving on, but one night was enough for me. I was glad I stopped, because it was a fascinating part of the trail experience and a perfect example of someone choosing his lifestyle without regard to how the rest of the world lives. Rusty didn't want a telephone, electricity, or running water; he'd found Nirvana in the mountains of Virginia, living the simple life.

Back on the trail, I endured a very bad day. The gnats and flies were the worst they had been, buzzing around me incessantly. I was hot, sticky, and miserable. All day I was on the verge of tears, letting my mind dwell on the discomfort and finding it hard to focus on anything positive. Even when I stopped for lunch, I couldn't enjoy the break because the gnats immediately honed in on my sweaty face, using their unfailing sonar. I often couldn't tell whether I was wiping away sweat or tears—somehow all the droplets ran together. "What's the point of this? Why am I here?" I repeated the questions again and again.

By mid-afternoon it was raining and my bandanna had a third kind of moisture to deal with. Thankfully, though, the rain drove away the flies. (I wondered if horses and cows find that a compensation for having to stand in the rain is *not* having to swish away flies.) The rain made the footing treacherous, and I slipped on a wet rock. I went sprawling down, bruising my elbow, which immediately swelled and started aching. "Does it have to be this uncomfortable? Why am I here?"

In the afternoon, Frenchy came charging up the trail, hiking twice as fast as I could ever go. I hoped he couldn't tell I'd been crying. We talked for awhile before he moved on. His boots had recently blown out and he was hoping the new pair he had ordered would be waiting for him in Waynesboro. In the meantime, he was hiking in his sandals. I worried about him. He could so easily injure his feet or twist an ankle hiking in sandals on this rocky terrain with a heavy backpack. I hoped he has being careful.

My mood improved after seeing Frenchy. These young men seemed to take everything in stride, both literally and figuratively.

The trail provided a soothing salve for my weary spirit that night in the form of companionship with my fellow hikers. And yet another trail town offered up a friendly welcome for the thru-hiker clan: The Waynesboro Fire Department had, for several years, made a small patch of grass behind their station available to thru-hikers for tenting. It was a novelty I hadn't expected: sleeping in a tent in the middle of a town.

I hitched a ride into Waynesboro at the end of the day and joined several of my friends already at the fire station. Gophermagne had been experiencing movie withdrawal for weeks and decided he had to see one; he didn't care what it was. He and Otter asked if I wanted to go along. I did, so I quickly showered in the large communal shower stall, using the sign for the door that announced "Lady in Restroom." No towel...oh well. I found one on a chair that was cleaner than I had been upon arrival, so I used it—no time to stand and drip dry. I threw on my "town clothes" (the same shorts and T-shirt I slept in every night) and we were off, walking the six blocks to the theater. Everything's close by in a small town.

We saw *City Slickers 2.* I couldn't sit through it. My legs and knees couldn't stay in one place for that long without throbbing and cramping up, so I wandered around during the last half of the movie. (No problem, there were only about six of us in the theater.) Dinner that night was movie popcorn.

When we returned to the fire station and climbed into our tents, I found it wasn't easy to sleep. It was much hotter in civilization surrounded by pavement and buildings than up in the mountains encircled by trees and other vegetation. Town sounds seemed surreal when heard from inside a tent. There was one fire run during the night, with men running everywhere and sirens blaring. As I was falling back asleep, I thought how bizarre this experience would have seemed just a few months ago—sleeping in a tent in a small town behind a fire station with men and trucks whizzing by. But when you're trekking 2,000 miles through mountains and villages, you find yourself in some unusual situations along the way. It was all part of the adventure.

I had cried often on the Appalachian Trail, usually because I wasn't sure if I could take the physical and mental demands of the journey, but once for a very different reason. I was watching the sun's rays streaming through the trees and wishing, as I often did, that I could see my dad's face shimmering among the brilliant streaks of sunlight. Then I remembered a joke that Shelter Boy had told:

"There was a man who lived by a river, and after days of rain the river started to flood. As the water rose to the first floor of his house, a man in a rowboat came by and said, 'You'd better come with me. I'll take you to safety.' 'No, no,' replied the man. 'Thanks anyway, but I'll put my trust in the Lord.'

"Soon the water rose to the second floor and someone in a motorboat came by calling, 'Come with me. I'll take you to safety.'

'No, no. I'll put my trust in the Lord,' the man answered again.

"Soon the water was nearly over the house, and as the man sat on his roof a rescue team in a helicopter came by, and they yelled to him, 'We've come to rescue you. You'd better come with us!' The answer was the same as before: 'No, no, I'm putting my trust in the Lord. He'll save me.'

"The water continued to rise and soon the man drowned. When he got to heaven, he said angrily to God: 'Lord, I put my trust in you. I thought you would save me!' And the Lord said, 'I *sent* two boats and a helicopter. . .' "

And as I remembered that story, I thought that I didn't need to see my father's—my Father's?—face reflected in the sunlight through the trees. His face was all around me. It was the face of Drifter when he came upon me as I sat on the trail in a state of exhaustion and he stayed with me all the way to camp. It was the face of Feather as she hugged me and said, "How're you feeling? I hear you had a rough day." It was the friendliness of Wood Rat when I came upon him as he sat by the side of the trail eating lunch, just when I was feeling tired and lonely. His face was all around me on the trail, if I was observant enough each day to notice.

For I had come to believe that my dad was my guardian angel on my quest. I believed he caught me when I stumbled and blew cool breezes on my face when I was weary. Mom told me that he wouldn't have been strong enough to make a trip of this sort; an undiagnosed disease of the intestine in college left him somewhat frail, and later, that's where the cancer struck. I was sure he helped plant the seed for the journey in my mind so that we could spend these months together to make up a little for all the years we didn't have. My strong legs could carry us and his spirit could guide us. I decided to dedicate my odyssey to my dad.

The Appalachian Trail

16

I finally spotted a bear!

Denton Shelter, Virginia
946 miles hiked
June 23, 1994

*T*he Shenandoah National Park was a much more "civilized" wilderness than we had experienced so far, with Skyline Drive never too far away and the campgrounds and restaurants (called waysides) often close enough to offer a respite from life out of a backpack. Translation: Hamburgers and milk shakes. It also had the easiest terrain to date. There were very few places where tenting was allowed, however, and the guidebook warned of stiff fines for violations. I stayed in the shelters (called huts in the park), but that meant the distance I hiked each day was determined by where the huts were placed instead of by how far I wanted to go. I registered and filled out an itinerary as I entered and received a hiking permit.

I inadvertently hiked my first 20-mile day in the Shenandoahs. I had planned to hike 13 miles and stop at a hut, because the next opportunity to stop was seven miles beyond that, which seemed farther than I could go in one day. (I think I had a psychological barrier about 20 miles. My longest day to date had been 18, which proved a very grueling 13-hour day.)

It was my first full day in the park, and not being familiar with the markers that pointed the way to the shelters, I missed Blackrock Hut. I kept hiking and hiking, thinking, "Where's the marker? Where's the shelter?" I finally concluded I must have passed it. About that time, I came to a trail marker and found that I was 1.7 miles *beyond* the hut. So my choices were to go back (never a pleasant thought on the trail) or to head on and hike another 5.3 miles to a campground.

Just as I sat down and took off my backpack to make this major decision of the day, a thunderstorm set in. The idea of turning back was even less appealing in the rain, so I trudged ahead. The trail quickly became a small stream, and I sloshed through water halfway up my boots. But the rain ended as quickly as it had begun, and I had dried out by the time I got to the campground. I had hiked through weeds up to my head, which, although uncomfortable, had produced the sighting of two deer right on the trail, very close to me. They hadn't spotted me as I plowed my way through the dense underbrush.

The disagreeable day turned into a delightful evening at Loft Mountain Campground, where the amenities included pay showers, a camp store, and washers and dryers for your clothes. It was the most beautiful campground I had ever seen: acres and acres of wooded campsites, each with its own picnic table and grill. I selected one and set up my tent.

A troop of Boy Scouts and their leader stopped by to talk and ask questions about my journey. I guess I did look a little out of the ordinary—a woman all by herself with a backpack, pitching a tent, without any means of transportation—among all the families and their campers. The boys, about a dozen of them, and their leaders had been carefully planning their five-day hike for months, but it turned out to be more difficult than they had anticipated, especially with the heat. They'd had a rough day. A couple of the boys had become dehydrated and several were not feeling well, so they were cutting their trip short and were waiting to be picked up the following morning.

A few of the boys, however, were really into backpacking and thought perhaps someday they'd like to try a thru-hike. It was fun to hear their questions and see their enthusiasm for spending time in the woods. I hoped I provided some additional inspiration for them during our encounter.

I developed new respect for campers and for the camping experience. What a wonderful way to spend time with family or friends in a relaxed, healthful environment. Some of those around me had very elaborate setups with recreation vehicles, tarps, mosquito netting, tables, chairs, grills, and lights. But once everything was in place, they just lounged around and talked or strolled through the woods. No deadlines, no pressures, just time spent outside with fresh air filling their lungs. It seemed a nice way to connect with each other. No television to be the focus of everyone's attention—just togetherness, conversation, and Mother Nature.

In the next hut register after Loft Mountain Campground, I

wrote that I had achieved my first 20-mile day. Many hikers congratulated me when I next saw them. Although I was probably one of the last thru-hikers to break that barrier, it was a supportive group and they made me feel good about my accomplishment.

One day in the Shenandoahs, I came upon a mother and her 6-year-old son, both with backpacks, sitting by the side of the trail. They were eating blueberries they had gathered alongside the path.

I stopped to chat with them and found that the family had three children, ages 3, 6, and 8. Mom brought them out to start backpacking "as soon as they're out of diapers." She and her son were in their second day of the weekend (evidently Dad was home with the other two) and they were enjoying their time together in the woods. His only disappointment was that he hadn't seen a bear. However, he *had* seen a rattlesnake that morning and he was very excited about that: He would have a story to tell when they got home that night! How nice for the little boy that his mother was starting him out so young. Perhaps I met a future thru-hiker that day.

Another day in the Shenandoahs, several of us—Bohemian, Flare, Howdy, Del Doc, Gophermagne, Phineus, and I—passed by a wayside late in the afternoon and stopped for a meal. Most of us were preparing to head on to a shelter about a mile up the trail when a severe thunderstorm struck. The wayside had just closed. The evening manager came out as we were fighting the wind and downpour to get our protective gear and packs on. She yelled, "You shouldn't go out in this storm! It's dangerous to be on the mountain in this!" We didn't disagree. The storm was fierce with driving rain, and constant thunder and lightning. She told us that we could go under the overhang behind the building and wait it out.

Phineus and Gopher had already left, so we hoped they'd make it to the hut without being harmed. Howdy, Bo, Flare, Del Doc, and I stayed, and while we waited for the storm to pass, we discovered that, among his many other bases of knowledge, Del Doc was a self-proclaimed meteorologist! He explained how weather systems work and eventually he convinced us that we should just stay there all night, because we couldn't be sure that the lightning was gone. (We had asked the manager earlier whether we could spend the night out back if the storm didn't clear. She was hesitant, but said we could if we were gone by 7 a.m. when the day manager arrived.) As the evening wore on, it became less appealing to start out in the rain and gathering dusk, so Del Doc had little trouble convincing us to stay.

Bo and Flare had free-standing tents that they set up on the concrete under the overhang. Howdy and Del Doc put their sleeping bags alongside, and I pitched my tent in the grass. Howdy rigged his tarp so it would provide protection for those on the concrete as well as for my tent. For some reason that narrow little chunk of cement under the overhang seemed one step up from what we'd find in the woods, and we were all grateful to be there.

In the morning we were up at dawn, wanting to be away before the manager arrived. Del Doc left early, about 6 a.m. (he was still setting daily "world records" for early departure), and Howdy, Bo, Flare, and I headed out at 6:30. I'd gone no more than 30 yards when I spotted a mama bear and her cub running through the woods. They were black and furry, and the cub, although small, was large enough to keep up with its mom. I motioned to the rest to be quiet, and we all had a fleeting glimpse of them as they bounded down the mountainside. My first bear sighting! I was very excited, as I'd been wanting to see one since the Smokies.

Hoping to spot them again, we tiptoed down the path, looking as if we were stalking wild game. A few minutes later we saw another bear, larger than the others, no more than 50 feet from us. We all stood completely still and watched as he proceeded to eat something—we couldn't tell what. It seemed sinewy, because he would pull on it and move around it, sometimes lying down to eat and sometimes standing up and yanking on it.

Eventually we began taking pictures like mad and he was very aware of our presence, but he was in no hurry to leave his breakfast. We watched for about 40 minutes before he wandered off into the woods. I looked in another direction and saw a doe with her spotted fawn nearby, and I thought how wonderful it was to be with these animals in their natural habitat instead of seeing them caged in a zoo.

About a mile away, we stopped by the shelter. Gophermagne was still there—he wasn't an early riser—and we were relieved to find he hadn't been struck by lightning or a falling tree the previous evening. He was very disappointed to have missed the bear encounters because he had been eager to see one. But he had his own sighting to report: The evening before, after making it to the hut in the raging thunderstorm, he heard a hiker approach, looked up, and saw Phineus arriving, completely nude! It was Nude Hiking Day (June 21) and, thank goodness, Phineus had decided to wait until after he left the restaurant to participate in this thru-hiker event.

There had been messages in various registers encouraging hikers to doff their clothes on June 21, the longest day of the year. Word had it that at least a few hiked sans clothes for much of the day. Most of us had forgotten about it, since we weren't planning to participate. Gopher was pretty taken aback by the sight of Phineus sporting a backpack, boots, and nothing else and I think he didn't know whether to ignore him, throw him a towel, or run screaming into the woods.

At one of the waysides, I was using the restroom to sponge off and brush my teeth when several ladies approached with the usual questions. They started quizzing me about how far I was going, how long it would take, where I was from, and why I was doing this. They were very excited and one said, "Oh, I was *hoping* I'd meet a thru-hiker!" (I knew how she felt. I finally got to see a bear.)

As I came out of the restroom, another woman asked if I would be willing to be interviewed on her video camera. She was eager to show her friends at home that she had met a thru-hiker, so we did a 10-minute interview in the parking lot and she went away happy. At times like that, I always felt like an endangered species or a rare animal of some sort. But it also renewed my awareness of the uniqueness of my adventure and helped me appreciate how lucky I was to be hiking the Appalachian Trail.

The next week promised to be one of the highlights of my journey. My son Brad and his friend Lisa would join me for five days of hiking. I had planned relatively short days while they would be with me, because even though the terrain by now seemed pretty mellow to me, they hadn't been on the AT for three months like I had and their definition might not be the same as mine. I wanted us to enjoy our time together and not push too hard.

I had been told before starting this trek that having someone join you to hike a section of the trail would slow you down, which could be frustrating if you had established distance goals and wanted to be churning out the miles. As a staff member at the ATC had said to me, "After the first month or two on the trail, your body will become a hiking machine." (What a wonderful image. I wasn't sure mine had reached that evolutionary stage, but I was certainly in better physical condition than at any other time in my life.)

At this point in my journey, I definitely preferred to spend time with Brad and Lisa rather than churn out miles, and since they were half my age, I thought perhaps we'd be compatible in our stamina and pace. I was thrilled that Brad wanted to join me; Greg was to hike with me for a few days over Labor Day. The interest and support of my two sons had been one of the best rewards of my journey. I don't know anything that could make a mother happier than to have her sons say, "Mom, I'm so proud of you!"

We often hear that if we take care of our own needs, we'll be able to do more for the other people in our lives. I was discovering that pursuing this dream for myself was adding much to the lives of those I loved and to our relationships.

I was hiking the Appalachian Trail because it felt like something I was meant to do. I had little choice in the matter; the decision seemed to have been made for me. And because of that feeling, I knew that everything about this odyssey was going to turn out in a way that would have meaning for me and for my family, whether I made it to Maine or had to quit the following day.

Many people don't believe in fate or in life events that are "meant to be," but those concepts have more meaning for me each year that I live. And that feels like a release—to be able to trust that my life is evolving in the way that it should. It removes a pressure that many of us feel as we deal with the decisions, options, and events that we encounter every day.

On the trail, I felt like a character in Benjamin Hoff's *The Tao of Pooh*, one of my favorite books. In the world of Pooh, things happen in the right way if you let them. Hoff tells us that we should work with circumstances instead of fighting against them. He says we should listen to our intuition and develop the ability to be sensitive to circumstances, which is sometimes known as having a sixth sense. Our reward is that we won't have to make so many difficult decisions, because they will make themselves.

Since deciding to hike the Appalachian Trail, everything had fallen into place for me. I was just following my intuition north, and that felt like the right thing to do.

Moses, Methuselah, and ChooChoo at a shelter in the Smokies (4/21/94).

The southern terminus of the Appalachian Trail, atop Springer Mountain, Georgia. It took me several hours on a wet, chilly day to reach the top (3/28/94).

My first night on the trail, I shared a shelter with Swan Song, Denver Dan and John (3/28/94).

Flaming azaleas added spring beauty to the trail (4/94).

Suds, Poet, and Denver Dan at the hiker hostel in Fontana Village (4/16/94).

A perfect night camping with (left to right) Sally, Flare, Charlie, Jabberwocky, White Rabbit, and Sunday (4/24/94).

A mountaintop view in the Smoky Mountains (4/94).

A hut in the Shenandoahs. Clockwise from bottom left: Bohemian, Flare, Howdy, Sourball, Otter, Gophermagne, and Del Doc (6/22/94).

Bad DNA was the only thru-hiker who carried a fly swatter. Sher Bear and JettButt know he's harmless (7/15/94).

The Goatherders in the Trail Days parade: Phishstick, Ox, Pigeon (holding the goat), Frenchy. Jester looks on (5/15/94).

My first state line was marked by this magnificent tree; notice the white blaze on the trunk (4/6/94).

A deer in the Shenandoahs (6/94).

Model-T wades through Vernie Swamp in New Jersey (7/23/94).

The trail sometimes traverses mountaintop ridges for miles in the White Mountains (8/94).

Greg squeezes through a crevice in the Mahoosuc Notch (9/6/94).

I was glad to be back on the trail in the beauty of Maine (9/95).

Geezer (front) and Greene King (middle) took the ferry—a canoe—across the Kennebeck River in Maine (9/12/95).

Reaching the top of Mt. Katahdin on a snowy, treacherous day were Getoverit and JettButt (back), Big John, Sher Bear, Magoo, and Dreamcatcher (front) (10/7/94).

Thanks to Sole Power for this magnificent picture of Pierce Pond, Maine (9/94).

Mt. Katahdin looming in the distance can bring tears to the eyes of a thru-hiker (9/23/95).

The summit—an unparalleled feeling of exultation (9/26/95).

17

The first thru-hiker

Dayton, Maryland
1,018 miles hiked
June 30, 1994

*J*n the past week, I had hiked 70 miles, but felt like I had been on vacation. Brad and Lisa seemed to have a wonderful time backpacking on the Appalachian Trail. We spent three days hiking into Harpers Ferry and then another two going north from there.

Our first day together was perfect. The terrain was fairly easy but had some challenging ascents and descents, we found lovely spots for lunch and rest stops, the weather was great, and the bugs left us alone. We had a shelter all to ourselves that first night and time to enjoy the evening in a beautiful mountain setting.

Most of the second day was spent in the pouring rain, so they saw that side of the experience, too. They quickly realized it was best to just keep hiking once we got wet, because if we stopped, we would get chilled. That night we stayed at a hiker hostel—eight of us in a big room with bunks—so they met several of my trail buddies and we didn't have to tent in the downpour.

I was pleased to meet two new thru-hikers at the hostel: Bad DNA and 'Toonman. They had both been ahead of me much of the way, and I had been reading their entries in the trail registers. DNA wrote philosophical messages and always had an interesting insight or analogy about life on the trail. 'Toonman drew cartoons! He was very good and his 'toons consistently hit the mark, showing the funny and poignant moments in the life of a thru-hiker. It was always a treat finding a register with his artwork inside. He was in his 20s; Bad DNA, a chemist who acquired his nickname in college, was 31.

On our third day together, Brad, Lisa, and I hiked 12 miles into Harpers Ferry, where we stayed at the Hilltop House Hotel, with its magnificent view of the Potomac and Shenandoah rivers. By that time their muscles were aching enough to let them know they'd had a good workout. When I walked into our room after supper, it smelled like a nursing home or an athletic training room! They had bought Icy Hot and rubbed it on their aching legs. I thought we'd all pass out from the fumes.

It seemed to me we'd had three pretty easy days, but they were feeling the effects. It was a nice gauge for me to realize that perhaps, after nearly three months, I *had* become "a hiking machine."

Harpers Ferry, West Virginia, founded in 1747, was the site of the John Brown Museum. Many Civil War battles were fought in the area and the AT paralleled the trenches where hundreds of soldiers were killed. The Shenandoah and Potomac rivers converged at this town of 1,500 people, and the trail crossed each on a footbridge. When leaving town, the AT followed the C&O Canal towpath for three miles (the only part of the trail thus far that was flat, level ground). The towpath was used by mules to pull barges through the canal in the early 1800s.

Most thru-hikers looked forward to stopping by the national headquarters of the Appalachian Trail Conference in Harpers Ferry. After talking to the staff several times during my year of preparation, I was eager to see the people who had provided all that good information. The staff took pictures of thru-hikers for its scrapbook, and some even stopped off for a couple of days and did volunteer work at the office. A huge 11-foot relief map of the trail along the back wall of the ATC gave the best overall impression of the terrain that I had seen. It was rather daunting, however, to see the great variations in altitude!

The center was also a source of thru-hiker information. I was pleased to find that Denver Dan and Strider had both left messages with the staff for me. I hoped either or both of them would catch up; there was no one with whom I'd rather climb that final mountain.

Another plan came together: Friends from Washington, D.C., took the evening commuter train to Harpers Ferry when Brad, Lisa, and I were there, to have dinner with us and stay overnight in the hotel. The train left the city at about 5 p.m. and returned by 8 a.m. Susie, Todd, and their son Jonathan had been intending to take this little excursion as a family outing, and my passage through the town provided the incentive to do it. We shared a lively evening with a sumptuous buffet (Brad: "Mom, I've never seen you eat three desserts!") and Jonathan entertained us with stories of a documentary he'd seen about the Civil War. After dinner we strolled through the town before saying good night. The next morning they took the train home, and we headed north on the AT.

I passed the 1,000-mile mark while Brad and Lisa were with me; I would be at the halfway point within the next week. Some pretty significant milestones! It seemed incredible to me that I had already carried my backpack over 1,000 miles of mountainous terrain. I gained more confidence with each passing day that I would make it all the way to Maine.

The first night north of Harpers Ferry, Brad, Lisa, and I stayed in the woods. A group of teenagers were tenting several hundred yards away. They were celebrating a birthday—someone's eighteenth, I think. At one point long after dark, two of them came to the shelter and said loudly, "Hello? Hello? Is anyone here?" One of the men roused himself and asked what they wanted. They were scared. They'd heard noises in the woods and thought there was a bear nearby. "What should we do? Will bears attack us?" The man assured them that the best thing to do was to make noise to scare the bear away, but not to worry. It was unlikely that a bear would attack a group of people in tents. They reluctantly went back to their tent site, and judging from the noise they made for the next hour, they were taking his advice. Silly people. Who would be afraid of bears in the night?

We spent our last night together with a longtime friend, Cynnie, and her family in their restored country home in Maryland, before Brad and Lisa headed back to Indiana. Cynnie and I had spoken on the phone and agreed to meet at the Dogpatch Tavern, which was about a third of a mile from the trail. It was listed in *The Thru-hiker's Handbook* as a place to avoid, because of the local motorcycle gangs that hung out there. We couldn't figure out anywhere else to meet, though; the choices weren't many when trying to find a place on a road crossing the Appalachian Trail.

The three of us arrived on foot with our backpacks at the tavern in the late afternoon, about a half-hour before Cynnie would appear. When we ordered a beer, the bartender said gruffly, "Sorry, no hiker trash in here. We only serve biker trash. Don't you know what we do to hikers?"

Two large patrons who were bellied up to the bar ignored us, and the men in leather vests at the pool table seemed much more interested in their billiards game than in three smelly backpackers. No record needles scratching; no threatening stares; just some bikers enjoying a sunny afternoon in a dark bar.

"I guess we'll risk it," I said. The bartender frowned at me for a minute, and then broke into an easy grin. "Budweiser all right, ma'am?"

He'd heard about the handbook's reference to his bar as a dangerous place, so he was giving us a hard time, but "Big Jim" turned out to be hiker-friendly when you got beneath the surface gruffness. We ordered pizza, beer, and chips, a total of six items in all, and it cost just $6! We thought there must be some mistake, but Big Jim assured us that he didn't "rip off" his customers like so many places. We discovered that the beer was just 50 cents a glass. The trail from Georgia to Maine was taking some interesting detours.

I was seeing many more day hikers and weekenders on the Appalachian Trail. Knowing that people were using this wonderful national resource was reassuring. Early on, it seemed the only ones out on the AT were thru-hikers. I realized, though, that millions of people have walked on that footpath, sometimes just long enough to go out into the woods and have a picnic.

I thought Benton MacKaye would be happy to see how the trail he envisioned more than 70 years ago had become a true wilderness escape for so many. Families used it for a day or a weekend, friends came out to give it a try, and a few fanatics tried to go all the way from Georgia to Maine. I wondered if Mr. MacKaye imagined in 1921 that anyone would try to hike the whole trail in one continuous journey. By the time he died in 1976 at age 96, several hundred people had done just that.

Following the trail's completion in 1936, the first person to thru-hike it was Earl Shaffer in '48. When he returned from serving in World War II, he decided to hike the AT to clear his head of wartime traumas. It was a much bigger challenge then: Thousands of downed trees blocked the path. The trail was so poorly marked in areas that he would sometimes hike a whole day without seeing a trace of it. Evidently he just headed north.

Shaffer carried mostly military surplus gear—about 40 pounds—and endured much discomfort to keep his pack that light. Tents were heavy and bulky then; he made do with his Marine Corps poncho, huddling under it during rainy nights. His sleeping bag was a medium-weight blanket with a zipper, and he often wrapped his feet in a burlap sack to help keep them warm. He wore moccasin boots, which he resoled twice. His feet were rarely dry. But even with the added trials of the trail, Shaffer averaged 17 miles a day. In 1965, he backpacked the trail again, going south, becoming the first person to thru-hike the Appalachian Trail in both directions. He used much of his original equipment. Today he lives in Pennsylvania near the trail. Now in his 70s, he talks of perhaps doing a third thru-hike. When my gear seemed bulky and the trail difficult, I tried to think of Earl Shaffer and the comparisons helped lighten my load.

By now there was the feeling among thru-hikers that most of us who were still on the trail would make it all the way to Katahdin. The camaraderie was growing. We had had the time to get beneath the surface conversation and discover a little about each other. A real bond develops when you share such intense experiences with people, and I was seeking the company of other hikers more those days. Perhaps I had spent enough time alone to be getting tired of my own.

The five days with Brad and Lisa had nourished me. The slower pace, easier terrain, and lighter pack gave my knees time to heal, and I reached a new level of relaxation, confidence, and enjoyment of my Appalachian Trail adventure. By seeing the beauty of the forest through the newness of their eyes, I was able to expand my own vision of the AT. And because I was more relaxed while they were here, the trail felt more benign.

I was finding there were two very distinct aspects of thru-hiking: the mountains and the miles. Perhaps the human distinction was the physical vs. the mental challenge. Or, the difference in the characteristics of a sprinter vs. a long distance runner. It takes very different qualities to succeed in those two events. On the trail, we needed both.

First we had to be equal to the physical endeavor. During the most rigorous of the steep mountain climbs, our physical ability was tested and stretched. We had to concentrate on the task at hand; without focus, there was the danger of injury. Adrenaline kicked in and helped us through the roughest spots.

When we reached the less arduous sections, the challenge was enduring the miles. As we spent months on the trail, mental stamina had to take over. Day after day, week after week, month after month—that was when we had to dig the deepest to just keep picking up those boots, step after step, mile after mile. The trail probably defeated more people with its daily grind than its physical trial.

It felt like the overall key to success for me was to relax, both mentally and physically, while remaining alert and focused. Not to struggle against the trail, but to flow with it. To see the joy in it. To see the image of myself successfully meeting the challenges involved. I was now more relaxed. That felt important as I continued up the Appalachian Trail.

18

Passing the halfway mark

Duncannon, Pennsylvania
1,118 miles hiked
July 8, 1994

I was halfway there. One of my steps on July 5 took me to mile 1,077.5, leaving an equal number of miles left to traverse before the large, wooden sign at the top of Mt. Katahdin gave me permission to lay down my backpack and go home. It seemed like a time to do some serious evaluation of what the trip had involved so far, how I felt about continuing, and whether I should make any adjustments.

But in reality, all those kinds of evaluations happened daily, and there wasn't a lot of trail conversation about passing the halfway point. In fact, instead of a philosophical discussion, acknowledging that milestone centered on the thru-hiker tradition of trying to eat a half-gallon of ice cream at one sitting. Nourishment for the body seemed more important by now than nourishment for the soul. (Perhaps that wasn't unusual, since I had thought from the beginning of my journey that it put us on the lowest level of Maslow's hierarchy of human needs, right down there at the food and shelter level.)

I couldn't finish my half-gallon and gave the remainder to Sher Bear and JettButt. Magoo couldn't do it, either, but Dreamcatcher succeeded, as did Bad DNA. (Dreamcatcher probably didn't weigh 100 pounds, even with a half-gallon of ice cream in her tummy, but she had the typical thru-hiker appetite.)

Certainly the significance of the halfway point was all in the mind: The trail wasn't any different than it had been the day before; the terrain hadn't gotten any harder—or easier. If a marker on the trail hadn't announced the milestone, no one would have been the wiser. Just one more step, one more mile, one more day. We could crank ourselves up to be reflective and emotional or we could just keep on hiking. I felt the need to be reflective.

It seemed to me the midway point could be compared to a fiftieth birthday, if you assumed you'd live to be roughly 100, or to a fortieth birthday if you were less optimistic. I think we bring to those birthday milestones the wisdom, insight, and calmness of having survived years of life's challenges—many terribly painful, many exhilarating and rewarding. We've tried various methods of coping with what life (or the trail) has thrown at us, with varying degrees of success. We've learned some lessons; we've repeated some mistakes. We've seen that no matter how we dealt with each situation, it was soon behind us. The next day arrived, and the next. The excruciating moments passed, as did the moments of ecstasy. If we recognize the wisdom and insight we've gained, the calmness is there for us to draw on. If not, the struggles don't really become any easier.

It's our choice. Can we put our fears to rest? I think life is supposed to be joyful. And it can be, if we draw on our strength and experience. Could I remember that when the next formidable peak rose before me?

When Brad dropped me off at the trail, I prepared myself to fight off waves of loneliness after enjoying five days of constant companionship. It was an emotional scene as Brad and Lisa drove me to a road that crossed the trail. We all hugged by the van, and then I had to scramble down the side of a hill and go under a viaduct to get back on the AT. Brad walked with me, holding my hand tightly all the way. I didn't know if he was providing support for me or for himself as he clung to my hand until I was ready to start off up the path. I hadn't anticipated there would be so many painful goodbyes during the course of my journey.

As I headed away from Brad, I kept turning around to wave until a dip in the trail cut him from my view. At times like that, I was reminded how closely our emotions are linked to our sensation of pain. I felt like I'd been punched in the stomach; loneliness struck the blow. My breath caught in my throat, and I wasn't sure I could inhale without sobbing. I tried to close my mind to the crushing feeling of aloneness, of knowing that I'd be hiking by myself until Greg joined me on Labor Day and that I wouldn't see Brad again until October, some 1,150 miles later. When I stopped for lunch that day and reached into my backpack where I kept my food, I found a note that Brad had tucked there: "Mom—I'm so proud to be your son. Hike on! Love Brad." Ah, the good fortune in my life still overwhelms me.

A letter at my mail drop in Harpers Ferry gave me something

to hang onto in the days that followed. One of my bridge club members at home had written to confirm that several of the group were driving out to spend a day with me. It helped tremendously to know they were coming. I think they wanted to make sure I hadn't turned into some kind of mountain creature and that I still remembered how to bid a short club.

The collective mindset of my bridge club is about as far removed from the wilderness experience as Montavani is from The Rolling Stones. We had all vacationed together at Sanibel Island in Florida, and half the group had never set foot in the Ding Darling Wildlife Refuge on the island. They would rather see their wildlife in a movie or in photographs.

But it was a measure of their friendship that several of them were driving all the way from Indiana to Pennsylvania to provide moral support and make sure I had everything I needed for the second half of my odyssey. It would also become part of our shared history. We had played bridge together on the third Thursday of each month for 20 years. The evolution of our lives during that period certainly reflected the changing faces and values of society. I was a housewife with two small children when I joined the bridge club. Most of us were stay-at-home moms, and we volunteered, were active politically on a local level, and were involved in carpools and neighborhood activities.

Carmel, the suburb of Indianapolis that we lived in, was the target back then of reverse-snobbery jokes: "What does a Carmel housewife make for dinner? Reservations." "How can you tell the Carmel housewife at a funeral? She's the one in the black tennis dress."

But like the rest of society, we'd gone to work (there was only one "Carmel housewife" left in the group), changed careers, divorced, and remarried (only one single left—me). Some husbands owned companies and some had struggled through periods of unemployment. We survived our children's high school years, athletic and academic accomplishments and decisions about colleges, along with the usual trials and tribulations of raising teenagers. We either celebrated or tried to hide from the big birthdays: 40, 50, 55. We commiserated through divorces, approved—or disapproved—of the choices for remarriage, consoled each other on the death of parents, and rejoiced at the birth of grandchildren. (Look out, here come the pictures!)

Our time together each month evolved also: From several rounds of bridge plus coffee and dessert. . .to some bridge, lots of conversation, and a few glasses of wine. . .to lots of wine and conversation plus a few hands of bridge, if we got around to it. . .to a more even mix of bridge, conversation, and wine. We'd taken trips together and then spent years laughing about the crazy things that happened. We'd joked about sharing a wing of a nursing home some day and hiring an aide who would take good care of us and bring us wine with our dinner.

Even though the bridge club thought I was crazy when I embarked on this bizarre wilderness adventure, they were supporting me. They gave me going-away gifts, helped me pack my boxes, sent my mail drops to me, and wrote notes of encouragement. One was even taking care of Elwood, my cat. And now they were coming to see me.

My journey pointed out how dissimilar I was from most of my friends. We shared some strong commonalities, but the differences were just as strong. Of course none of us fits any mold completely. We're all individuals, on the trail, as well as in life.

I had spent time recently with a variety of hikers who were adding interest and diversity to the trail mix. Del Doc had reappeared and we were progressing north at about the same rate. He was doing a survey on "numb toe syndrome," which most of us had. Evidently constant pounding on the soles of the feet could deaden the nerves running to the toes, causing numbness. The nerves usually regenerated gradually when the abuse stopped, although it could take up to a year. My toes had been numb for months; I hoped they would recover.

Del Doc was the ultimate strategist. He recorded every aspect of the trip from weather to the exact timing at road crossings and other landmarks, and he created various charts and graphs. I was grateful that he was willing to answer our medical questions. Back in the Shenandoahs, he had advised me to take megadoses of ibuprofen every day to keep my knee pain at a tolerable level. It helped tremendously. His other suggestion was to get off the trail temporarily and go home to have my knees checked out at a sports medicine clinic, but psychologically, I couldn't do that. I was afraid I wouldn't return.

Sourball provided comic relief on the trail. He looked amazingly like Bill the Cat from *Bloom County* and did right-on impersonations of Christopher Lloyd and Jack Nicholson. He entertained us with his wit and threw in flute solos in the shelters at night. The sound of a flute merged perfectly into a forest setting, as the light, airy notes gently drifted up into the trees. Sourball's diversity was apparent when he broke into a geology lesson. He was from Maine, where he'd hiked extensively on the AT, and he let us know daily that *the best part of the trail is in Maine!*

We sometimes referred to Sourball as Snoreball, a name that reflected his well-earned reputation as the loudest snorer on the trail. I always wore my ear plugs when he was sleeping nearby.

Memphis was traveling with Sourball; they were a good example of hikers who hooked up on the trail because they were compatible in goals, hiking style, and personality. Memphis was a quiet, low-key Southern gentleman, the opposite of Sourball's often-frenzied state, and he was the perfect foil for Sourball's comedy routines.

Dreamcatcher and Magoo also started traveling together after meeting on the trail. With very different personalities which nevertheless meshed well in the hiking experience, they had become romantically involved. I thought it would be interesting to see if their relationship lasted beyond Mt. Katahdin. I imagined that rapport on the trail wouldn't always translate to compatibility in the other parts of your life.

At the other end of that relationship spectrum were Sher Bear and JettButt, who had been friends for several years before dating and becoming engaged to be married following their recent college graduation. They had many similar interests, philosophies, and life goals and had struggled through the adjustments of traveling on the trail together, making the necessary compromises. They were finding their bond deepening as a result.

The members of this younger generation seemed willing to just be themselves without keeping up pretenses. I doubt that I would have had the nerve before marriage to spend six months, 24 hours a day, with my fiancé—pushing myself to my limits, dealing with the raw emotions that surface from constant pain and exhaustion, letting my future husband see me at my physical and emotional worst. No barriers. No hiding behind makeup or flattering clothes. No role distinctions. Come to think of it, perhaps if more couples put their relationship to such an arduous test before marrying, there wouldn't be such a high divorce rate. I admired Sher Bear and JettButt for their courage. They reflected the best qualities of their generation.

Two of the Goatherders, Frenchy and Phishstick, were still heading north and I intersected with them periodically. It fascinated me that the young men on the trail could hike so much faster than I, but our paths crossed over and over again. That's because they were always taking little sidetrips—hitchhiking to Memphis for a Bob Dylan concert, renting a van to drive to Virginia Beach for Memorial Day weekend, hitching into D.C. for sightseeing—and then they would go right back to where they left the trail and head north again. Some, like Slacker, seemed to be stopped whenever I saw them, often in a hiker hostel or perhaps at a beautiful location. Slacker appeared to be drinking in every moment of his journey, and his register entries indicated there was a lot of processing going on in that young mind of his.

I just kept plodding along. I was like a tortoise surrounded by dozens of hares, and I had the feeling we'd all reach the end of the trail about the same time.

One of the most unexpected, and sometimes funniest, aspects of the journey was sharing motel rooms with a variety of people. Every week or two, when an opportunity arose, it was nice to sleep in a bed and take a shower. But with many hikers on limited budgets, we often looked for someone to share a room, perhaps even a bed.

Recently the trail had crossed a highway where there was a motel just a few hundred yards down the interstate. The timing and location were too perfect to pass up. It had been a beastly hot day spent crossing several fields and pastures unprotected by the usual forest canopy. A late afternoon thunderstorm and continuing torrent of rain made the prospect of tenting grim. Several of us decided to stay at the motel. I shared a room with Del Doc and Bad DNA. Now, Del Doc liked to split the cost of a room, but he wasn't about to share his bed, so that left DNA and me together. The other alternative was for someone to sleep on the floor, but no one volunteered.

By 9 o'clock, we were ready to hit the sack. In one bed was Del Doc, controlling the remote to the TV. He'd found a station featuring classical music, and being a huge symphony buff, he was thoroughly enjoying it, lying in bed drinking a beer and loving the music—even laughing in certain parts. I had never seen anyone enjoy a performance more.

In the other double bed were Bad DNA and me. I was reading the newspaper and DNA was writing in his journal. He asked,

"Indiana Jean, what's your last name and address?" It suddenly struck me so funny that I was in a motel room with two men, we didn't even know each other's names, and we were all getting ready to spend the night together. I tried not to burst out laughing as I gave him my name and address. I just lay there smiling to myself and thinking as I had so many times on the trail, "I'll never do any of this again!"

It was hard not to get nostalgic and a little homesick on holidays when I knew my family and friends were probably together doing something special and I was off by myself in a strange environment. The Fourth of July weekend was like that for me. I hiked through Caledonia State Park on July 3. It was filled with picnickers: families and friends with their tables full of food and volleyball games in full swing. I knew my sons were at a lake with their dad, so I called from a pay phone and talked with them. I also talked to my mom. And then, one of the vacationing families invited me to their table and heaped huge helpings of food on my plate before filling a container for me to take along for my evening meal in the woods. Trail magic always appeared just when my spirits needed a boost.

Although I was sometimes melancholy, I could usually get beyond the feeling because I believed so strongly that this journey on the Appalachian Trail was a life-changing experience for me. I think we all need life-changing experiences. They don't have to be six-month adventures; they can come in much smaller increments. But we each need to be building a lifetime of significant events. They can be as simple as reading a book that causes a shift in our thinking, or hearing a speech that redefines our values, or spending a little time in the woods and coming away with new insights.

Or, on another level, they can involve conquering a fear, setting a challenging goal that makes us push ourselves to achieve it, doing something we've never done before, or making friends with someone totally unlike us. Or perhaps spending time away from our family and friends, giving them time to miss us and ourselves time to miss them. I missed my family and friends terribly sometimes, but I was sure that when we reconnected, the bonds would be stronger than before.

My journey was adding so much to my life in many different ways. It was much more than just a hike along a narrow footpath in the mountains; in fact that was probably the least of it for me. It was deepening my relationships with family and friends, providing encounters with many wonderful people both on and off the trail, giving me time for reflection and personal growth, and offering a look at very different kinds of lifestyles and geography than I was used to seeing in the Midwest—plus a chance to see nature at its best.

I headed into the second half of my trek knowing that the newness and excitement had worn off and the long days of summer were ahead. Sometimes I tried to think about what I had learned and how to apply it. Other times I had to stop all the thinking and just keep on hiking.

19

Reunions and companionship

Eckville Hiker's Center, Pennsylvania
1,204 miles hiked
July 15, 1994

*M*y day with the bridge club provided the laughter, sharing, and sense of normalcy I needed to reassure me that I'd be able to reconnect with dear friends upon my return home. And it was another opportunity to feel the warmth of friendship surrounding and supporting me.

When the bridge club picked me up, we drove to Harrisburg, 40 miles away, where we stayed at a Residence Inn—a perfect choice with its kitchen and living space. We spent 24 hours together, and during that time they helped me pick out my summer wardrobe at a local sporting goods store. I'd decided to buy a sports bra and try hiking in that since it had been so hot that my T-shirt was constantly soaked with perspiration. I also wanted a pair of thinner, lighter shorts. I bought those two items and that was all, everything I'd need for the whole summer. I sent home more weight than I acquired so ended up with a net loss in my backpack. Hallelujah!

One of my most peculiar off-trail experiences occurred in the post office in Duncannon when I was picking up my mail while waiting for the bridge club to arrive. A man walked in and began to quiz me about my journey. He introduced himself as Siggy. Having done some backpacking, he was interested to meet a thru-hiker and eager to talk. He went on and on and on. I needed to get my mail sorted and organized, so I started to fidget.

During our conversation, he mentioned that he was a writer and that the large manila envelope he had with him contained all of the poems and short essays he had written. He was planning to mail his collection of works to a friend, but impulsively decided he wanted *me* to have it so I could read his work. I tried to protest since I wouldn't have time to read it in town and certainly didn't intend to carry it with me on the trail, but he was persistent. I ended up with the manila envelope.

True to my nature, I then offered to mail it to the person he'd addressed it to after I had read it. Siggy thought that was a great idea, because, as he said, "That would save me something that I don't have much of: money!" He also invited me to his home for lunch. His wife and kids would be back from the park soon and they wouldn't mind if I came over for a sandwich. Besides, he said, his home was air-conditioned.

Siggy's next comment was, "Don't pay any attention to the white spots on the rugs. We have a new puppy that isn't housebroken yet, and that's just the baking soda we sprinkle on the rug whenever he has an accident."

I finally extricated myself from him and lugged my backpack down the block to the laundromat. It was extremely hot and I was feeling very uncomfortable. I was sweating profusely, more than I usually did out on the trail, and was in the hottest place in town: the laundromat. As I was putting my clothes into the washer, along came Siggy. He'd followed me there. Once again he encouraged me to stop by for lunch, and he now gave me his phone number. He'd already given me his address.

I didn't go to his house, and when the bridge club picked me up, I still had the manila envelope with all his compositions. During the evening, we decided we should see what kinds of things he had written before mailing it on to his friend.

We were impressed. His writing was excellent. Very poignant stuff—about his childhood, his marriage, his kids, his father, himself. One really funny essay on an ongoing battle with his wife about washing his underwear. Several lovely poems about his children, and a very telling piece about his father never paying any attention to him when he was a child.

Carol took the envelope home and promised to put it in the mail. I'll always remember how Siggy reinforced the lesson: You can find talent in the most unusual places, tucked away in the most unlikely people. Some day I expect I'll see his name in print.

I was glad I had the warm memories of being with my friends to carry me through the next week, because it was a rough one. One day I got lost. I couldn't find a white blaze anywhere. As I searched and searched, the far-off sound of traffic started to seep into my consciousness. A quick check of my data book confirmed that the trail would cross a road soon. So I decided to bushwhack down the side of the mountain, tracking the sounds to the road. Then I'd be able to follow the road until I found where the trail crossed it. That was my plan.

I started carefully picking my way through the undergrowth straight down the mountainside, grabbing onto branches and sliding down through the brush. When the ground leveled out, I was confronted with a huge briar patch, completely filled with jagged brambles. It was the only way to get to the road. I should have stopped right then and dug through my backpack for my long underwear to keep my legs from being shredded. But I didn't realize what I was getting into. Once I started through the briars, I realized my mistake, but it seemed impossible to stop, and going back would have sent me right back up the mountain. The razor-sharp briars sliced my legs, inflicting an additional wound with each step. By the time I reached the other side, my legs were covered with blood. I had depleted my repertoire of profanities, which didn't help the outcome, but released some of the frustration.

Upon reaching the road, I hiked back and forth for a full two hours before finding the trail. It had paralleled the road for more than a mile, high on the side of the mountain, before dipping down to cross it. What would have been an easy 15-mile day had turned into a 20-mile bad dream.

The lesson for me: Keep my eyes on the blazes, and if I lost my way, look for the familiar trail markings to put me back on the path instead of heading off into unchartered territory.

The night before I reached Eckville Hiker's Center was one of the nastiest nights of my journey. It had been a rainy, dreary day, and I had hiked 20 miles. I decided to head for a campground with a grocery store, 1.5 miles from the AT via a blue-blazed side trail. Unfortunately, it was the steepest, worst footpath I'd seen yet. At one point I slid for about 50 yards down the side of a mountain, right through gravel and rocks, in the pouring rain. The precipitation had turned the trail into a river. I walked along fuming, up to my ankles in water, furious that the route was marked as a trail when it was virtually impassable.

When I finally reached the campground, darkness was descending and I was still a quarter-mile from the store/registration center. It struck me as odd that so many of the campers and RVs looked like they weren't going anywhere. They were established for the summer, all decorated with electric lights and Chinese lanterns. Some even had radios and televisions. It seemed more like a wooded town than a campground.

The store was about to close when I arrived, so I quickly bought a little food and asked where I could tent. They pointed out the hikers' shelter on a map, another quarter-mile away, where I could stay for $9.

I trudged along in the darkness and rain, sloshing through puddles on a rutted road, hoping for a nice dry shelter. Not to be. It was just three walls and a sloping roof covering the bumpy dirt ground, and the roof leaked almost everywhere. So I pitched my tent in the darkness and drizzle and dirt, wearing the little headlamp that I carried, trying to avoid all the drips and rivulets running along the ground. It was grungy and spooky, I was the only hiker there, and I knew I would have to retrace that treacherous trail in the morning unless I could find an alternate route. I was not a happy camper.

The next morning I awoke determined not to take that same trail back to the AT, because I wasn't sure if I could make it back up the steep area where I'd slid down. I asked some people in an RV nearby if they knew another way to the Appalachian Trail. Sure enough, there was another blue-blazed trail to the AT. It wasn't as treacherous as the other one; however, it put me back on the trail two miles *south* of where I'd left it, so I had to re-hike the section I'd already done the previous afternoon.

But on the trail, something always happened to redeem a bad experience. When I arrived at Eckville Hiker's Center, Sher Bear, JettButt, and DNA were here. I was thrilled to reconnect with them because I hadn't seen any hiker friends since Duncannon. The only unwelcome guests were the bugs, which were biting badly.

It was the second night at Eckville for DNA, Sher Bear, and JettButt. DNA had planned to leave that morning, but just never got around to it. Sher Bear and JettButt were trying to decide what to do. JettButt had developed terrible blisters on both heels from walking in the rain in his new boots. He couldn't hike with those blisters, so that posed a dilemma: Should Sher Bear hike to Delaware Water Gap while he hitchhiked there to wait for her, allowing his blisters time to heal? Should they both hitch ahead and then come back and make up this section? Or should they just stay there for a few days until he could hike again? They were having a difficult time deciding what to do, and he was really in pain.

Many hikers had needed a second—or third—pair of boots by this point, and breaking them in on the trail often caused serious blister problems, especially with frequent rain. For that reason, many people broke in two or three pairs before they left home and had them sent out to the trail as their boots wore out. The danger there was that some of us found our feet expanding on the trail, and we needed a larger size. I was lucky; I hadn't had a blister yet, even when I broke in my new boots with 14 miles my first day back from Los Angeles.

The past week had shown me once again how rapidly circumstances could deteriorate or improve on the trail, and how crucial attitude was in getting through the hard times and leaving the unpleasantness a few steps behind on the trail. Yesterday was over. Tomorrow I would cross Blue Mountain, Hawk Mountain, Bear Rocks, The Cliffs and Bake Oven Knob. Sounded like a good day ahead.

The Appalachian Trail

20

"I am not afraid"

Delaware Water Gap, Pennsylvania
1,265 miles hiked
July 21, 1994

I was about to enter New Jersey—my eighth state, and a long way from Georgia! I would hit New York within two days, then crisscross the state lines a few times before leaving New Jersey for good 70 miles later. About 90 miles farther on, I would cross the New York line into Connecticut. This was beginning to feel a long way north.

Pennsylvania seemed to whiz by even though the trail traversed 232 miles in the state. I had been on a high from passing the halfway mark and riding on the memories of all my visits with family and friends. Although the terrain in Pennsylvania was beautiful, the trail there was infamous for its rocky, uneven surface. In some sections, the path was simply a jumble of rocks—uneven, irregular rocks—that went on for miles. We were forced to slow our pace and keep our eyes on the ground with every step, for an unwary hiker could easily twist a knee or ankle. Many of the entries in the trail registers protested the latest challenge that Mother Nature had thrown our way.

At Eckville, JettButt had decided to hitch a ride to Delaware Water Gap, 63 trail-miles north, where he would wait for Sher Bear and give his feet time to heal. She was extremely nervous about going on alone because they had been hiking together from the beginning. I was very proud of her for deciding to do it.

The first day she was by herself, Sher Bear caught up to DNA and me as we were stopping for lunch. We agreed to stick together for the four days it would take to get to Delaware Water Gap. It gave her confidence to travel for a few days without her fiancé, but she liked the security of having a hiking partner.

It was the first time I'd spent several full days with another thru-hiker. And it was my first time of extended conversation on the trail with another woman. We enjoyed our time together. During the many hours each day, we talked about our values and ideals, relationships with family, raising kids, and making marriages work—the kinds of conversations I have with women friends at home. It was a welcome and refreshing change from the masculine environment in which I'd been living.

Although Sher Bear is almost 30 years younger than I, she became a friend. On the trail as in life, age doesn't have much to do with anything. It doesn't tell what your interests and priorities are, how much wisdom or insight you've gained, how you deal with people or life situations, and what you're capable of physically, mentally, or emotionally. It just indicates what year you were born.

Our second day together, we stopped in a small community, Palmerton, for a couple of hours in the afternoon. We went to the local police station, known as the jailhouse hostel, where thru-hikers were invited to use the shower and stay overnight. After photocopying our driver's licenses, they allowed us free access to the building through a back door that was propped open. It was Sunday afternoon and there didn't seem to be any staff members around. The friendliness and security of a small town can renew your faith in the goodness of people.

We stayed in Palmerton long enough to hit the shower and grocery store before heading back to the trail to get in a few more miles before nightfall. Several of our hiker friends were planning to spend the night, and it was a temptation to do the same. Sometimes it was hard to leave when the company was good and the sleeping was under roof. But Sher Bear was eager to reconnect with JettButt, and I just wanted to keep putting miles behind me.

On our way out of town, we passed Memphis and Sourball in the park talking to a group of teenagers. With a little prodding, one of the teens agreed to drive us back to the trail and went to get his vehicle. Pretty soon he pulled up driving a car decorated with garish, psychedelic patterns and colors, loud music blasting from the radio, and a condom hanging from the antenna! It was a wild ride back to the trailhead.

As Sher Bear and I hiked up Lehigh Gap that afternoon, we encountered our steepest rock climb to date. We pulled ourselves up from boulder to boulder, and there were places where I wasn't sure I could stretch far enough to find a handhold, with my backpack weighing me down. I was very nervous and proceeded slowly, trying to keep my fear of heights under control. Sher Bear was reassuring and helpful; she had worked through her own fears with hours of backpacking above treeline in the Adirondacks. We then walked along a steep, rocky section where I felt like I would fall to my death if I slipped. I knew I was being irrational and that if I would just stand up straight and walk as if I were on flat ground, I would be in no danger. But I couldn't put logic into practice, and I inched along in a crouched position, adding more trauma to the experience than necessary. I tried to keep my peripheral vision in check and not focus on how far above the valley we were and how steeply the earth seemed to drop away toward the river below. When we made it beyond the rocks, I suddenly burst into tears, as a release from the tension and fear. Sher Bear said, "Oh, I'm so glad to see someone else get emotional!" It reminded us both that we were, for the most part, surrounded by men on the Appalachian Trail.

I had been talking through this fear with some of the other backpackers because I knew I would face many steep rock climbs above treeline in New Hampshire and Maine, and for a while I was rather panicked about that. But I listened to what people said and decided it wouldn't help to worry about it. Instead, I was trying to build my hand and arm strength and use every rocky section along the way as practice so I would gain confidence as I went. Others had done it; I could too: "I am *not* afraid," she said fearfully.

JettButt was waiting for Sher Bear at the church in Delaware Water Gap when we arrived. It was a tearful reunion. His blisters were healing and they would head north in a day or two.

I had intended to hike out of Delaware Water Gap the day after arriving but was stopped dead in my tracks by all the mail I received and the emotions it evoked. When I arrived at the post office, the clerk said, "Oh, I'm so glad you arrived when I was working. I've been hoping to meet you. I've never seen a thru-hiker get so much mail!" (There were 34 letters plus packages.) "I'm really happy I got to meet you." Excitement must be hard to find at the post office.

My faithful correspondents—family and friends—had made me a post office celebrity. The letters were a constant source of inspiration and motivation to continue. I often wondered if I could have continued on the Appalachian Trail if it hadn't been for the wonderful, loving support that was reaching me each month through the U.S. mail. Here's a sampling of what awaited me when I arrived at a post office:

Homemade cookies from a lady in Illinois who had never met me but heard about my journey from a mutual friend.

Correspondence from people who hadn't missed a mail drop since my journey began.

Letters from relatives with whom I had never corresponded before.

Notes of encouragement from acquaintances in Indianapolis and people I had never met who were reading about my journey in *The Indianapolis Star*, including typed letters from a 100-year-old woman who prayed for my safety every day. I was eager to meet her when I returned.

Carefully written letters from schoolchildren whose teachers were sharing my story with them.

Many expressions of love from family and friends so dear to me.

Absorbing this outpouring of support and taking time to enjoy the warm feelings had become a treasured part of my months away from home. I stayed in town to savor it. By the next morning when I once again planned to leave, I became immobilized with the anticipation of a pitch-in dinner at a local church. So I put off leaving a second time. I wondered if I would ever get out of this town.

I continued to be amazed at the generosity of people who lived near the Appalachian Trail. The Presbyterian Church in Delaware Water Gap had a long-standing tradition of serving as a hiker hostel, with a bunk room, sitting room, restroom, and shower available to thru-hikers. If the bunks were full, tenting was allowed in the back yard. Parishioners provided fresh, fluffy towels and washcloths, which they replenished daily.

But that wasn't the best part. Every Thursday evening all summer long, the congregation provided a dinner for thru-hikers. They brought in tables full of food and an invitation to hikers to go through the line first. With the voracious appetites of those on the trail, the parishioners were taking a big chance there would be anything at all left for them.

Since this pitch-in dinner tradition was published in *The Thru-hiker's Handbook*, many hikers tried to be in Delaware Water Gap on a Thursday evening. Nothing was a stronger magnet for thru-hikers than free food, especially if it was home-cooked.

I sat with some of the church members during the meal—people of all ages, including a 90-year-old woman who came to the hiker dinner each week. She was vital, fascinating, and doing the nonagenarian version of living life to its fullest. I loved talking with her.

An unexpected benefit of the pitch-in dinner was that it became a mini-reunion for thru-hikers. With some staying for days and others rushing into town on Thursday afternoon, we ended up with 24 hikers at the table, and tents everywhere. I'd not seen so many trail friends since Trail Days in Damascus.

Delaware Water Gap was missing just one hiker amenity: a laundromat. Therefore, DNA and I found a ride to Stroudsburg, several miles away. After washing our clothes, we bought groceries and decided to catch a movie. *Forrest Gump* was playing at a theater a couple of miles from the laundromat. We didn't have much time before the movie began, so we ran through town, both with arms full of laundry and groceries, with our thumbs out. It was a very hot day and we were both dripping with sweat, but we kept hustling along, and eventually someone took mercy on us and gave us a ride. We each had to use an extra seat in the theater for our food and clothes. I was impressed with the character of Forrest Gump, running back and forth across the country like that, except it took him just 10 minutes to do it in the movie. It had taken me almost four months to get from Georgia to the border of New Jersey. It always seems easier in the movies!

I experienced yet another enjoyable off-trail encounter in Delaware Water Gap, which had become one of my favorite trail towns: Childhood friends, whom I hadn't seen in 29 years, joined me for dinner. I was in their wedding after high school. They had been living in Pennsylvania for a number of years, and when they heard about my AT thru-hike, they wrote me at an earlier mail drop suggesting we get together. I called them from a pay phone as I hiked through Port Clinton and we arranged to meet.

We spent the evening reminiscing about our childhood and catching up on the events of our lives for the past three decades. They had brought our high school yearbooks, and after dinner we went back to the church, where my hiking buddies enjoyed seeing what high school looked like back in the '50s (the era of most of their parents).

My time in Delaware Water Gap had been very special, mainly because of a congregation that provided food and shelter for strangers who happened to be passing through their town. What a wonderful way of putting their Christian beliefs into practice. How many of us make time to perform acts of kindness, expecting nothing in return? Surely people who do have many rewards in their lives simply from living the way we were taught. We were blessed by their generosity, but truly, they were the blessed ones.

In a discussion the night before leaving town, several of us talked about why we were still on the trail when so many others had gone home. Gophermagne, age 22, shared two stories which showed the measure of this young man. One was an incident within his first month on the Appalachian Trail, in the Smokies. He had developed shin splints and had gone home for several days to recover before returning to the trail. As he was leaving, he overheard another hiker say, "He won't be back!" But instead of discouraging him, it just made him more determined. He wasn't the kind of person who would look for an excuse to quit. He *would* be back, and he'd complete the trail. I think the young people like Gophermagne were developing the perseverance to stick it out through the rough times and they were pleased with themselves—and sometimes surprised. It took much more than muscles, strength, and physical stamina to hike the trail. It also took grit, determination, and mental discipline. I had tremendous admiration for these young people who were developing those qualities so early in life.

We all agreed that emotions were raw and close to the surface on the trail. Some of the men admitted crying at various times. Gopher also told us about a time in Virginia when he'd gotten lost. It was late in the day and it was raining; he was exhausted, frustrated, and off on the wrong trail. He sat down, took his pack off, and started crying. What made me think he was such a mature young man was that he had told his girlfriend about the incident, including the crying part. I hoped she appreciated him.

21

An encounter with lightning

Bear Mountain, New York
1,375 miles hiked
July 28, 1994

*F*ewer than 800 miles remained on my journey, and given the initial number, that was beginning to sound small. It was four months to the day since I started my trek, and I planned to reach the end of the trail in just over two months. There were times when I felt like I had spent my entire life on this narrow footpath through the mountains. My equipment was holding up well and my backpack had become such an accepted extension of my body that I could barely remember the early days when I struggled mightily just to hoist it onto my back. That's not to say it was a welcome addition. It was more like a huge growth—unpleasant, but necessary for survival. It had all my life-support systems. The weight was still a factor, always a factor, but less so than before.

I had spent time recently with Model-T. He was a retired Marine and the trail seemed to have worked its magic on him, for he was very un-Marine-like. After thru-hiking the trail in 1990, he was doing it again. He said the effects of the trail had started to wear off, so he needed another dose. I couldn't imagine doing this a second time!

Model-T told me that when he was in the Marines, he was typical career military: He had to be better than anyone else to progress up through the ranks, so he was very competitive and hard-core. But now he was one of the most laid-back, low-key hikers on the trail. He had rigged bug netting to surround his sleeping bag, and while other hikers swatted bugs throughout the nights in the shelters, he slept in comfort with nary a bite. He carried a very light frying pan, spread butter on English muffins and sautéed them for breakfast— producing a tantalizing aroma which made my cold toaster pastries even more unappetizing than usual.

While Model-T and I were hiking together one morning, we suddenly noticed that we were following the blue blazes of a side trail instead of the AT's white marks. But Model-T was confident that if we stayed on that blue-blazed trail, we'd get back to the AT fairly soon. Sure enough, within 15 minutes, the trails reconnected and we were back on track. If I'd been by myself, I would have turned around immediately when I discovered I was off the trail and searched until I found the white blazes. No more bushwhacking through briar patches for me! But I trusted Model-T's instincts, and he was right on target. He inspired confidence; nothing seemed to faze him. At 58, he was closer to my age than most. I was impressed with the wives who were understanding enough to allow their husbands to go off on a six-month trek. Perhaps they didn't have a choice.

A close encounter with lightning had recently produced another glimpse at the fury of Earth's natural elements. One day I was crossing the top of a mountain in a downpour, with lightning flashes all around. I made it safely across the open space and into the relative security of the downward descent, surrounded by trees. As I made my way down the mountain into a gap, a fire alarm and sirens started to blare from a nearby town, signaling a lightning strike, I thought.

Suddenly I heard a clap of thunder and immediately saw or felt the lightning very close by. My body involuntarily hit the ground and I felt myself praying fervently as I went down. When I sat up and looked around, I began to smell a very strange odor, like a sulfur aroma. After looking for smoke, flames, or fallen trees, I scrambled up and hurried on down the mountain, trying to get as far from the top as possible. The forest took on an eerie feeling, and I felt the trees and I were equally vulnerable to nature's whims. It was a disconcerting experience and a solemn reminder of the awesome power of the physical world.

When I reached a shelter later that afternoon, the rain had stopped, so I spread my equipment out to dry on the ground and over the bushes. Model T was already there and, as always, seemed completely calm and self-contained. I spent about two hours trying to get my stuff dried out, while he sat quietly in the shelter. I thought, "His gear doesn't even get wet!"

The next day was sunny and gorgeous, and I stopped at a beautiful lake with a beach, lifeguard, and concession stand at High Point State Park in New Jersey. Otter, Poet, and I arrived about the same time, and we all went for a refreshing swim. It seemed like such a traditional summer scene, with families vacationing together in the warm sand, that I felt like an observer instead of a participant. I didn't fit into this picture with my backpack, hiking boots, and stick, and I must have looked as out of place as I felt. My shorts and T-shirt doubled as a swimming suit, and I felt very odd walking into the lake wearing them. However, the water was cool and invigorating, and no one came along to tell me that I couldn't swim without proper attire. I floated on the surface for a long time, with my face to the sky, enjoying the therapeutic effects of the water on my always-sore knees and feet. After the sun dried me off, I slipped back into the woods, feeling more refreshed than at any time since my journey began.

Picture this: You hear there's a swamp ahead, and people warn you that the water level is higher than usual, you won't get through it without sinking into murky water above your boot level, and you're better off to take an extended road walk around the perimeter. I was prepared to heed the advice, but when I approached Vernie Swamp in New Jersey with Model-T and DNA, they were planning to be more adventurous. They convinced me that I shouldn't be a wimp and that I would regret it if I missed this opportunity to do a "swamp walk." It was another occasion when the trail provided other hikers at just the right time, because they were right: I loved it.

The guidebook said that 112 bog bridges would allow us to go through Vernie Swamp without wading, but that must have been when it hadn't rained for a long time. The water was often calf deep. DNA and I took off our boots and waded through in our sandals. Model-T wore his boots, proving my theory that he didn't get wet.

The bog bridges were two boards about six feet long, nailed together with a couple of logs underneath them so they would float. But when we would step onto one, it would promptly sink and we'd walk under the water until we came to the next one, which would sink, too. The boards were very slippery and we had to be extremely cautious so we wouldn't slip off and end up getting sucked down into the muck. DNA led the way, pretending he was riding a series of surfboards, and Model-T brought up the rear. I felt secure in the middle. We laughed, took pictures of each other, and generally acted like a bunch of kids. It was one of the most entertaining episodes on the trail. And no one got leeches.

People often asked what I did when it rained. I got wet. When planning for the trip, I often heard the phrase "No pain, no rain, no Maine." My experience bore out the validity of that warning. I had gotten caught in a lot of rain, and I *hated* having wet boots. After 16 miles of walking in wet foot gear, at the end of the day my feet ached even more than usual. But if I tried to complete the trail without hiking in the rain, I'd never get to Maine.

By New Jersey I had realized I probably couldn't continue my journey without ibuprofen, or some other pain-killing, antiinflammatory drug. Each night, I counted out enough pills for the next day and put them in my waist pack so they'd be accessible. I took two in the morning, two before lunch, two at mid-afternoon, and two with dinner. Sometimes I took a fifth dose in the evening. I always carried enough in my backpack to last until the next town.

One day, I took my morning dose and by lunch noticed that the day's supply had fallen out of my waist pack somewhere along the trail. Instead of rummaging through all of my gear to get more, I decided to wait until I unloaded my pack that evening. That was a big mistake, but an important learning experience.

By 5 o'clock I was in misery, with my knees, feet, and toes hurting more than they had since the Shenandoahs, when I used to cry almost daily before I began taking round-the-clock doses of ibuprofen. I was hiking that afternoon with Poet and Newsman, and by late afternoon I was back in the pain cage. When we reached a road where we stopped to rest, I broke down right there and started sobbing! ("We are thru-hikers, MIGHTY thru-hikers. . .") Sometimes I really embarrassed myself.

But it made me aware of what a miracle drug ibuprofen is, and I was grateful it was available. Without it I doubt I could have stood the pain. I had heard before starting my trek that ibuprofen was the drug of choice on the trail, but I didn't realize that I would become so dependent on it. I wished I'd bought stock in the company before leaving.

When I passed through Harriman State Park in New York, I spent a tranquil evening camping by myself. The park was 46,000 acres of rolling, wooded terrain. It was absolutely beautiful and unlike anything I had seen on the trail—kind of wide-open in a closed-in sort of way. I found a secluded lake where I could spend the night, and I was careful not to leave any trace I'd been there. Unfortunately, others who had used the area before me had not been so considerate, and litter was strewn everywhere. I found it remarkable that people who appreciated the natural world enough to spend time in the woods were so self-centered that they left their trash behind.

After finally finding an unlittered area to pitch my tent, I sponged off in the lake, rinsed out my clothes, and hung them on tree branches to dry. I was content to be alone, completely and happily alone.

A large rock jutting out over the water made a perfect place to cook and eat my dinner. As I was enjoying my solitude, I suddenly realized someone was swimming across the water, with powerful, even strokes, right toward the rock where I was sitting. Eventually I could tell it was a man, a very strong swimmer. I watched him approach for about 15 minutes. This was no casual swim.

As he came closer and closer, I had this romantic notion that the man of my dreams would swim right up to my rock, emerge from the water, and we would discover over Ramen noodles and candlelight that we were soulmates, meant to discover each other in a fateful encounter on the Appalachian Trail. But alas, the young man swam almost to the rock I was sitting on, reversed course, and started swimming back, without breaking his stroke or concentration. Perhaps if I'd been 25 years younger, he would have come all the way, climbed up onto the rock, and the happily-ever-after would have begun.

It was a serene evening by the lake spent all alone, gazing at the stars and watching the rippling patterns the breeze made on the water as darkness quietly closed in around me. Finding solitude in the open air has always felt important to me. It provides thinking time, time to discover if I feel all right in my own skin and with my own life patterns. Nature provides a mirror with a glass clearer than any made by humankind. "Who am I? What am I doing with my life? Is this the right direction for me?" On the trail, I knew immediately if I veered off in the wrong direction. I wish life were as simple.

That evening was also a strong reminder that living modestly, without what are often considered the "necessities of life," grows on you. Everything needed for that perfect evening was either provided by the outdoors or had been carried on my back from Georgia. We can get along in life with little if we choose to, because the sights, sounds, and smells of nature are available to us—free of charge.

The Appalachian Trail

0   Miles   100

Sharon Mountain Campsite,
Connecticut

CANADA

VERMONT

White
Mountain
National Forest

MAINE

Mt. Katahdin

Green Mountain
National Forest

NEW
HAMPSHIRE

NEW YORK

Hudson River

MASSACHUSETTS

RI

CONNECTICUT

Delaware Water Gap
National Recreation Area

New York City

PENNSYLVANIA

OHIO

Harrisburg

NEW
JERSEY

MARYLAND

DEL

Harpers
Ferry

C&O
Canal National
Historical Park

WEST VIRGINIA

George Washington
National Forest

Shenandoah
National Park

VIRGINIA

KENTUCKY

Roanoke

Jefferson
National Forest

Cherokee
National Forest

TENNESSEE

Pisgah
National Forest

Great Smoky
Mountains
National Park

Asheville

NORTH CAROLINA

Nanatahala
National Forest

Springer
Mountain

Chattahoochee
National Forest

SOUTH CAROLINA

GEORGIA

N

W   E

S

APPALACHIAN TRAIL

MAINE TO GEORGIA

22

A mountaintop movie

Sharon Mountain Campsite, Connecticut
1,469 miles hiked
August 4, 1994

efore leaving New York, I had crossed the Hudson River south of West Point on the Bear Mountain Bridge. The very first sections of the footpath that would become the Appalachian Trail were constructed in Bear Mountain State Park during 1922 and 1923. The trail goes right through the middle of the Trailside Museum and Zoo that was built in 1927, partly at the urging of the AT's inspirational father, Benton MacKaye.

Although the zoo, which featured plants and animals native to the area, was supposed to inspire an appreciation of nature, several thru-hikers complained loudly about the animals being kept in cages. Juxtaposed next to months in the wilderness seeing animals in their natural habitat, man's practice of capturing them and putting them in cages so we could look at them seemed particularly cruel.

Gophermagne had another of his kismet experiences. The strap on his backpack had broken, and the manufacturer agreed by phone to send a new one via UPS to a small town near the trail. But a delivery mix-up occurred and through a bizarre set of circumstances, Gopher spent most of one day riding around with a UPS driver while he made deliveries.

They delivered a package to Mary Tyler Moore's house near Kent, Connecticut, and drove by Henry Kissinger's place. At one point during their travels, they drove under a pedestrian overpass on a highway and the driver pointed out a hiker crossing the overpass. Gopher recognized me and rolled down the window, yelling, "Indiana Jean! Indiana Jean!" I didn't hear him (he told me about it later), but I would have thought I were imagining things if I'd heard my name being called from a UPS truck! I shouldn't have been surprised, though. It was a compressed little world on the Appalachian Trail, and that was the kind of coincidence that happened regularly.

I spent a night at Graymoor, historic home of the Franciscan Friars and Sisters of the Atonement in New York. For 20 years, continuing the centuries-old tradition of Franciscan hospitality for the travel-weary, Graymoor had provided free lodging, dinner, and breakfast for thru-hikers. An unobtrusive donation box left each hiker's conscience to be his or her guide. I had heard about Graymoor before even beginning my journey. It was a favorite stop of thru-hikers, and I had been looking forward to it for months.

I stayed in my own little room with a bed, dresser, and washbasin. A table was reserved for thru-hikers in the large dining room, with generous quantities of food served family-style. The night I was there, a lively gathering of priests and church lay leaders were attending a conference. Most were wearing regular street clothes during dinner, but when I saw them later going to their worship service, they were fully robed. They were an impressive sight as they passed me in a narrow corridor on their way to the chapel.

The grounds were beautiful and after dinner I strolled on the pathways, encountering gardens, statues, and quiet places to sit and contemplate. Franciscan friars are masters at creating an aura of peace and serenity for themselves and for those who come into their circle.

The most poignant moment of that week was drifting off to sleep in the monastery to the sound of the friars singing at their 9 p.m. vespers. It was an incredibly peaceful chant and I wanted to lie awake and hear that repetitious refrain all night. It occurred to me as I was falling asleep in my little monk-like room that, with few exceptions, I had not slept in the same place two nights in a row in the past four months.

My friend Gail drove over from Connecticut to pick me up at the monastery so we could spend a day together. Gail was our next-door neighbor in Carmel while my sons were young, and she was like a second mother to them. Although she moved to New England a dozen years ago, she had remained a dear friend. She provided one more bit of motivation in the past month to keep hiking through the bugs and the heat and the pain: How could I quit when I knew I would see Gail if I could just make it to New York? The last time we were together had been three years before, so it was another very special day for me.

When Gail dropped me off at the trail near the monastery, we were hugging and saying goodbye just as Gophermagne and Slacker hiked by. Gopher laughed when he saw us. He'd been there when Zelma dropped me off in Virginia, and here was the same scene being repeated in New York. "Another Hallmark moment," he said. Within a half-hour DNA came along, so he and I hiked together for a couple of hours. I was getting good at orchestrating these goodbyes to muffle the pain.

I had been averaging between 15 and 20 miles a day for several weeks, and that had become comfortable mileage for me. I had no desire to go any faster; I was pushing my physical limits as it was. Although I was, in some ways, in the best physical condition of my life, I had begun to think that our bodies weren't meant to take this kind of abuse. Carrying a heavy backpack over rugged, uneven terrain for 10 hours a day, month after month, didn't seem like any way to treat a body. And, although our diet reflected the need for enormous amounts of calories to provide the necessary energy for our constant exertion, it couldn't be considered nutritionally sound, with its lack of fruits and vegetables. I hoped none of us would incur permanent damage to the knees, feet, or digestive systems.

I had recently met a few southbounders (those who start at Mt. Katahdin and hike south to Springer Mountain). Their experiences confirmed why most thru-hikers travel north: With Mt. Katahdin's trails closed from October 15 until May 15, the southbounders had to wait until mid-May to begin their journey, and they risked running into winter weather late in the fall at the high elevations of the southern Appalachian Mountains. The rivers that crossed the trail in Maine were swollen with the spring thaws when southbounders were there, and that could add several feet of depth, making river crossings much more treacherous. The black fly season was also in full swing as the southbounders came through Maine and New Hampshire. They told horror stories about waking up in the morning to a sound like hail on their tents: It was black flies on their early-morning bombing missions.

Southern Maine and the White Mountains had the most challenging rock scrambles and terrain on the whole AT. Going north, we built our fitness, stamina, experience, and courage before we reached it. The southbounders faced it within their first month. I admired them, but I wouldn't want to try it their way.

I had spent several nights with Dreamcatcher and Magoo, and I liked them more every time I saw them. I learned that Magoo hadn't planned to thru-hike the AT; he had gotten on the AT at Fontana Dam, intending to backpack for awhile with a friend. But he met Dreamcatcher, who was thru-hiking with another young woman. When Dreamcatcher's friend had to leave the trail, she and Magoo continued on together. Now he intended to finish the trail with her. Talk about going the extra mile(s) to show someone you care!

One night I had stopped at a camping area and set up my tent so I could rest a little before cooking dinner. When it started to sprinkle, I crawled inside and dozed off. Pretty soon I heard my name being called. It was Dreamcatcher and Magoo returning my sunglasses, which I had dropped that afternoon on the trail. Somehow they recognized them as being mine; I was grateful for their sharp eyes. So far on the trip, my camera, hiking stick, and two bandannas had also been returned to me by observant friends.

Dreamcatcher and Magoo chose a campsite near a viewpoint overlooking the valley. After dinner, they came over and invited me up to their front porch to watch a movie (you have to use your imagination in the woods). They had popped some corn on their stove. For almost an hour, we sat on the rocks munching popcorn and watching the colors of the setting sun spread out across the sky and fade into the horizon. We thought it was Academy Award-winning caliber: no dialogue, but beautiful choreography, exquisite cinematography, and a story line that flowed along naturally toward a fitting conclusion. The movie ended, the theater grew dark, and the audience went home to bed.

One of the things I was learning on the AT was how to be— how to just *be*. How to slow down from the fast pace I set for myself in life and just exist on a more leisurely level. I'd probably missed a lot, always whizzing along at breakneck speed. I remember one time when I was driving to Michigan and the kids were small, Brad asked, "Mom, why do we always pass all the other cars and no one ever passes us?" It was one of those innocent questions of children that makes you stop and think. I thought, but I didn't slow down for long.

Out on the AT, I was moving slowly. There was no alternative. I spent day after day just walking a few miles—sometimes only eight or ten. That's all I did all day. I was either walking or not walking. Watching the world go by. Existing. Not causing anything to happen, not influencing other people, not trying to cram one more thing into an already busy day. Just letting the days roll by.

The world was getting along fine without me. I hoped I could carry the lesson home that it's okay, sometimes, to just sit. And watch. And think. And be a part of the world, without altering it in any way. Perhaps Indianapolis had slowed just a fraction, without one more whirling dervish adding to the frenzy of activity. I guess just one fewer makes no impact. But what if a hundred people left and went to the woods . . . a thousand . . . a hundred thousand? Could the world please slow down?

There were so many lessons to be learned in the wilderness. Perhaps members of the government should go to the trail and head north for a while, just to watch the cycles of nature and observe the wildlife as they take care of their own needs without someone else to smooth the way for them or make rules for them or fill their nests for them. Self-sufficiency. What a concept.

One of my goals in life has always been to tread lightly on this earth. Not to negatively impact the environment any more than I have to. Not to be an overconsumer, an overuser of the world's natural resources. While I was on the AT, I was living out that goal more clearly than ever before. I generated almost no garbage. As I ate my food, I put the trash—the plastic and cellophane wrappers—into a ziplock bag and carried it until I found a garbage can in a town or at a road crossing. At the end of a week, the ziplock wasn't very full, and that was all the trash I had generated. I liked that. If we could all live that simply, we'd have a lot fewer landfills.

The Appalachian Trail

23

I've never felt so pitiful

Cheshire, Massachusetts
1,552 miles hiked
August 11, 1994

*T*he week before reaching Cheshire had been a real potpourri of moments I'd remember forever and ones I was already trying to forget. One day in particular stands out in my mind because it encompassed both the highs and the lows. The first couple of hours, the mosquitoes were relentless in spite of my repellent. I was afraid I might be killing off brain cells by breathing in so much Deet, but it was better than losing my sanity getting eaten alive by bugs.

At one point in the early morning, the deer flies came in swarms and tried to dive-bomb my hair. They reminded me of the minnows, as they all seemed to be trying to land on the same place on my head and start munching. I finally covered my hair with a bandanna, which helped. The power of positive thinking often had trouble kicking in when I was fighting my way through the never-ending supply of insects. I saw Dreamcatcher and Magoo mid-morning and they'd also been attacked. They could see the deer flies swarming in each other's hair.

By 10:30 a.m., it had started raining, which helped drive away the bugs, but then I spent several hours slogging along in a downpour. My two least favorite things on the trail were bugs and rain, and it was a morning filled with both. There was probably some beautiful scenery, but that day I missed it.

Eventually I came to Salisbury, Connecticut, a picture-book New England town. I arrived at the road around 2 p.m. and walked a mile into town from the trail to get groceries. Because I was so miserable from the rain and bugs and hadn't had a shower in six days, I decided I would treat myself to a motel where I could get dry and clean.

I first stopped at what turned out to be a very elegant inn to see if they had a room. Leaving my pack outside (I figured no one in town was going to steal that wet, grimy thing), I sloshed into the carpeted lobby with drenched hair and soaked clothes plastered to my body. I stood there dripping on the carpet while asking about vacancies. The clerk didn't even flinch when she said they had one room left: a suite for $180 that she'd be happy to show me. (If I had been her, I would have taken one look and put out the "no vacancy" sign. She was more polite, but the price was one I wasn't willing to pay.) She checked other places in town for me, but they were all equally expensive or full. No low-end motel in *this* town.

When it became clear I wouldn't be spending the night in Salisbury, I trudged back outside and wandered around town looking for a grocery store. I soon found one—the most upscale market imaginable. Once again, I left my backpack outside. Still soaked to the skin, I now was freezing as well in the store's air-conditioning. I had stepped into another cliché, with movie set written all over it, but at the other end of the sophistication scale from those in the South. Everyone was dressed in casual chic, buying expensive gourmet cookies, imported deli cheeses, fresh fish, and perfectly ripened fruits and vegetables. They moved elegantly and self-assuredly and seemed at ease filling those slots reserved for the comfortably rich. I was shivering in my wet T-shirt and shorts, buying peanut butter and Ramen noodles. I've never felt so pitiful in all my life.

I walked back to the inn, hoping for a hot meal in the cozy restaurant with its blazing fire and needing a place to pack my food before heading into the woods. But they didn't serve again until the dinner hour, and besides, they wouldn't let me bring my backpack in. The bartender pointed out a little tearoom a couple doors away and suggested I try it.

Thinking I wouldn't fit in any better in a tearoom than anywhere else in this town, but desperate enough to throw away my pride, I went in and asked if they were serving in the mid-afternoon.

Bless their hearts. They were my salvation that day. It was a quaint little restaurant, with antique tables and chairs and two teen-age girls wearing floor-length dresses and aprons, cooking apple pies in the open kitchen. Everyone looked like they belonged in a Laura Ashley catalogue. They let me repack my backpack and didn't even blanch when I sat on a beautiful antique chair in my still-wet clothes (after covering it with something dry from my pack). They served their own variety of tea steeped in a special cylinder teapot, delicious gourmet sandwiches, and *huge* pieces of dessert.

The owner, also looking like a Laura Ashley model, was drinking tea and discussing paintings for the walls with an artist, and two young men were chatting with the waitresses. One of them had been on his own wilderness trip, and he was enthusiastic about mine. The combination of the quietly elegant setting with the rejuvenating food, steaming hot drink, and friendly conversation was mesmerizing. The whole room seemed to glow with good will. By the time I left, everyone in the tearoom was discussing my adventure, showing genuine interest and encouragement. These people were sincerely pleased I had stopped by and they wished me Godspeed on my journey. They will never know what they meant to me that day. But it reminded me how each of us can, through simple acts of kindness, so easily lift the gloom from someone's day.

By 5 p.m., I was hiking in the rain again, feeling *much* better, with a warmth in my heart to cut the late-afternoon chill. Four miles later I came to a shelter where I planned to spend the night. But there were two very large Buddha-like characters sitting in it (they were even sitting in Buddha-like poses), so I decided to pitch my tent. I found a little spot off in the woods and spent another night in the rain.

It turned very cold that night and a brisk breeze blowing by morning drove away the humidity and bugs, so the next day was glorious for hiking. The weather was so perfect that my spirits immediately lifted. I felt like singing as I walked through the forest and over the mountains. "Oh, what a beautiful morning. . ." What a difference the weather makes when you spend 24 hours a day outside!

The forests in this area were enchanting and the views as beautiful as anything I had seen along the trail. The woods had started to include many pines and hemlocks, sometimes very dense and a little eerie, but in a beautiful, not intimidating, way. They reminded me of a line from a song that was in my fifth-grade operetta—"This is the forest primeval." I often sang it as I hiked. I liked to think how much of the world must have looked this way before mankind came along and started chopping away.

Since I've complained so often about the bugs, and since they were, for many of us, the most annoying feature of life on the trail, I offer a bug rundown:

Gnats: were the worst in Virginia, not as bad up north. They didn't bite but were very annoying, especially when they swarmed around my face and into my eyes as I was hiking. They seemed to love sweat. Letting a bandanna hang down over my face helped with the gnats, but it didn't do much for the scenic views.

Horseflies: ditto. Like the gnats, only bigger!

Deer flies: nasty little devils; they drew blood when they bit, and the bites stung. They were not very quick, though, so I could often kill them by hitting them while they were biting me, which was some consolation at least. They didn't appear until Pennsylvania.

Mosquitoes: really bad in the summer. When I was all sprayed up with Deet, sometimes they landed on my arm, then dropped dead. Although that brought me much glee, I hoped I wasn't poisoning myself along with them.

No-see-ums: so tiny, they couldn't be seen, hence their name. They bit—especially during the night—and were the main reason many of us tented. Their bites itched. Part of the fly family, they're just one-twentieth inch long.

Deer ticks: so small they were hard to spot, and they sometimes carried Lyme disease. Massachusetts was particularly infested; there are warning signs everywhere and local residents mentioned them often, encouraging us to check our bodies carefully every day.

Black flies: They came in swarms in New Hampshire and Maine in the spring and early summer, but I hoped they would be gone by the time I got there.

I was still finding that my trail name worked well as an identifier. One day, I met Frightwig, another thru-hiker. When I told him my trail name, he asked, "Aren't you related to George. . ." His uncle was my brother's law partner in Illinois. Frightwig had heard George's sister from Indiana was thru-hiking and sure enough, eventually we intersected. From my trail name, he figured out who I was. I saw him several evenings at shelters, and we had dinner together in Cheshire. Once again, the trail provided a connection to people in the real world.

Cheshire was a quiet residential community with lovely old homes and manicured yards and the Appalachian Trail running right through the middle of town. I took a day off there. Since my last bed and shower, I had hiked 168 mountainous miles through three states—New York, Connecticut and Massachusetts—swatted a lot of bugs and endured days of rain and mud. A bed would feel good. The guidebook mentioned a bed-and-breakfast in Cheshire so before arriving I had called from a pay phone in Dalton, a little town nine miles away with just a couple of mountains in between. When the proprietor answered, I asked if I could make a reservation. At first he said no. After 16 straight nights of guests, he needed a day to do errands and clean the rooms. An admitted perfectionist, he hated to have anyone stay when all the bedrooms weren't completely ready for the white-glove test.

When he asked if I were in the area, I told him I was a thru-hiker and would get to Cheshire by mid-afternoon. He either loved thru-hikers or knew they didn't have anything white to administer the test with, because he immediately said I was welcome to stay. He wouldn't be home when I arrived, he said, but he would leave the key on the front porch under an ashtray and I could use the room at the top of the stairs. I should just go in and make myself at home, and he'd be back eventually. Now *that* was a trusting soul!

At the end of the conversation, I said, "By the way, my name's Jean" and he said, "Oh yes, I'm Peter." So that was all he knew about me, but when I arrived, greeted on the porch by a cat sporting a bow tie, I found the key and entered a home filled with a fortune in antiques. I'm no connoisseur, but even I could tell that this was no ordinary collection. The dining room was filled with more china, silver, and crystal than I'd ever seen in one home. Peter had left me a welcoming note, and I spent the next two hours before he returned getting showered and settled. (He had also said I could use his washer and dryer when he got home.)

Then I curled up on the front porch with the cat to read all the mail I'd just picked up at the post office. Before long my emotions took over and tears started streaming as I read a letter from Bunny, my 100-year-old correspondent, who said she planned to mail me a little angel to protect me as I traveled. I couldn't believe that this lady whom I had never met was feeling such a strong connection with me that, even at her age, she was going to find a way to buy and mail me a gift!

Her letter made me cry because it epitomized all the love and encouragement I was receiving from so many dear people. Sometimes it just bowled me over. I felt that I was being entrusted with so much good will and support that I didn't know what I was supposed to do with it all. I needed to live up to the expectations that were pouring forth. I felt I must make it all the way to Maine. I didn't even know why anymore, except so many people wanted me to.

Sometimes I wasn't sure it was just me out there backpacking. Maybe it was all of us together, everyone's dreams and aspirations for their own adventures that I was carrying in my backpack and in my heart. Maybe it wasn't my dream, but a dream that belonged to everyone and I had just taken the baton for a while. Someone else would take over with a new and very different life adventure when I was through, and I would become the armchair supporter. I was looking forward to that role and hoped I could be as supportive of those new adventurers as everyone else had been for me.

The next morning Peter fixed me an exquisite breakfast, served with style and elegance. Since I was his only guest, I felt like the Queen of England sitting all alone at a huge oak table surrounded by opulence, with my own antique silver coffeepot, and cups, saucers, bowls, and small plates spread all around my place setting. I ate fresh fruit sprinkled with powdered sugar, eggs Benedict, and buttermilk pancakes, just one day after choking down two cold Pop Tarts in the middle of the woods. From hiker to Her Highness in 24 hours. And, unfortunately, back again just as quickly.

It was a busy day: I waterproofed my boots again; resealed my tent seams; cleaned my water filter and stove; washed water bottles, pan, and spoon (my total kitchen); did laundry; bought food; and showered. I felt refreshed and ready to go again.

I was wondering how much I would slow down as I reached New Hampshire and Maine. I hiked very tentatively on the rocky ascents and descents, and the worst of that terrain was ahead. As I picked my way very carefully up or down, sometimes it took me 30 seconds just to decide where to put my foot next. I often went down the rocks sideways or even backwards, using my hands and knees, sometimes just sitting down and scooting. I must have looked pretty awkward, not exactly my image of a macho thru-hiker, but it was the only way I could do it. I really didn't want an injury to end my trip, because I wanted to find out if I had the mental fortitude to go all the way. It felt like that's what this trip was all about for me.

I hoped to reach Mt. Katahdin by October 7 but really couldn't tell if that was feasible until I discovered how much the upcoming terrain would affect my pace. I was getting very eager to tackle all the parts that scared me: the White Mountains, the Presidentials,

Maine. Some people, particularly the New Englanders, said that the most spectacular part of the trail was still to come. Many of us felt we had used up our bodies' extra resources and we were running on no reserves. And so it had just come down to whether we wanted it bad enough to stick it out. It helped to know we were nearly three-quarters of the way there. Perhaps if we had been as mentally and physically depleted when we still had a thousand miles to go, the trail would have dispatched even more of us.

Even though I was prepared for a half-year of demanding challenges beyond any I'd faced before, there was no way I could have anticipated the variety of unique, enlightening struggles and the wearing down of my physical and mental resources, just from the daily grind.

Each part of the Appalachian Trail presented a new kind of challenge. Sometimes the trail felt like a stern taskmaster saying, "Well, you dealt with the steep ups and downs, now I'll throw in a little rain and see if you can take that. Okay, so you handled the rain; let's try 95 degrees and 90 percent humidity. Thought that was tough? How about some mosquitoes and gnats? Hmmm, now I'll add ticks and deer flies. You still here? Well, let's add a dose of rocks and throw in some hand-over-hand climbing. Rest? No, you can rest when it's over."

The trail was always testing you, pushing you, stretching you, making you work harder and harder. And the harder you worked, the better shape you were in and the more confident you became. And eventually you were doing things you never thought you could do and your progress had been so gradual that you hadn't even noticed how far you'd come and how much you'd grown. You always had the option to just sit down and say, "I don't want to go any farther. I don't want to learn any more. I've had enough!" On the Appalachian Trail, that's when you go home. I think in life, that's when you die.

The Appalachian Trail

24

Not a princess among us

Manchester Center, Vermont
1,623 miles hiked
August 16, 1994

After my wonderful respite at Cheshire, I had three really nasty nights in a row. Is the best always followed by the worst, or does it just seem that way?

The first day out of Cheshire, I crossed Mt. Greylock, at 3,500 feet the highest point in Massachusetts, with a large distinctive war memorial at the summit. The AT was a rigorous climb up and back down again on the other side. There were other trails leading to the top, and I talked with several day hikers and weekenders who had taken an easier route and were enjoying the summit.

That evening, I stopped at a camping area deep in the forest, with several tent platforms. Unfortunately, I couldn't use them since my tent needs to be staked, so I anchored it in the dirt. It was a rather creepy area, and when the insects started biting, I climbed into my tent. I was all alone. It was one of the few nights I had felt a little uncomfortable being by myself. The trail was littered and unkempt coming out of North Adams; it was one of the least attractive stretches I had seen. There was no one around and nothing to be afraid of; I just wasn't used to litter and graffiti near the Appalachian Trail. It made me realize that one of the sources of my secure feeling on the trail was the pristine nature of the forest.

During the night the rains began, and by morning it was really pouring. When I awoke at 6:30 a.m., I found that the water had leaked into my tent. I could either get up, pack everything in the pouring rain, and start the day soaked to the skin, or go back to sleep for a while and hope the rain would quit. I'm glad that I sometimes did the reasonable thing: I slept for another hour until the rain was just a drizzle, able then to break camp and take off without the discomfort of being drenched.

Unfortunately, I had pitched my tent where the rain washed down a slope, splashing dirt onto it, so in addition to being wet both inside and out, it was muddy. Several days passed before I was able to get it dried out. Why hadn't I learned by now that I needed to assume it would rain *every* night and place my tent accordingly? (Even though I had resealed my tent, it had started to leak around the edges during major rains, perhaps because it had been rained on so often.)

That cool, dreary day gradually turned into a cooler, drearier evening. I crossed the state line into Vermont, and although it was a beautiful stretch of the trail, the weather wasn't very welcoming. At the Vermont border, the AT connected with the Long Trail, the nation's first long-distance footpath, and they together stretched for 100 miles before the AT veered east toward Maine and the Long Trail headed north to Canada. The Long Trail was some 300 miles long, and challenged its own set of thru-hikers annually.

I stayed in a shelter that night and hung my tent outside in a futile attempt to get it clean and dry. Even though it was still raining, I figured it would at least wash the dirt off, which perhaps it did; I had hoped the rain would stop by morning so the tent could begin to dry a little, which it didn't. I was chilly and uncomfortable, most of the night and all the next day. I thought often as I was hiking, "When I get back to civilization, I will *never* be outside in the rain, ever again!"

The next night was one of my coldest on the trail. It had been another drizzly, cold, gloomy day and I decided to stay in a shelter once again instead of pitching my tent, which was still wet inside and out. When the shelter finally appeared through the rain, it was on top of Glastenbury Mountain and the wind was blasting right into the open side. The clouds and mist were so thick I could almost feel them hit me in the face. Everything on my body was soaked, as usual, but it was no use trying to spread things out to dry. The humidity was 100 percent.

The shelter was filled with weekenders, but they made room for me. I felt sorry for them, because in their few days on the trail they were being hit with some really bitter weather. They seemed to be taking it in stride, though. A father/teenage daughter duo were on their annual backpacking trek. A number of men and boys out for the weekend together were having a good time in spite of the elements. (Whenever I saw someone in blue jeans, I knew they were just out for a few days.)

One of the weekenders had spread his tarp across part of the shelter's open side in an attempt to keep out some of the wind. It was flapping mightily as the gusts whipped it back and forth, but it helped keep out a little of the biting cold. I was chagrined to discover that these weekenders were better equipped than I to deal with the frigid temperature. Since I didn't have my winter gear back yet, I wasn't really prepared for bitter weather. My winter layers (waterproof pants and jacket plus a fleece jacket) would arrive at Hanover the following week, so I hoped I wouldn't hit any more of those cold nights.

I climbed into my sleeping bag, changed into dry clothes and tried to cook, eat, and get organized for the evening from its warm confines. It *was* possible, but not easy, to change clothes while inside a mummy sleeping bag. I didn't have a lot of choice, with the freezing temperatures and six men within a few feet of me. Boots arrived shortly after I did, and the two of us made up the thru-hiker contingency, outnumbered by weekenders 8 to 2. I had met Boots just recently. He was somewhere in my age range and because he was having severe foot pain, he hiked even more slowly than I. He was a skinny guy with a beard—a description that fit 90 percent of my trail friends—and he wore a cool cowboy hat.

With 10 of us in the shelter, we were stacked shoulder to shoulder, but perhaps that helped to keep us warm. Boots' sleeping bag was very big and puffy, and he was only inches away. I woke up several times during the night coveting his toasty-looking bag while I lay shivering in mine.

The next morning was even worse. It was frigid, and with nothing dry to change into, I dreaded getting out of a relatively warm sleeping bag into damp clothes and wet boots. The best plan was to get on the trail and start burning energy. I moved quickly that morning.

The following night, however, was a warm, wonderful contrast to that chilling experience, appropriately enough at Stratton Mountain, where Benton MacKaye is said to have first thought of his vision for what became the Appalachian Trail. It was another "thru-hiker special," with the staff at the ski resort allowing us to stay in the warming hut at the mountain summit, near the chairlifts and gondola. The lifts were staffed in the summer so tourists could ride to the top for a breathtaking view of surrounding valleys and faraway peaks. If hikers arrived by mid-afternoon, they could ride free on the gondola down to Stratton Village.

I'd put in another grueling 16-mile day, but with the temperature dropping rapidly in the late afternoon, I decided to go the seven-tenths of a mile off the trail to the warming hut.

The side trail wound tightly through the trees and was flooded in several areas, necessitating some fancy footwork to avoid sinking up to ankle depth. The wind was blowing fiercely at the summit, creating a brace-yourself-or-you'll-be-blown-over experience. As I stumbled across the open mountaintop to the hut, I appreciated what good protection trees offered from the elements and realized how much I missed them when there weren't any.

When I reached the warming hut, it already had one occupant, Sara, a Long Trail thru-hiker. Sara was glad to have company, and she and I shared our dinners—rice and tea.

The hut was like a cozy cocoon, a complete contrast to my inhospitable lodgings the previous nights. A space heater and one little electric light made it seem like a palace compared to the cold, dark shelters. The next pleasant surprise was that when we fought our way through the wind another 100 yards across the summit to the restrooms and turned on the tap, out came *hot water!*

Pretty soon Boots arrived and we strung clotheslines to hang our wet things near the space heater in the hope they would dry by morning. All of the large pads wrapped around the lift towers during ski season were stacked into the hut for the summer, piles up to eight feet high, and they took up most of the floor space. Instead of sleeping on the floor, we climbed up on top of the huge piles of foam padding with our sleeping bags. We must have looked like the princess-wannabees in the fairy tale "The Princess and the Pea." Even though the pads were uneven and we had to avoid deep crevices, it was better than being on the hard floor. And I guess there wasn't a princess among us, because we all slept like babies in our high, cushiony beds.

Vermont was gorgeous, with thick, lush forests and moderately high mountains. It was a real treat to have the kind of terrain where I could average 2.5 miles per hour with a backpack. The day I went into Manchester Center, I hiked 12.5 miles on gentle trail and then hitched a ride into town, still arriving with plenty of time to complete my chores before dinner. I spread out all my gear in the bright sunlight in back of a church, and it dried out for the first time in days.

I was a little uneasy about going into Manchester Center because it was 5.5 miles off the trail. Once you commit to a distance that far, it would be a very long walk if you didn't get a ride. But I had heard it was usually an easy hitch into town and that proved true for me. The local people knew that hikers brought business and were often willing to give them rides. I didn't have my thumb out for more than five minutes before someone stopped.

The Zion Episcopal Church where I stayed was yet another example of a congregation opening their doors to thru-hikers. I shared floor space with 10 others, and we were allowed to use a shower and the kitchen. We had to vacate the premises for a few hours in the evening while a bridge group played cards in our room. (Or were we in their room?) I wondered if our gear made the room smell, since backpackers aren't the most fragrant group of people.

Everyone scattered as the bridge players arrived and we walked downtown to eat at various restaurants. The Tres Gourmet were in the mood for a good steak, and they were headed for what sounded like an expensive place. (Gourmet John's dad and brother were hiking with him for a few days, so their combined trail name was Tres Gourmet.) Water Boy was on a tighter budget; he and I ate at a restaurant where one of my favorite artists, Norman Rockwell, used to hang out. With us were two Long Trail hikers; it was fun to meet a different group and hear about their adventures.

After dinner, Water Boy and the others took in a movie; I stopped at a drugstore, made a couple of phone calls, then went back to the church. A lounge with comfortable overstuffed furniture looked inviting, but an Alcoholics Anonymous meeting was being held there. It was a strange feeling to be in a town and not have any place at all to go—not even a motel room. There was a swing set in the back yard of the church so I swung until the AA meeting broke up and I was able to go inside. The Gourmets came back soon and we relaxed in the sitting room until the card game broke up. Hikers go to bed early, and as soon as the card players left, we all crashed, knowing that we'd be getting up with the dawn and heading back to the trail.

Gourmet John was a super young man. I first met him and his fiancée, Dr. Becky, at a shelter outside Duncannon, Pennsylvania. Dr. Becky was hiking with Gourmet John for a short time before going home to begin medical school, while he continued north to Mt. Katahdin. John had recently graduated from college and after finishing the AT, he would look for a job near her school.

I thought it was wonderful that Gourmet John's father and older brother had joined him for several days. He said the three of them hadn't had this kind of experience together since the boys were young. His dad and brother decided to seize this opportunity for all of them to share an adventure, while John's mom spent the week with his sister. It was obvious his father could have afforded a motel for the three of them, but they wanted to have the full thru-hiker experience, so they were on the floor of the church with the rest of us.

The ordeals of the past week receded as I lay on the church floor, surrounded by fellow backpackers. Even though the surface was hard, I was under a roof, warm and dry. I recently had seen a funny bit of graffiti on a shelter wall: "I was miserable here." Written in a moment of honesty, no doubt. I imagined that a year down the road, that person would be telling the story of his night there, both the good and the bad, with great flourish. Making it sound both better and worse than it was.

25

I was becoming a tree

I must tell you about my hitchhiking experience going back to the trail from Manchester Center. As I stood by the road with my thumb out, a car screeched to a stop right ahead of me. After I piled my pack and myself into the back seat, the lady at the wheel peeled out like an Indy 500 driver. I hung on and hoped I wouldn't be flung out as we went around curves.

The driver was a woman about my age with her mother-in-law in the passenger seat. They were classic New Yorkers in their speech and mannerisms, and they argued the whole time I was in the car. Initially, I was surprised that two women would pick up a hitchhiker, but somehow I guessed these two could take care of themselves and wouldn't have anything to fear from a lady with a backpack.

When they started questioning me about my destination, I told them I was hiking from Georgia to Maine. The mother-in-law turned around, looked straight at me, and asked, *"What's the point?"* The driver said, "Oh, don't pay any attention to her!" and she tried to explain to the older lady that my journey was a noble thing.

The mother-in-law was not impressed. She asked, "Aren't you afraid of getting attacked by someone?" When I said no, she huffed, "Well! You're *surely* not from New York. People in New York *know* how dangerous it is to be out by yourself where someone could attack you!" And she asked, "What if you get sick or hurt?" Every time she said anything at all, the driver would interrupt with, "Just ignore her!" or "She doesn't mean that."

The lady was driving so fast and they were both talking so rapidly that we whizzed by the trailhead before I could tell her to stop. I was finally able to break in and yell, "We just passed the trail! That's where I needed to get off." She slammed on the brakes and we stopped in a shower of gravel about 100 yards beyond where the trail crossed the road. As I was closing the car door, the mother-in-law was saying, "Well, I hope you stay *safe* and *healthy*," and the driver said, "Oh, don't pay any attention to her!" before she sped off up the road. I laughed all the way back to the trail.

It was another week of real ups and downs (by now you know that's meant figuratively as well as literally). Vermont would have been my favorite state on the trail, but it rained so much that it wasn't easy to enjoy the beauty. But it *was* beautiful! I loved the pine forests; and the mountains, although challenging, weren't as difficult as what was ahead, so I was enjoying the relative ease of the terrain.

I saw my first coyote. He was very close but not intimidating. In fact CC and the Mule were there (remember CC's dog, whose trail name is Mule?). The dog and the coyote left each other alone, although they weren't separated by more than 25 yards. The Mule looks like he's part wolf, so maybe they felt like kindred spirits.

It was fun to meet up with CC again. After seeing him fairly regularly in Virginia, we hadn't crossed paths for a couple of months. One day there he was, just coming up behind me on the trail. He was so much thinner that he looked very different. We were all losing weight. On some it was more obvious than on others. I couldn't tell how much I'd lost because my shorts had elastic around the waist. Some of the guys who lost up to 50 pounds had to buy a new pair.

Because it had rained so much, the trail in Vermont was more like a creek than a path. Even when it wasn't raining, I still walked in mud and water; most of the trail was covered with one or the other. There are signs saying sections of the trail are closed in the spring because of the rain, but August was acting like spring. My boots hadn't been dry for days.

CC's traveling partner, Moonshine, developed a fungus on her feet, probably from being constantly wet. She was so uncomfortable that she left the trail temporarily to get it cleared up. She planned to meet CC at a town up ahead, and he started off early in the morning to do a 30-plus-mile day—just because he wanted to. I had seen him practically run down the trail. On his mother's 50th birthday, he hiked 50 miles in her honor. How's that for a birthday tribute!

A few days before reaching Hanover I crossed a river swollen from all the downpours. It was knee-deep and the current was very strong. I could find nothing to hold onto. When I would try to put my hiking stick down to brace myself, the current would sweep it up to the surface as if it were merely a toothpick.

Without all the recent rains, I could have just waded across with no problem, but with the pounding current, I wasn't sure I could even stand up against it. I was as nervous as I had been at any time on the trail. I had heard about a woman who drowned trying to cross a river on the AT in Maine when she was pinned under the water by her load. I unhooked the waist belt of my backpack in case I fell into the water and started inching my way across.

Looking back it surprises me, but I suddenly realized there were some small branches hanging down from a large tree overhead. I was sure they hadn't been there when I started across. I was able to reach up and grab onto them to help keep my balance as my feet searched among the slippery rocks for secure footing. I honestly don't know how I would have gotten across without those branches, but I was finding that the trail (or Dad?) always provided what I needed for survival.

What a relief it was to be on the other side. Another tense situation, where all it took was one step at a time to put it behind me. I took off my boots, poured out the water, wrung out my socks and insoles, and put them back on. No point in putting on dry socks; they'd be wet in minutes.

Later that day, my friend Joyce from Indianapolis picked me up by the side of the trail. In another perfect coincidence of timing, Joyce had written me that she was planning to visit relatives in Killington, Vermont. She would be there from August 18 through 23, and she hoped we could plan a rendezvous. It turned out I would be reaching the Killington area right at that time! So I left a message on her machine that I'd wait for her where the Appalachian Trail crossed State Road 103 at 5:30 p.m. on the eighteenth.

I arrived around 5 o'clock after a 15.5-mile day, and Joyce pulled up right at 5:30. She was amazed that she actually found me in the middle of Vermont by the side of a road, but there I was, sitting on my backpack in the drizzling rain. And I couldn't believe she was really there. My friends always hugged me in spite of the odor.

I noticed one thing immediately: She was wearing summer clothes; last time I'd seen her, at the end of March before leaving home, she'd been in winter fabrics. Suddenly I became confused and wondered if it was the same season on the trail as in civilization. I asked her what month it was at home, with the feeling it might be different on the trail. It's strange how discombobulated I became when the two worlds intersected.

That night Joyce and I talked for hours before bed. I had so much catching up to do. She was one of my closest single friends, and hearing her talk about the past five months made me realize how many things happen in people's lives in that time span. I felt like I was in some sort of strange time warp where time was just standing still for me. I realized more than at any time on the trip that when I returned home, I would have missed half a year in the lives of my friends and family. Everyone else was going on with their activities, and I was on a different planet.

A couple of days later, the rain actually rewarded me with one of my nicest afternoons on the trail. I had arrived at a shelter around 1 p.m., where I planned to stop for a brief lunch break after a nine-mile morning. A southbound thru-hiker was there who had already decided he was finished for the day.

Just as I was preparing to head out for the afternoon, another deluge set in. Somehow the thought of hiking six to eight more miles in a downpour was more than I could bear, so I decided to stay at the shelter and take the afternoon off. It was a good decision. The shelter was in a beautiful pine forest with a waterfall nearby and for once, I had the chance to really enjoy the magnificent natural setting.

It was hard to believe, but that was the first time I had taken a half-day off in the woods since starting the trail. Way back in North Carolina, Sunday told me that he planned to rest every Sunday in the woods, where it was much more relaxing and rejuvenating than in a town, with the pressure of numerous chores to do. And now I wished I'd allowed myself a few full days to just sit and rest in the forest.

By the way, I never saw Sunday again after Erwin, Tennessee, and it had been months since I'd seen a register entry by him. He usually wrote in the registers, so I assumed he was no longer on the trail. Since I didn't even know his name, I probably would never find out what happened to him. I hadn't realized the importance of collecting names and addresses until later in my journey.

The southbounder and I looked at maps and plotted our next several days; we were able to advise each other about what to expect since we were going in opposite directions. I also spent several hours reading a book I had been carrying since Harpers Ferry. There was something so pleasant about reading in the woods; it was the perfect setting for absorbing the words and the subtleties of their meanings. The air was clearer, the sounds were more soothing. Sometimes I thought my biorhythms were changing. I'd always had a special affinity for trees, and I thought that spending so much time among them was causing me to take on the cadence of their life forces. I felt I was becoming a tree. I hoped they didn't cut down any of my relatives to print that book.

That week I spent a blissful night by myself in the woods near Podunk Road (its real name) right outside West Hartford, Vermont—population 198. The trail had gone by a little deli/grocery store where they knew how to treat thru-hikers. They offered free bottled spring water, as much as I could carry. I ordered goulash and drank fresh coffee that the owner made for me, while I sat on the front porch, about two feet from the dirt road. The creaking wooden floor and old cash register were from another era. Local folks in pickup trucks stopped by for a variety of staples; I think 'most everyone in town must have come by during the hour I spent rocking on the porch.

Three miles later I came to Podunk Road. Beyond the road and out of sight of the trail, I found a level spot to pitch my tent. I was in one of Vermont's majestic pine forests with a dense canopy overhead, rolling elevation, and ground softened by fallen pine needles. My favorite kind of place to sleep. The early evening sunlight slanted through the trees, and I laid down flat upon the ground and enjoyed the solitude of the forest. There wasn't a soul around, no sounds, nothing to break the pattern of the trees shooting up against the sky. Sometimes I just loved tenting entirely alone.

I spent most of every day hiking by myself, which gave me lots of time to think. The trick was keeping my mind focused on positive things instead of on the discomfort I was feeling. Sometimes I just trolled through my mind for someone I hadn't thought about in years, then I reminisced about that person for a while. I tried to remember the books I'd read, plays and movies I'd seen, concerts I'd attended. Why did I like them? What did I learn? Sometimes I tried to imagine what I wanted to do when I returned home, but my mind usually blocked there. I would start thinking about that in Maine. Until then, it didn't seem relevant.

It was a glorious, sunny day when I reached Hanover, and oh, did I need it. My boots hadn't been dry for days, and all my gear was damp. I was also happy to be in New Hampshire—my second-to-last state and home of the infamous White Mountains. I started out with 14 states to cross, and I was down to the last two. Amazing. But it was too soon to celebrate. The most difficult part of the trail was ahead.

I felt a special affinity for Hanover because Greg graduated from Dartmouth College, which is located there, and I visited several times during his four-year stay. It's a classic little Ivy League town. I expect few of the students know they're on the Appalachian Trail each time they walk down the main street of Hanover.

Several fraternities made space available to thru-hikers, along with the Foley House, a co-op where several members of the Dartmouth Outing Club lived. I decided to stay there. They let thru-hikers sleep on the floor in a room with a television, a lamp, and a rug. I shared the space with Water Boy and Boots.

I went to the post office and picked up my mail, about 30 letters, put on clean shorts and T-shirt, and headed to a restaurant for dinner. I was finding that shorts and a T-shirt could suffice for everything from hiking to sleeping to swimming to dining in a restaurant. I thought I should empty my closet at home and just keep my shorts, T-shirts and long underwear. I could save a lot of money.

Since it was a gorgeous evening, I ate out on the patio and enjoyed watching young people and families stroll by. However, as I relished the setting in this idyllic college town, I suddenly looked around and felt inadequate and out of place. All of the other diners seemed to be professors and their spouses—erudite, sporty, well-read. I wanted to be like the lady with the smooth hair and sweater tied around her shoulders who looked like she had spent the afternoon on the tennis court, probably after reading *The New York Times* over breakfast, teaching classes in the morning, and serving an elaborate lunch to a visiting dignitary.

It occurred to me that I probably couldn't even participate in the conversations at those tables. I was sure they were discussing the important events happening around the globe and debating the most recent political developments at home and abroad. I had no idea what was going on in the world. I assumed I'd have heard if someone dropped a bomb on a major country, but short of that, I didn't have a clue what the important news was.

But as I sat there beginning to feel ill at ease, the realization dawned that I was the only one dining there that evening who had hiked all the way to the restaurant from Georgia. They knew about world events, but I knew about hiking the Appalachian Trail. Perhaps I *could* add something to the conversation. We all have our own value in the world, and we bring different experiences and talents to the table.

I had been pondering the New York mother-in-law's query, "What's the point?" It was a valid question, and I wished I had a definitive answer for her. I didn't know when I made the decision to hike the trail what the driving force was, and now that I had been on it for almost five months, I still wasn't entirely sure I had it figured out.

The pat answers were easy: To see a new slice of life, to challenge myself and push my personal limits, and to create a transition that would point me in uncharted directions in the next phase of my life. But one thing I knew: It wasn't to have fun. It always surprised me before I left home when people would say in parting, "Have lots of fun on your journey!" Does this have anything to do with fun? I wondered. It never felt to me like that was what this odyssey was all about. And although I had enjoyed many good times on the trail, they are relatively few in the total scheme of things.

But if it was seldom about having fun, it was often about something much deeper and much more important. It was about growing, and learning, and evolving, and understanding. It was about seeing if there's a different way to think and finding my own place in the world. It was about becoming one with the trees and creatures of the forest and cramming years worth of life lessons into a journey on one little path that had become, for me, a metaphor for the journey through life.

The Appalachian Trail

26

The rocks went straight up

North Woodstock, New Hampshire
1,785 miles hiked
August 29, 1994

I had reached the White Mountains! For weeks, it seemed everything in my mind had centered around "When the Whites begin. . ." and now I'd had my first taste of them. Mt. Moosilauke, the official beginning, rose to 4,802 feet and was the first mountain for northbounders that soared above treeline. On a clear day, you could see five states from the summit, but since the states didn't have huge signs rising above them, I had no idea whether I saw them all. My map showed that Canada was closer than any states other than Vermont and Maine, so perhaps I saw our sister nation, too.

The White Mountains provide some of the most majestic scenery anywhere in the world, according to our guidebook—written by an obsessive AT hiker, so perhaps the opinion was slightly prejudiced. I hadn't been all over the world, but being above the timber with a 360-degree unobstructed view allowed my mind to expand and fill up with the wide open spaces. The United States didn't seem big enough to contain this expanse of mountain peaks for miles in every direction. Although I loved the Midwest, I had to admit that we had nothing to compare with the incredible majesty of those mountains.

The climb up Mt. Moosilauke wasn't as rough as I had anticipated, but of course everything is relative. It would have seemed a lot worse five months before, and once again, I found that if I prepared myself mentally for the worst, the reality was tolerable. I was by myself heading up that first mountain of the Whites, and as with the earlier parts of the journey, I found that all I had to do was take it one step at a time.

One rather remarkable coincidence occurred as I was on my

way up the mountain: I encountered a hiker coming the other direction, whose trail name was Wolf. Although he was only in his twenties, he was already becoming well-known on the AT because he spent so much time on the trail. Since thru-hiking several years ago, he had backpacked numerous sections. You never knew where you'd see him or what direction he would be going. Perhaps he was one of those people who was just more comfortable out in the woods than in society.

Exactly five months earlier, Wolf had been the very first hiker I met, my first day on the trail. As I started up the approach trail to the top of Springer Mountain in Georgia, he was finishing a section hike and stopped to introduce himself. "Hello, I'm Wolf. What's your trail name?" (Geez, I don't know, I'm not even to the beginning of the trail yet. I haven't got that figured out. Why is my pack so heavy when yours looks so light?) "Good luck. You'll love it. It's a great trail."

On August 28, five months later, I saw him again on my way up Mt. Moosilauke. Wolf remembered meeting me and congratulated me on making it all the way to the Whites. As we talked for a few minutes, my mind flickered over the thought, "I hope I'm not seeing him on both my first and last days on the trail!"

Wolf was an ethereal sort of figure; his trail name fit him well. He had long dark hair, seemed as at ease in the forest as his namesake, carried no more than 16 pounds on his back. He was the trail's ultimate minimalist. He glided along with light, easy steps as I watched him disappear down the mountainside.

Seeing Wolf caused me to reflect on the contrast from the first time I met him. And it seemed appropriate that now I was seeing him on a bright, sunny day when I was feeling optimistic and confident. For I remembered so clearly that the first time we met, it was rainy and dreary and my mood matched the weather. I was alone, anxious, and frightened, and the immediate future held experiences that I had no way to visualize. What would it feel like to carry my backpack over the mountains for the next six months, day after day, sleeping in the woods at night? How would I get into and out of the small towns to get food? How would I handle the cold, the rain, the bugs, the blisters? The days ahead were a blank slate with no familiar patterns to grab.

Wolf had seemed like such a confident figure, so alien to me with his comfort on the trail. And now, five months later, I was one of his peers. Admittedly, I would never become as comfortable in the forests and mountains as Wolf was, but that was not my goal. My goal was simply to complete this journey, to become a long-distance hiker for as long as it took me to travel from Georgia to Maine.

And I was making it. I was living in the mountains, getting into and out of the small towns, carrying my backpack, dealing with the hardships and feeling more confident each day. And even though I slipped back temporarily into anxiety when faced with rock climbs and other new territory, that felt familiar. It was really just like living in the "real world" and facing new experiences—a new job, new relationships, buying a house—all those things we do for the first time with a combination of excitement and anxiety. The challenges on the trail were simply reduced to a much more physical and elemental level. And just as I was able to become comfortable wearing the mantle of all my different roles in life, I had been able to accept the role of long-distance backpacker. I was grateful that the trail showed me, through two brief encounters with Wolf, the progress I had made in the past five months.

Let me tell you about one of my favorite evenings of the whole trip. I was a few days north of Hanover, on one of my last nights before the White Mountains. Late in the day, I arrived at Hexacuba Shelter, which was aptly named: It was hexagon-shaped, with walls on four of the sides and two sides open. I swept out the shelter with a broom someone had left, laid out my gear in one corner, and found the water source at the bottom of a steep decline. Soon Earth Frog, Boots, and Knothole Willy arrived.

You may remember Earth Frog from my first meeting with him in the Smokies when we tented in bear country. I had also seen him in Damascus and again in Harpers Ferry. He had just returned to the trail after spending several days at the Woodstock reunion concert.

Knothole Willy was a young southbounder, traveling alone. When he realized that Earth Frog had been a Navy SEAL, he was in awe. Meeting Earth Frog was surely a high point of Knothole Willy's hike. He immediately began asking questions about the program because he was considering joining a hard-core branch of the service. (His dad, a former Green Beret, wanted a legacy.) At one point he said, "Boy, *my friends* would sure be impressed if they met you!"

And Earth Frog was impressive: in his late twenties, knockout handsome, unassuming but obviously competent, built like a quarterback. Not flashy. He just seemed rock solid, physically, mentally, and emotionally.

It was fun to hear about some of the rigors of his SEAL training: Their program tried to weed out anyone who might crack under any circumstances. The percentage of those who completed the training was about the same as those who completed the Appalachian Trail: 10 to 15 percent. The SEALs did everything they could to help the 90 percent decide to leave.

One of their exercises was to link arms, walk out into the ocean, and, as the waves crashed in about them, stay there until someone dropped out. They would go to the ocean in the evening and, if no one dropped out, stay in the water most of the night. Every so often the trainers would bring them back up onto the beach to "make sure we were all still alive," let them do some pushups, and then send them back out again. Boots: "What happens when someone drops out?" Earth Frog: "They're out of the SEAL program. They're still in the Navy." "Oh. I thought they'd just rejoin the group in the morning."

Also, at one point in the training, they had to do a certain number of pullups before dinner, and if they failed to do it, they didn't get to eat. Then they had to keep trying until they succeeded. Naturally, the longer they went without eating, the weaker they became, so the incentive was there to do it the first time.

So you can see that Earth Frog was one tough cookie, but you'd never know it from talking to him. He was as low-key and humble a guy as I had met. Every time Knothole Willy would tell us about something coming up on the trail that sounded intimidating, Earth Frog would quietly say, "Geez, that sounds really rough. I'm outta here!"

I'm getting to the best part of the evening, provided by Earth Frog. He carried a very small guitar with him in a padded case on the side of his backpack. It weighed about three pounds. When he was a student at MIT, he sang in the coffeehouses on Harvard Square. As it was getting dark, he pulled out his guitar, sat down, and started singing and playing. He was good, really good.

Boots, Knothole Willy, and I each lit a candle and lay down in our sleeping bags, and for about an hour, Earth Frog sang. He had a wide repertoire and was able to honor most of our requests, even mine for Kingston Trio songs—my favorite group from my college days. He did his own version, kind of a jazz style, of many old favorites. He sang "Charlie on the MTA," threw in some country songs with great story lines, and ended his concert with "American Pie." It was the perfect way to spend an evening in the woods, hearing my favorite songs sung in the darkness with just a candle to silhouette the musician and no other sounds to compete with the tunes.

I decided to stay at a bed and breakfast in North Woodstock, so I called from Hanover to make a reservation. It was so inexpensive that I couldn't pass it up. The days of $5 hiker hostels that we had found in the South were long past; New England had been tougher on the pocketbook. When making the reservation, I had asked the owner of the B&B if he'd pick me up at the trailhead—not an unusual request from a hiker, with North Woodstock six miles from the trail. When I called from a tourist spot near the trail, he said he'd be there in a half-hour. How would I recognize him? "I'll be the one in fur-lined skivvies and a leather vest!" Right.

Soon he showed up in a big old dilapidated car with litter everywhere, an overflowing ashtray, and a cigarette hanging out of his mouth. With his girth, his round smiling face, white whiskers, and a twinkle in his eye, Bill reminded me of a cigarette-smoking Santa Claus. I could tell he would do anything he could to make my stay comfortable. The people in small towns were the best.

Bill would have shuttled me back to the trailhead the next morning, but he wanted to take his grandson to school on his first day of the fall term. (School's starting? Another brief touch of reality.) He found someone else to take me.

We agreed that I would leave most of my gear with him and slack-pack (hike with a small day pack) the 15.5 miles to the next road crossing, where I would call him from a pay phone to pick me up again. Bill liked to arrange slacking for hikers so they'd spend another night with him. I guess you could call it trail-side marketing.

Just as I reached the AT, Gourmet John was crossing the road, so I yelled to him. He waited and we went on together. He'd already hiked a couple of miles that morning after sleeping in a shelter. His dad and brother had gone home.

Pretty soon we hooked up with Steve, the British guy, who had stopped at a stream for some water. Steve didn't have a trail name, so we called him Steve, the British guy. My theory was that he was too classy to succumb to the AT trail-name nonsense. Steve began the trail with his dog Pemba, but Pemba became ill and Steve arranged for friends to keep him while he finished the trail. He would tour the United States after his thru-hike before returning to England. He and Gourmet John were hiking together during the Whites; their pace and stamina seemed compatible.

The three of us spent the whole day together, and I was thrilled that I had found them. Another godsend. They, of course, had their full packs, and if I'd had mine, I couldn't have kept up with them for five minutes. But with me carrying 10 pounds and them carrying about 50 pounds each, our paces were similar.

The climb up Kinsman Mountain was, for me, the most difficult part of the trail so far. This was what the Whites were all about. In the very steep areas, the rocks went straight up and we had to search for handholds and pull ourselves up while stretching to find a foothold. I followed the two guys, so I was able to see how they were doing it. They were struggling, often grunting with the effort, but their strong legs and arms allowed them to make progress. I followed along and could barely keep up. I wondered several times, "Could I have done this with a full backpack on?" The next day I would find out.

When we finally arrived at the summit, the magnificent view really was a worthy reward, and to add to the thrill of the moment, we saw two glider planes overhead. One of them swooped low over us and wiggled its wings as we waved and took pictures. We would have loved to spend more time up there enjoying the clear air and far-reaching vistas, but we knew there were many difficult miles ahead.

We had a full day of conversation, discussing everything from what fairy tales Steve grew up with in England to how each of the men wanted to raise his children someday. However, we always kept pressing on, and by the end of the day we were hurrying to beat the darkness. Steve and Gourmet John decided they wanted to go into North Woodstock and stay at the B&B. I told them Bill would pick me up when I called so they would have a ready-made ride into town.

Steve had been having problems with his boots, and by the last few miles that day, his feet were miserable. I knew every step was putting him in agony. It was a rough day for me, too, but the men had hiked two miles farther and their packs were full, so I was very sympathetic to their exhaustion and pain. It was approaching 7 p.m. as we arrived at the road where we would find a telephone. If I hadn't been with Steve and Gourmet John, I would have been extremely nervous in the gathering darkness.

I knew Bill would be worried about me. He had told me a story the previous night about a man who had slackpacked that same section but had been stupid enough to go without a flashlight. (I quietly slipped mine into my day pack.) The man had ended up on the trail after dark trying to make it to the road. The police had gone out to look for him because someone in town knew he didn't have what he needed to spend the night in the woods. Sometimes it's not smart to slack-pack, but often God takes care of those who haven't planned sufficiently for themselves. I wouldn't count on it too often, though.

That night Boots, Steve, Gourmet John, and I ate a late dinner in a restaurant across the street from the B&B. When I went to the restroom, a young lady stopped me and asked if I were a thru-hiker. She said she could tell by the way I walked—painfully. She came back with me to the table. (I knew she'd already spotted those handsome young men I was with from across the room.) She had been thru-hiking the trail several years ago, reached North Woodstock, fell in love with the area, stopped hiking, and stayed! She obviously enjoyed encountering hikers and offered to take the guys into Lincoln in the morning to an outfitter's store. Trail magic at its best.

In one day the Whites had certainly lived up to their reputation of difficulty. I was very grateful that I had been able to hike the most difficult day of my journey so far without a full pack and with Steve and Gourmet John. It helped me gain confidence, and now I could head into the rest of these mountains without as much fear. If my ride had been ten minutes later that morning, I never would have caught up with the men. Once again, the trail had taken care of me.

I was off in the morning to tackle more of the White Mountains. I knew it would be the hardest part of the journey for me, but I was confident I could do it. I didn't expect to enjoy it, but I also knew that the best rewards in life are often those that we have to work hardest for. The memories we savor the most are often of the times when there was anxiety, risk, challenge, and danger. I expected to face all of those in the weeks ahead.

The Appalachian Trail

27

Life-expanding experiences

Gorham, New Hampshire
1,838 miles hiked
September 4, 1994

*T*he White Mountains were unbelievable, and the best part about them was that they were behind me. I felt like celebrating! I knew that some of the most hazardous trail was still ahead in southern Maine, but if I could make it through the White Mountains, I could do Maine too. Isn't it funny how you can say, "Wow, that was wonderful!" about something you've done, when what you really mean is, "That was the hardest thing I've ever done, but boy, do I have stories to tell and memories for my treasure chest."

Although the trail was harsh and the weather often brutal, walking along a ridge 5,000 feet up in the sky when you have hiked all the way there was a mind-blowing experience. Often when I was traversing a field of rocks, there was no discernible path at all, just a direction. The trail above treeline was often marked with cairns—man-made piles of rocks, easily distinguishable from those placed by nature. (With the frequent snow, rain, and cloud cover, the white blazes on the ground could be difficult to see.) The hand-over-hand climbing up or down huge slabs of rock was, as I expected, difficult for me. But I actually found myself sometimes *enjoying* the ascents—never the descents!—and was pleased to see how much confidence and expertise I had gained through the weeks and months on the trail.

The Whites were known for their severe weather. Temperature changes could be dramatic and unexpected, with snow possible every month of the year. Winds often ranged up to 80 miles per hour, and the highest wind speed ever recorded on Earth, 231 miles per hour, was at the top of Mt. Washington. And although it had been the most challenging part of the trip so far, I think other thru-hikers would agree that the most difficult parts were what we'd remember and cherish the most. Those were the life-expanding experiences.

However, I admit my first day out of North Woodstock was a life-expander I could have done without. I made it just 10 miles that day and worked harder than I often had going twice that far. I went over Little Haystack Mountain (4,760 feet), Mt. Lincoln (5,089 feet), Mt. Lafayette (5,249 feet), and Mt. Garfield (4,488 feet). Most of the hiking was above timberline with no protection from the elements, and the wind was brisk.

The last mountain of the day was Mt. Garfield. As I struggled up its rocky face, there was one spot I'll always remember, where I had to inch forward, sliding my boots along a narrow ledge about three inches wide, looking for a handhold to hoist myself up the rocks and hoping my backpack wouldn't tip me off balance. It was the kind of terrain I'd been dreading for months, and I kept thinking, "Now how do they expect us to do this?" But I did it. In fact, I'd found that everything on the Appalachian Trail was doable. I'd known that in my mind for months, now I finally knew it in my heart. Others had done it; I could too. (Some of these things I had to keep telling myself over and over.)

When I reached the top of Mt. Garfield, I thought the worst was over. The data book said there would be a shelter and campsite just two-tenths of a mile from the summit, but that was the longest fifth of a mile I'd ever backpacked.

The trail went down-mountain steeply. I had to lower myself down the rocks, stretching for the next place to put my foot and trying to keep from falling. As always late in the day, the pain in my knees was becoming intense. I was on the verge of tears, thinking I must have missed the sign for the shelter because it *couldn't* be this far, and if I did miss it, I was not going to sleep that night because the terrain offered no level spot anywhere to pitch a tent. All of these negative and anxious thoughts kept pouring through my mind, and I became more and more nervous and upset as I picked my way down through the rocks.

By the time I reached the turnoff for the shelter (I hadn't passed it), I was too mentally exhausted to enjoy the relief. At times like that, I was usually surprised how one moment I could be on the verge of panic, and then I would spot a sign or a blaze, and in the space of an instant, my panic would be gone. By the time I exhaled, the relief had settled in. But this time, I was so overwrought that I just stood in a stupor until my breathing returned to normal.

The water source was a little spring right near the trail, and I thought I might as well get water first and then head for the shelter. A young man was also there for water, someone I didn't know. We greeted each other and I asked him if he would take my water bag from the side of my backpack so I could fill it without taking my pack off. Just as he was reaching for it, I broke into uncontrolled sobbing. Another embarrassing moment. ("We are thru-hikers, MIGHTY thru-hikers...") The poor guy. He felt so sorry for me, he filled my water bag before filling his own, while I stood there blubbering. All I could force out of my mouth was, "It's been a rough day..." He seemed to understand that the mountains can do that to a person.

I had recovered my equilibrium by the time I reached the shelter, and I set up my sleeping gear at one end, while the young man and his girlfriend arranged theirs at the other. It became cold very quickly as we cooked our dinners and settled into our sleeping bags.

As darkness fell that night, a group of Brown University students—a freshman orientation group, the first of several I'd meet—arrived at the shelter. It was a bitterly cold and windy night. Some of them were really suffering from the effects of the long day with harsh weather and demanding terrain. They all crowded into the shelter to cook their dinner, long after dark, when I wanted to be asleep.

Their plan had been to tent, but the student leaders decided to give the group the option of staying in the shelter instead, given the wind and temperature. Some, but not all, could have squeezed in and several wanted to stay there. But many felt they should all stick together as a group. While they were cooking, one of them tipped over a stove, spreading fire out into the middle of the shelter, which caused some quick extinguishing action. Perhaps that persuaded them to pitch their tents rather than sleep in a fuel-soaked area.

They said another group of students had lost some food to a bear the night before, not far from where we were. They had hung the food in a net bag, but not quite high enough, and the bear was able to snag it with his claws, spilling the food to the ground.

I was intrigued to hear the interaction among the students and to watch the decision-making as it took place. This was the most strenuous physical challenge many of them had ever faced, and some were able to shake it off better than others. A few were still immersed in the feelings and exhaustion they'd experienced on the trail and couldn't get beyond that. They were all with people they'd met just a few days before, but the bonds of shared adversity were already visible. I imagined those few days in the mountains forged some friendships that would last throughout college, and some self-realizations that would carry them through a few difficult final exams.

When I hiked over Mt. Washington, the highest point in New England with an altitude of 6,288 feet, it had its usual cloud cover and visibility of just a few yards. Ice was on the ground, the temperature was in the 30s, and the wind was blowing about 40 to 50 miles per hour. I had seen it from afar for several days, looking like a huge mother mountain, watching over all the rest. With its top almost always in the clouds, there was a mystique surrounding it, giving it an unapproachable aura. Stories about how it created its own weather systems, how the temperature could drop dramatically in a very short period, and how people died there every year when they were unprepared for the weather had kept my apprehension level high.

Many people drive up an eight-mile road to the top of Mt. Washington, or they take a train that cuts its way up the mountainside. The day I crossed, I could hear the train approaching, sounding its warning whistle, but was able to catch just a brief glimpse as it went by in the clouds and mist. I could visualize the tour guide saying to his passengers, "Oh look. We're lucky today. I've spotted an Appalachian Trail thru-hiker. Over on your left, about 30 yards away. You can tell it's a thru-hiker by its large backpack, hiking stick, and weathered clothing. This one is heading north, which means it's been on the trail for 1,825 miles and probably for about five months. It looks like a female, but I can't tell for sure since it's wearing a hooded jacket and pants to shield itself from the wind. It's probably not a young one; look at the slow, tentative way it's making its way down through the rocks. It's probably suffering from sore knees, a typical thru-hiker ailment, especially in the older ones. If you hurry you can get a picture before the mist rolls back in. Now over to your right..."

The Appalachian Mountain Club (AMC), which maintained that section of the AT, allowed no camping above treeline except at designated sites. They were trying to protect the delicate ecosystems, as well as the lives of ill-prepared campers. This necessitated careful planning, since the trail was above treeline in some areas for miles at a time.

I had read and heard much about the AMC's hut system in the White Mountains. The huts were large buildings, with no heat or electricity, where hikers paid $60 to sleep in a bunk room with as many as a dozen other people. The crews cooked huge dinners and breakfasts, which guests ate family-style at large wooden tables. The huts were very popular with scores of backpackers who planned two- or three-day hiking expeditions in the mountains. But for a thru-hiker, they could be a nuisance. At the huts, we either paid the hefty fee or worked for our food and lodging. Most of us worked. The shelters and campsites also had fees, so we couldn't get through the White Mountains without paying.

A typical example was Madison Springs Hut. I arrived late in the afternoon and asked the crew if I could work. They needed only a few workers, so if too many thru-hikers arrived ahead of you, you were out of luck. I was the first one there that day.

After awhile, Sher Bear and JettButt arrived. We shouted and hugged each other. I was thrilled to see them! I had been ahead of them since Delaware Water Gap, Pennsylvania, and they seemed like long-lost friends. Other hikers were now becoming those treasured familiar faces.

There was a gorgeous sunset that night, and many people rushed outside to take pictures. It was one of the most beautiful I'd seen, with the clouds and mountaintops teaming up to provide fascinating shapes and colors. It was a perfect backdrop for my reunion with hiker friends, and a chance to say an evening hello to my dad.

After the hut's paying customers had eaten, we were given a free dinner—leftovers with the crew. We slept on the floor because all the bunks were filled. In the morning, after the guests had left, we started on our chores. I was assigned the task of scrubbing out the toilets and sinks in the restrooms. I could see why the crews were willing to let us stay: They gave us the chores they didn't want to do! As I was completing my tasks so I could get back out on the trail, I kept thinking, "I came out here to hike the Appalachian Trail. What am I doing cleaning toilets?"

That day included my least favorite mountain of the whole Appalachian Trail: Mt. Madison. It was one huge pile of rocks, one mile up and two miles down the other side. The rocks were treacherous; my knees were grieving and longing for the days before I'd ever thought of hiking the Appalachian Trail; my backpack was adding its bulk to my insecure feeling; and my hiking stick, as always, was providing the one anchor which kept me upright. It took me four hours to traverse that three miles. If I hadn't had a hiking stick to help me keep my balance, I think I'd still be out there.

My off-trail good fortune continued to connect me with friends who lived within driving distance of the Appalachian Trail. My most recent rendezvous had come at Crawford Notch, right before the Presidential Range began. Ruth, the same friend who put me on the trail at Springer Mountain, drove over from Portland, Maine, to spend a night with me. Of all my friends, she was probably one of the few who would really have loved to attempt a thru-hike of the Appalachian Trail. (Many would put it first on a list of 100 things they *wouldn't* want to do.) So instead of waiting for me at the road crossing, Ruth headed up the trail to meet me. I was tramping along with my head down, checking the ground as usual for rocks and roots. Suddenly I looked up and there she was, coming toward me. Here was one of my "real life" friends actually out on the trail, in the middle of the woods. I tried not to cry.

It always seemed like such a surreal experience when I connected with a friend. I was able to see the towns a little farther from the AT and get a broader feel for the regional geography, apart from the mountains. However, it was disconcerting to be riding in a car, going to a restaurant, and sleeping in a motel, all the while knowing that the next day I'd be back in the mountains carrying my backpack, cooking dehydrated food, and sleeping on the ground.

When Ruth deposited me back at the trail in the morning, she spent two hours climbing up Mt. Webster with me before turning back as I continued on ahead. Once again, she took pictures of me as I waved goodbye and headed up a mountainside, this one 1,800 miles north of Springer. She also left me with the best trail-treat of the trip: Fresh lobster that she had cooked and brought along. We put it in a plastic bag, I took it with me, and that day, I sat on top of Mt. Jackson and ate lobster—my favorite food. I think my taste buds were thrown into a state of confusion, after months of peanut butter as my lunch fare.

Many of my emotions and reactions to situations on the trail reminded me of life. (Why did I always feel as if being on the AT was like being on a different planet or dimension, and I was viewing "real life" from afar?) One day in the White Mountains I was trudging along the top of a very high ridge, bundled up in my jacket to keep warm, and battling the wind. I was going very slowly and hurting with every step, questioning my sanity as usual. Suddenly the strap from my backpack flipped up in the wind and smacked me in the cheek with such a sharp sting that I immediately burst into tears. It was so completely a reflex reaction from the sharp pain that I was reminded of a baby who bursts into tears instantly when falling. It almost made me laugh to observe my own reaction, but I was so miserable that instead, I just sat down behind a rock to shield myself from the wind and cried for a while. I think crying is such a natural reaction to pain and other types of misery that I'm surprised we don't do more of it. Have we trained ourselves not to? At home I rarely cry; on the trail, I cried a lot.

At times like that I was glad to be alone, because I'd probably have felt the need to explain what was the matter if anyone were with me. And usually the only thing the matter was that I was in pain, exhausted, frustrated, or scared. Or maybe I'm just a crybaby.

I was very excited waiting for my son Greg to arrive. He was driving out from Chicago to join me for four days on the trail. I would find someone to take us up to Route 26 at Grafton Notch in Maine, 40 miles north of Gorham, and then we would follow the AT south back to the town.

That may seem a little complicated, but if we traveled north from Gorham, there wouldn't be a way for Greg to get off the trail after four days of hiking. Although Route 26 went by the trailhead, it was in an isolated area, and I didn't want to take a chance that we could hitch a 40-mile ride back to town on remote roads. So we'd still be hiking the trail, but going south. I wondered if it would feel any different. We'd do short mileage each day, because that section included some of the most difficult terrain on the whole Appalachian Trail.

I was eager to share my experience with Greg and thrilled that he wanted to participate in my venture. We'd have the memories of this time together for the rest of our lives, and it would be one more bond in the years to come. I was feeling very, very lucky to have two sons who meant so much to me and who had shown their support in so many ways.

And I was almost to my last state! Just 300 miles from home. After such a long journey, I could almost hear Mt. Katahdin calling my name.

Indianapolis,
Indiana

28

My guardian angel

Indianapolis, Indiana
1,853 miles hiked
September 10, 1994

*B*ad news. My grand adventure had come to a screeching halt (literally), and I was back home again in Indiana. My thru-hike was over. I never expected such an abrupt ending to my journey. I didn't know whether to cry or say, "Thank God, it's over." But I really didn't want it to be over until I reached my goal. The end of the trail. The mighty Mt. Katahdin.

Just days before, I had been in the home stretch—the last leg, so to speak—of the most adventurous journey of my life; now I was stretched out on a couch with my leg in a cast. But even at the end, the trail provided what I needed, and my guardian angel was watching over me. I'll go back and fill you in on my time with Greg, because we had quite an adventure, right up to the end.

On our first day together, Greg and I started out in a cool, misty rain. You'll remember we were in Maine, heading back south towards Gorham, New Hampshire. The trail was mostly up, with a lot of hand-over-hand climbing on very hazardous terrain. It was as difficult and treacherous as any part of the trail I'd seen so far, and with the rain thrown in, I could see why Greg was struggling. It was his first day on the trail; I was into my sixth month. I led the way most of the time, and being the pacesetter gave me a confidence I wouldn't have felt had I been alone.

As the afternoon wore on, it became colder and rained harder. The wind had picked up and was blowing fiercely when we approached the top of one mountain. We crossed the top, above tree line, with no protection. The rain felt like hail as it pelted our faces.

We were fighting our way across the peak when the wind picked me up and threw me down into a bush, backpack and all. Greg was a few yards behind me. He yelled, "Give me your hand; I'll pull you up!" He had to shout; the wind was blowing so hard, we could barely hear one another. As I was struggling to get up and stagger on, I started laughing rather hysterically. It suddenly seemed insane to me that Greg had taken vacation time from his job to join me on the trail, and on his first day we were caught in a rainstorm on top of a mountain—miserable, wet, chilled, and wondering how we were going to get through this. But I knew his sense of humor hadn't left him when he shouted in frustration, "They didn't mention hail in the brochure!"

When we finally reached the shelter, we were cold, soaked, and tired. It was a relief to have refuge from the weather. There were several lumps in the shelter, which turned out to be Model T, Shirt & Ty, Earth Dawg (not to be confused with Earth Frog), and Oliver huddled into their sleeping bags trying to stay warm. I made introductions and they squeezed together to make room for us. Greg seemed to be in a daze, wondering, I expect, what in the world he was doing out here.

I immediately went to the river to get water for our dinner. It was flowing fast over a log; I just held my water bag under the flow and it poured right in, looking very brown and unappetizing. I didn't tell Greg about the color.

Upon returning to the shelter, I changed clothes, hung my wet gear on a couple of nails, and snuggled into my sleeping bag, as Greg already had. No one said much; we all just huddled down for warmth. Soon I got out my stove and made hot chocolate to warm us up. (Just like all those times at home when the kids used to play in the snow and then come in to mugs of steaming cocoa.) Eventually we cooked our dinner and settled in for the night. Greg told me later that he was so cold when we arrived at the shelter, he couldn't even think until he drank the hot chocolate. It just felt like a normal day on the trail to me.

The next morning we packed up and struggled into our wet clothes and boots. We were headed for Mahoosuc Notch. I had warned Greg that it was considered the most difficult mile on the trail—Maine's Murder Mile—and indeed it was a perilous section. The Notch was filled with truck- and house-sized boulders, all jumbled together, creating an enormous obstacle course. Because mountains rose so steeply on both sides that the sun had no entry to the cracks and crevices, there was ice in the water every day of the year. At times we had to take off our backpacks and stuff them through a small opening and then squeeze through ourselves. There were places where Greg went first because, being 6 feet tall, his legs were longer than mine. He would climb up a boulder and I'd lift our backpacks to him; then he'd pull me up. At one point we couldn't stop laughing because I got stuck crawling under a rock with my backpack on and it took awhile to wiggle my way out. Greg: "This is *hiking?*"

I knew I would have been able to do the Notch by myself if Greg hadn't been with me, but it would have taken me a lot longer to do that mile (it took us nearly three hours), and I would have been very apprehensive. In fact, one of the reasons I picked that section to have him hike with me was because I knew going through the Notch would be one of the most demanding segments of the trail, and I didn't want to do it alone.

As it turned out, the climbs down the mountain into the Notch and then back up the other side were almost as difficult as the Notch itself, so we had a strenuous workout that day—again in cold, wet weather. We were proud of ourselves, though, and felt quite a sense of accomplishment when we emerged from that ordeal. "We did it! Hallelujah!" Much later we decided it had been pretty cool. You couldn't have convinced us of that at the time, though.

That night we shared a shelter with Colorado SloGoes, Sole Power, Papillon Duo, and the Pink Panthers, couples in their 40s, 50s, and 60s. Although I'd met all of them before, it was the first time I'd spent an evening with any of them. I could tell from the conversation what a different experience I'd have had if I'd intersected with them more often. Not necessarily better, just different. They were of my generation, and it was comforting to see that their perceptions of the trail were similar to mine. (They were also popping ibuprofen at about the same rate as I. Greg thought we were a bunch of pill fiends.)

They were getting ready to do the Notch the next day since they were heading north, and it was a relief to know we had it behind us. They let us know, however, that the day they'd just finished, which we had coming up, was another grueling one. ("You can't call that hiking; 'mountaineering' would be a better name," said Colorado SloGoes.)

Sure enough, within an hour of starting out the next morning, we were struggling again. We ascended one stretch where the only way up was to find handholds in a crevice etched into a slab of rock pitched at a 70 degree angle. If you looked down, you realized that with one slip you'd fall a long way before you stopped rolling. We hugged the mountain and hoped our backpacks wouldn't pull us over. Soon I said, as I had the previous two days, "Greg, if *every* day were like this, I swear I wouldn't be out here." And he finally said, "Mom, for me every day *has* been like this!" I wondered again whether this experience was building his respect for me or whether he was just becoming convinced I was getting a little loony in my middle years.

We set a goal of 10 miles for our third day, which was ambitious given the ruggedness of the terrain, my slowness in the rocks, and Greg's lack of trail conditioning. Around 1 p.m., we crossed the Maine/New Hampshire state line heading back south into New Hampshire, with five miles to go until we reached the campsite where we intended to spend the night.

We stopped at the state line and took pictures of each other—of me by the Maine sign giving a victory cheer that I'd made it to my last state, and of Greg by the New Hampshire sign, home of his alma mater, pointing at it and laughing because it said "Your [*sic*] in New Hampshire now." It had been misty all morning, but now the sun was starting to poke its head out and it seemed as if the afternoon would finally give us a break from the rain. "All right, Greg! It's going to be a beautiful afternoon! Now you'll see how wonderful this trail can be."

The sunlight boosted our morale, as well as knowing that the worst terrain was behind us. Mt. Success was just two miles ahead. What a great name for a mountain! We decided to celebrate our success at surviving the last three days when we reached the top.

A hundred yards later, while we were chattering away, my left foot slipped out from under me on a wet rock—one of thousands of wet rocks I'd stepped on in the past five months. My right foot stayed behind, at an odd angle, and I heard a pop in my ankle as I went down.

The pain was immediate and intense, and I could feel the blood drain out of my face. I knew I was in trouble. Greg started to help me up, but I said, "No, I don't think so." I stayed on the ground and took my boot off. My ankle was already starting to swell and throb, and I felt certain it was sprained. "What do you think, Mom? Can you walk?" "I don't know, Greg. Give me a few minutes."

I took my elastic bandage from my knee and wrapped it around my ankle, put my boot back on, laced it tightly, and told Greg I'd try to continue. Using my hiking stick as a cane, I moved ahead very slowly, thinking perhaps the pain would subside. It didn't. Every step brought increased pain. Almost immediately, we came to a slab of rock where we had to climb straight up, and I could see I wouldn't be able to do it. Each time I took a step or tried to bend my ankle, the pain was sharp. "I can't do this, Greg. I can't go on."

We considered our options. There weren't many. We looked at the map. Greg could leave me there and hike out to find help, but the nearest road we could spot was 10 miles away. It was a gravel road with no likelihood there would be any traffic for him to hitchhike to Gorham. Since it was getting close to 2 o'clock, it didn't seem feasible for him to make it that far before dark—and certainly not there and back to where I was.

Greg asked what I thought we should do. I said, "Well, if I were a thru-hiker, I'd pitch my tent, stay overnight right here, and see if the ankle felt better in the morning." "Mom, you *are* a thru-hiker!" "Oh. . . yeah, you're right." I wasn't thinking very clearly.

Leaning on Greg for support, I hobbled back to the only level spot we had passed, where the trail crossed the state line. When we got there we realized the trail itself was the only level spot, with the ground on either side rocky and uneven. I sat down while Greg pitched our tent, right on the path. Our heads would be in Maine and our legs in New Hampshire. I think in football that would be considered a touchdown, but I didn't feel much like celebrating.

We decided we'd just have to explain to anyone who came along why we were camping in the middle of the AT. We had planned to stay at shelters each of our three nights together, but had brought the tent with us in case of emergency. It must have been my guardian angel that convinced us to carry the extra weight.

It was still cold and damp and Greg said we needed water to cook a hot dinner. He left his pack at the tent with me and took off with the water bag to find a shelter we'd passed about a mile back. I lay there with a mixture of pain and turmoil swirling through my brain; I already could tell my ankle wouldn't feel better by morning.

I tried to visualize what the immediate future would bring if my ankle were sprained. In years past, I'd had two sprains and I knew that they can take days—or weeks, depending on the severity of the sprain—to heal. Knowing how rugged the trail was in that section of Maine, I thought, "How am I going to be able to hike with this ankle? If I have to take a week or two off for it to heal, I'll be way behind everyone, the weather will get worse, it will still be painful when I start back on the trail, I might not make it to Mt. Katahdin before it closes."

I finally just numbed my mind to all the anxieties and waited for Greg's return. He had good news: He had found a work crew of Harvard students at the shelter, supervised by an AMC (Appalachian Mountain Club) member. Jim, the AMC member, had told Greg he'd help us get off the mountain. Within an hour he arrived, and we created a game plan.

Jim said that the next day an AMC van would be waiting for him at an old logging road that wasn't on the map, just three miles from our present location. The terrain between us and the road was rugged and steep, but if we could make it there, he could drive us to Gorham. He would bring one of the Harvard students with him in the morning and along with Greg, they would get me to the logging road somehow.

Whenever possible, Jim said they try to convey people off the mountain with the resources available rather than having to call in a rescue team. That can involve up to 24 people with a litter (a stretcher for use in the wilderness). Going down the steep rocks of the mountain, one crew of eight would hand the litter to the next crew positioned a little further down, then they would hand it down to the third crew while the first one scrambled by to get into position for the next hand-off. It seemed like much more volunteer effort than was warranted to get me to the road.

I couldn't face the prospect of trying to make it to the shelter that night, so Jim said he would be back for us in the morning. I took several more pain pills than usual and Greg cooked dinner. After spending a very melancholy evening wondering what the next day would bring, we squeezed into my little tent. Greg had hung our food and put all of our gear under rain covers. Thank goodness. It rained during the night.

I didn't sleep any more my last night on the trail than I had during my first. I kept remembering: No pain, no rain, no Maine. It was supposed to serve as a warning that if you weren't prepared to suffer, you'd never get to the final state. It took on a little different meaning as I lay there listening to the raindrops, with my head—after all these months—finally in Maine, feeling the dull ache in my ankle and wondering whether my journey would end at the state line instead of the finish line.

In the morning, promptly at 7:30, Jim and Kevin, the Harvard student, arrived. They carried our backpacks while Greg positioned himself by my side as a crutch. With my elastic bandage and tightly-laced boot again protecting my ankle, we started out. My hiking stick, having served so many roles for me in the past five months, now became a cane. The three young men took turns carrying the backpacks and acting as my crutch while I hopped along on one leg. When one of them became tired, he would switch with another. We moved very slowly, and they traded places often. On the steep rocky descents, one would lift me down to the next and they formed their own little two-person litter, always taking great care to protect me from further injury.

More than an hour later, we arrived at the shelter. We rested while Jim supervised the crew, finished up his tasks, and got his gear packed to leave the mountain. It was his last day working before heading home to start his junior year at Greg's alma mater, Dartmouth—the last of the trail's many coincidences. I wrote an entry in the shelter register, wishing my trail friends well and saying the future was uncertain for the continuation of my hike.

For the final two miles, we had all of Jim's equipment in addition to Greg's and mine. The two backpacks became much heavier, and I carried the third pack with some of the weight in it. Eventually we set off again, this time encountering rivers as well as more rocks. When we came to the streams, the men would stand in the water and hoist me across on the rocks. It was exhausting for them, but they worked well together. These young men were unbelievably solid and proficient in their roles as my rescue team.

Hours later, in the middle of the afternoon, we arrived at the logging road. I don't remember a more welcome sight, ever, than that AMC van sitting in the dirt. The first link to civilization. I laid down in the back seat, closed my eyes, and started to relax for the first time in more than 24 hours. The ordeal was almost over.

As the Harvard student started back up the mountain with our profound thanks sending him on his way, Greg, Jim, and I began a bumpy ride through miles of rutted back roads. I made a pillow of my clothes to protect my leg and spent the next half hour bouncing around in the back of the van. Jim dropped us off in Gorham, where we had left Greg's car, and we found the nearest hospital 10 miles away. Twenty-six hours after hearing that fateful pop in my leg, we arrived at the emergency room.

I guess this story ends when the ER physician returned from reading the X-ray with the news that my leg was broken just above the ankle. Greg and I just stared at each other blankly as he said, "I'm afraid you have a spiral fracture of the lower fibula."

Well. No decision to be made about whether or when I could return to the trail to finish the rest of my journey. A week of recovery wouldn't do it. My adventure was over. The orthopedic surgeon confirmed the diagnosis the next day and applied the cast.

To have my journey end so abruptly seemed inconceivable. My brain was as numb as my toes had been all these months. Emotionally, I couldn't feel a thing.

The next day and a half were spent with my leg propped up, to keep the swelling down, on the dashboard of Greg's little sports car, headed back to Indiana. I was still reeling from the shock of my early exit from the trail and Greg couldn't believe what had happened. "Geez, Mom, you got along just fine for more than five months until I arrived!"

"Greg, just think how much worse it would have been if I'd been alone. My guardian angel definitely orchestrated this scenario in the best way possible. Thank God you were with me."

I knew it wouldn't really sink in what a *huge* adventure I'd had until there was time to process it over the next several months. While I was on the trail, I just did what it took to accomplish the goal I'd set for myself, and I didn't really think much beyond taking the next step. Now I had no more steps to take. That made me very sad.

I had much to say and many people to thank, but that would come in a few weeks. In the meantime, my body was crying for some recuperation time. It had served me well for the past five and a half months. I'd lost 15 pounds and my clothes were hanging loosely on my frame. I couldn't feel my toes, and my knees hurt more than the broken bone. But I knew the pain was temporary and that my memories would last a lifetime.

I tried not to think about not reaching my goal. I *knew* in my heart from the very first moment I planned my journey that I would make it all the way. Knowing something in your heart doesn't always mean it will happen. Another life lesson, no doubt. I hoped that one day I would feel that not reaching Mt. Katahdin didn't negate the five months of accomplishment and life-changing experiences.

I'll leave you with a story of one of my favorite trail encounters. While I was hiking in Vermont one day, a man with a day pack came walking toward me on the trail. As he drew near, he called out, "Are you a thru-hiker?" When I said yes, he stopped right in front of me and started applauding! He stood there clapping and clapping, and then he said, "Way to go! You're almost there! What an accomplishment! Congratulations!"

He continued clapping while tears welled up in my eyes: my own personal cheering section right there on the Appalachian Trail. With a huge smile, I thanked him as he told me what an unbelievable accomplishment it was to hike all the way from Georgia to Maine. I'm not sure I had ever had a greater sense of pride than at that moment. No words of praise had ever meant more.

And that's when it began to sink in what an extraordinary adventure I'd been having for the past five months on the Appalachian Trail.

Indianapolis,
Indiana

29

The smile's still there

Indianapolis, Indiana
October 7, 1994

*I*t had been one month since I sat in the Berlin, New Hampshire, hospital while a cast was put on my leg. It would have taken me about 30 days to reach Mt. Katahdin. Snow, ice, bitter winds, and freezing temperatures had socked in the top of the mountain for the past week. Why did I wish I were there?

As the days went by, I found that my heart was still out on the trail, and I thought often about my trail friends. I felt out of their world and out of the mainstream. How odd that suddenly, for me, the mainstream of life felt like a little trail through the mountains of Maine, guiding a bunch of backpackers toward their destination after months of rigorous outdoor living. Not like my life at home, with a car in the garage, food in the refrigerator, comforter on the bed, and lock on the front door.

Perhaps I would finish the trail some day, but my heart was with this group, the thru-hiker class of '94, because they were my friends. I wished I could be at the summit to welcome each of them to the end of their journey and offer the congratulations they deserved.

News has a way of traveling on the trail, and many of my friends heard quickly about my broken leg. Several found ways to send me cards even before they reached the end of the trail. The reality and finality didn't hit me until I received a card from DNA a couple of weeks after returning home. I guess my mind was protecting me from dealing with the emotional pain until the physical pain had subsided. Or maybe my hiker friends just knew how to touch a chord within me that no one else could reach right then.

My disappointment remained strong, and it was mixed with a dose of disbelief. I was so sure that I was meant to reach Katahdin. I decided it was a lesson in goal setting. All those times when people asked me how far I was going on the trail, I said, "Maine." I should have said, "Mt. Katahdin." Visualize yourself crossing the finish line. Athletes do it all the time.

So what did I discover in all those months that filled the space between Georgia and Maine? Well, I think the brain doesn't process an experience of this magnitude in a day, a week, a month, or even a year, so the most important discoveries were yet to come. But I did reaffirm many things, gain important new insights, and reorder some priorities.

I learned that I could live outdoors 24 hours a day with minimal comforts and not really miss much of what we so often think of as necessities. I could live for nearly half a year without wearing makeup or deodorant, carrying a purse, watching TV, listening to a radio, reading newspapers, driving a car, using electricity, taking daily showers, or having a place to call home.

I discovered that bears, coyotes, rattlesnakes, spiders, and mice weren't so scary in their own environment.

I remembered how important it is to try new things. To stretch yourself beyond what you thought were your limits. To "get outside the box." To meet new people. To see new places. To do things you're afraid of doing. To expand your thinking and your horizons.

I realized that we don't all hike the trail, or live our lives, the same, and that's good. You find what works for you and do it. "Hike your own hike": a good rule to follow in life.

I discovered that people are looking for heroes.

I found that fortitude can get you through a lot of hard times. And even though days are filled with discomfort, pain, loneliness, or fear, when the next day dawns, you realize that though it was hard, now it's over. And the next time you're experiencing the same thing, you think, "I got through this before and I can get through it again. 'This too shall pass.'"

I recognized anew that you can't tell what people are made of by looking at them or listening to them. You have to watch what they do—over the long haul.

I found out that cows don't moo at night.

I saw that to get where you're going, you just have to keep putting one foot in front of the other. And sometimes when it's too scary to look down because the bottom is so far away and it's too intimidating to look up because the top is pretty far away as well, it works best to just look straight ahead and go.

I discovered that it felt good to live the life of an adventurer—getting water from streams, carrying all my supplies on my back, sleeping in the woods, hanging my food in the trees, and not seeing civilization for days at a time.

I found you can become friends with people with whom you have little in common but have shared an intense experience.

I learned how to spend time doing nothing that *looks* productive.

I discovered you can get 'most anywhere you want to go on foot. It just takes longer.

Perhaps the most poignant part of my time on the Appalachian Trail had been my strong feeling of connection with my dad. Checking in for a quick hello in the morning became a reassuring part of my routine, and whenever my personal resources flagged, his spirit was there to sustain me. His constant presence added to my feeling of destiny. I have never loved him more.

As my odyssey progressed, I began to realize I never could have made this journey without three groups of people:

Friends and family members helped me plan my adventure, took care of my things, mailed supplies to me, and came to see me, some driving hundreds of miles for a brief visit. The nearly 400 cards and letters I received along the way were my constant motivation to continue.

Fellow thru-hikers bestowed their friendship, mentoring, and assistance when needed. Just when I felt I could no longer stand up to the trail's punishment, a hiker would appear to shore up my courage and bolster my morale. Those new friends were my constant motivation to continue.

Strangers, the most unexpected support group, provided food, lodging, a ride, a drink of water, a word of encouragement. They'll never know about the role they played, but every thru-hiker recognized that without those unknown benefactors, the trail would take an even heavier toll. Those strangers were my constant motivation to continue.

How ironic that I left home thinking I was going out on my own, without any support systems, and I returned feeling that the only reason I was able to make it all the way to Maine was because of the people at home and those I met along the way. Will Rogers said, "People are what the world is all about." For me, people became what the Appalachian Trail was all about. It's curious that you can undertake a solitary journey and return more connected to people than ever before.

When I reached New England and the end of the trail started to feel close, I started thinking about those big smiles you always see on the faces of participants in the Special Olympics as they cross the finish line, and I began to understand what they're all about. I realized the smiles are there for two reasons: One, because the participants feel so good about just doing their best. It doesn't matter whether they're the fastest runners or have the best style; they've just done their best and that's all that matters. And they're smiling because they know their loved ones are proud of them.

As I was nearing Maine, I started thinking, "I'm not the fastest hiker out here (far from it!) and I don't have very good style, but I'm doing it the only way I can. I'm doing my best, and I'm getting there. And I know how proud of me my family and friends are."

And I realized that when hiking the trail, as in the Special Olympics, there were no losers; everyone out there was a winner just because we'd all made a gutsy decision to take a risk and face a challenge and see what we were individually made of. And I would get this huge smile on my face—and the smile's still there.

30

A second chance

Indianapolis, Indiana
March 28, 1995

I had decided to go back. I couldn't give up my goal of hiking the whole Appalachian Trail. To be so close to the end, less than 300 miles from the finish, and not to put forth that final burst of effort went against my beliefs. I've never settled, never said, "Oh well, it's not perfect, but it'll do." A way of showing respect—for your job, your volunteer activities, the people in your life—is to do your very best for each endeavor. There was a very important mountain still to be climbed at the end of the trail. I had to do it for myself and for a wilderness footpath that I had come to love and respect. I owed it that final salute.

I would return in September. It would take me approximately a month to finish the remaining miles, and my thru-hiker friends had convinced me that I should do it when I could witness the beauty of the fall colors. They said whole mountainsides full of oranges, reds, yellows, and purples are a sight I shouldn't miss. I trusted their judgment.

Exactly a year before, I had taken my first step on the Appalachian Trail. Since then, my life had taken many new and unexpected twists and turns. The first half of the year encompassed the biggest personal challenge of my life. The last half had been just as eventful, and a lot less painful. It had been the time during which I'd reaped the rewards of my labors on the trail.

I felt an unbelievable sense of peace in my life. I no longer worried about what the future might bring, or whether something would work out for the best, or if I were making a right decision, for I was more convinced than ever that all things are meant to be. If we accept that we are here to learn some fundamental lessons, then we can also accept that everything that happens in our lives causes that learning—even the uncomfortable or traumatic events. If we accept that we are here to grow, then we surely recognize that we don't grow spiritually while we're sitting around eating bonbons. We must sometimes create situations that allow spiritual growth. Peace rarely comes without a price, and the price tag is different for each of us.

By now I realized that breaking my leg was a positive, rather than a negative, life event. That slip on a wet rock launched a year of activity that I wouldn't have enjoyed had I put an end to my adventure.

In the past six months, I had spent most of my time making speeches and writing this book about my adventure. A newspaper columnist at *The Indianapolis Star* had chronicled my journey on the Appalachian Trail based on the letters I sent home from the trail. Thousands of readers had followed along to see if I would make it. Many thought I would quickly give up. When I didn't, they began pulling for me to make it all the way. There was an outpouring of sadness and sympathy when my journey ended. Everywhere I went, people told me they felt a personal loss when I broke my leg. Now they wanted to hear the trail stories straight from "the hiker."

I had already shared my slides and stories with thousands of people in organizations and schools, and I had speeches scheduled into the next year. My adventure was providing inspiration to others who wanted to find their own paths to follow and goals to pursue. Just as I found a role model in the young woman who was the inspiration for my journey, now I had become a role model for many others. The climate seemed right for people of all ages to hear the message: "Stretch your limits. Seek new adventures. The rewards will follow."

Speaking with schoolchildren had been especially rewarding. The kids were genuinely interested in the adventures of Indiana Jean. They tried on my backpack, listened to the stories, and asked intelligent and thoughtful questions. A sixth-grade boy said to me after hearing my speech, "You're my hero!" It's exciting to think that I may have stretched his mind a little in causing him to consider a middle-aged woman a hero. Of course, the boy next to him said, "I don't know how you could have hiked that trail at your age. I know *my* grandma couldn't have done it!" Kids can always keep you humble.

I might also have an even broader opportunity to share my story: A video production company had contacted me with the possibility of producing a documentary about my journey for airing on national television. They would send a cameraman with me to film portions of my final month on the trail. That wouldn't have happened had I reached the end of the trail when I'd planned to. When a door closes, a window opens. . .

In five more months, I would reenter the world of the Appalachian Trail, with its daily lessons, challenges, tests, and rewards. I was looking forward to it—especially to seeing whether I'd really learned anything, or whether I just thought I had. I would be able to put into practice the lessons I learned about life and about living on the trail. As my son Brad said, "How many of us get a second chance at a once-in-a-lifetime adventure?"

The Appalachian Trail

31

The fear was gone

Mt. Katahdin, Maine
2,155 miles hiked
September 26, 1995

On August 29, 1995, I returned to complete my journey on the Appalachian Trail. Had I finished the trail the year before, the pain, exhaustion, mental fatigue, and weather would have combined to make it simply an endurance test. This time, I was able to enjoy each day, each view, each challenge. And I discovered anew that the Appalachian Trail is a small community of people, and that I am still part of that community. It felt like going home.

The best part of going back was discovering that the life lessons of the year before became clearer in my mind. And I gained a new respect and appreciation for the trail itself.

During my year of speeches, I had gradually begun to put the difficulties, the pain, and the bad times into the far recesses of my memory banks. The people, the fun, the magnificence of the mountains, and the spiritual growth had risen to the top. By summer, I found myself sometimes forgetting to mention in a speech that hiking the trail was the hardest thing I'd ever done; that it was a grueling, rigorous journey, and not a goal to be set lightly or by very many people. It was sounding like five months of high points, both literally and figuratively, with good times at every turn on the trail.

And then I went back.

On the first day, in one of the most difficult sections of the trail, I was hit with the reality: The trail never, ever made it easy for a thru-hiker. With a heavy load of gear strapped to your back, every single day tested your spirit.

No one should attempt to thru-hike the Appalachian Trail unless they have a burning passion to do it. Otherwise, they won't find the mental resources necessary to sustain them through the rigors.

At the end of my first week back on the AT, I was enjoying

lunch one day on top of a mountain, soaking up energy from the sun. The realization suddenly dawned as I sat there with my face turned upward that I wasn't anxious or fearful anymore. The previous year I had lived every day on the trail with anxiety, never knowing if I could go as far as I wanted to that day, climb the next mountain without falling off, stave off the exhaustion and pain, or endure the discomfort of the heat, rain, bugs, and mice. I lived with that anxiety for five months, never becoming completely at ease on the trail, and knowing that the hardest part for me, scaling rocky peaks above treeline, was still to come. But those peaks appeared and I made it over every one of them. This time, I knew I had already taken the worst that the trail could throw at me.

Now, finally, I could enjoy spending an extra hour in the sun on a mountaintop without worrying if I'd find a place to pitch my tent by nightfall. If I had to tent above treeline, I could do that. If I crossed a peak during gale-force winds, I'd get through it. If I were cold, wet, and miserable, I'd feel better the next day.

I broke through my fear, discomfort, and anxiety and moved *beyond* them so that they didn't matter anymore. They didn't restrict my activities. I could truly relax and let the trail take care of me. And that was the most freeing emotion I'd ever felt. Freedom from anxiety, pain, and fear. Learning to live *with* those emotions was very different from going *beyond* them. That's taking the next step, and that's what I did this time around. Before, I worked at it; now, I enjoyed it.

Oh, there was still discomfort and pain, but the fear was gone. Climbing jagged rocks, enduring treacherous winds, hiking through chilling rains, and sleeping outside in 20-degree temperatures are not for the faint of heart. I endured them all in that last month on the trail, and some of the situations were intimidating, but the gut-level fear was gone. The rest of the journey just got better and better.

One day as I was hiking, a man and a woman approached, weighed down with backpacks that identified them as long-distance hikers. As they came near, she said, "You're Jean Deeds from Indianapolis!" They had heard two of my speeches, which helped convince them to make the trek. They had started at Mt. Katahdin and were going south to Harpers Ferry, with plans to finish the southern half of the AT the following year. And now here we were, meeting on the trail. We sat down right there on the rocks and talked for an hour. She said, "I wish someone had told us how difficult this trail is!" Oops.

I hiked on with a wonderful feeling of serendipity. Within 10 minutes, the trail turned nasty. I didn't see a ground nest of bees on the path before stepping on it. As the bees swarmed angrily about, one stung me on the cheek, another on the hand. Both stings immediately started to swell and burn. I'd been stung before, and I knew that days of itching, redness, and swelling were ahead.

A half-mile later, a hand-lettered sign on a tree warned of another ground nest of angry bees just ahead. The sign suggested climbing straight up the side of the mountain to avoid them, which I did, but the roots and mosses that I tried to hang on to weren't secure. I started sliding back down, right toward the nest, thinking I would land in their midst. When a bee stung me on the back of the neck, I panicked.

I hit the ground running and didn't stop until I was well outside their territory. That's the only time I remember running with my backpack on—not a pretty sight. Three more nests within the next two hours kept me nervous and cautious.

By the time I made it over that mountain, I was hot, sweaty, hurting, and ready for the day to end. Eventually I found a stream where I could soak my bee stings and a small clearing where I could pitch my tent.

As I put down my pack and started to unload my equipment, I saw a tent nearby with a man inside. The flap unzipped and a voice said, "Indiana Jean?" I turned around to see Wood Rat, one of my '94 hiker buddies! Wood Rat had made it to Harpers Ferry last year. When he left his pack near a road to walk to a store, it had been stolen. He went home and worked for the next nine months to resupply himself. This year he started back at Springer Mountain and was hiking the whole trail.

And now here he was, in a little clearing by a stream in the wilderness of Maine—on the exact same night that I was there. It was a great reunion. We spent the evening reminiscing and exchanging stories of our mutual trail friends. I fell asleep with a contented glow of good fortune. That and a Benadryl helped me sleep through the discomfort of the bee stings.

Another day, I stopped for lunch at one of the lean-tos and encountered a young man from Indianapolis who was hiking sections of the trail in Maine and New Hampshire. I asked him, "When did you start planning your hike on the Appalachian Trail?"

He responded, "Well, when did you speak at the Hiking Club?" My speech there the preceding March had prompted him to come to the trail. I couldn't believe that here was another person for whom I had served as an inspiration to plan his own adventure, and I just happened to encounter him on the trail.

Yet another experience made Maine seem like my second home: Halfway through the month, I took a day off to rest. While sitting in a boardinghouse in Monson, doing my laundry and talking with other hikers, in walked Sourball!

You may remember Sourball: He was a '94 thru-hiker who carried his flute, did great impersonations, snored louder than anyone else, and kept reminding everyone that the *best* part of the trail was in his home state, Maine.

Sourball lived in Bangor, about an hour from the AT. When he heard that I would be finishing the trail, he wanted to hike with me for a day. The timing worked out perfectly. He found me on a Friday evening, as I was getting ready to head into the Hundred Mile Wilderness the next morning. We hiked together on Saturday and stayed in a shelter that night. The next day, I continued north and he hiked back to Monson, where he had left his car. He drove home and was back at work on Monday.

That exquisite bit of timing was one more example of the trail weaving its magic for the faithful. I shouldn't have been surprised. I no longer believe in coincidence—on the trail or in life.

Northbound thru-hikers are often sentimental about the trail in Maine, and I imagine that has as much to do with its being the end of their long and arduous journey as with the personality of the trail itself. But Maine has many legitimate reasons for being one of the most memorable states for hikers. The woods were among the most beautiful, with moss and lichen adding a variety of greens to the array of trees and plants. A combination of spruce, firs, pines, and birches added their stately countenance. And since northbounders were usually in Maine during September, they were regaled by an unparalleled display of fall color.

Pennsylvania was noted for its knee- and ankle-twisting rocks, but sections of the trail in Maine rivaled it for rocky terrain. The roots that were so eager to trip us up along the whole route were ever-present. The rugged hand-over-hand climbing up or down huge slabs of rocks and boulders was unsurpassed anywhere on the AT, even in the mighty Whites.

Maine added ponds, waterfalls, bogs, marshes, and rivers to the trail mix, and they contributed their own challenges and rewards to the wilderness experience. Fording a river with knee-high rapids was a test of courage. But jumping into a pond with clear, cold water after a full day of backpacking was a refreshing antidote for weary and sore muscles.

Ponds (which would be called lakes by Indiana standards) were an excellent place to sight moose as they fed in the shallows at dawn and dusk. They were huge, majestic creatures, weighing 1,400 to 1,500 pounds. I found it amazing that they could navigate through the dense woods with their wide antlers.

There was a void of female thru-hikers again this time; I met just three while on the trail among dozens of men. I hooked up with two of the men, Geezer and Greene King, who were traveling together through Maine.

Geezer lived just 15 miles from the Appalachian Trail in Georgia, where he ran a campground with his family and led whitewater-rafting excursions. He was my age, a real outdoorsman, and one of those people who seem to have all the right skills for hiking the trail. It had been a 20-year dream of his.

And yet, he never expected to be one of the few who would finish the whole trail. So he set short goals for himself. "I think I can make it to Hot Springs, North Carolina." And then, "Well, I'll see if I can get to Damascus, Virginia." It wasn't until he crossed the Kennebeck River, 150 miles from Mt. Katahdin, that he finally said, "I'm going to make it all the way!" Once again, I was amazed that I had the naiveté to assume I could become a thru-hiker, with my lack of experience in the wilderness. And it gave me an internal sense of accomplishment to realize the caliber of the fraternity that had accepted me into its ranks.

Greene King was a delight. He was close to 70, British, and had hiked many places in England and Europe. His daughter lived in the United States. When Greene King came to visit her, he was always looking for something to do with his time, since she worked. So he decided to hike the AT. I guess that kept him out of her hair for a while!

I often stayed with Geezer and Greene King in lean-tos. Sometimes I would have dinner with them and pitch my tent nearby since the lean-tos were often infested with mice, squirrels, and chipmunks. We thought they must be storing up for winter, because they were more aggressive than any I'd seen since the Smokies. Even when I hung my food, they would still go through my backpack and chew holes in all my plastic bags. And they shredded my Handiwipe, which I used as both washcloth and towel.

One of the most emotional moments for a northbound thru-hiker was his or her first glimpse of Mt. Katahdin looming far off in the distance. Katahdin, named by the Indians, means "greatest mountain," and it was a fitting end to a journey of this magnitude. The highest mountain around, it could be seen from more than a hundred miles away. As they drew near, many backpackers changed their behavior. Some fairly flew along the trail, eager to be finished with the experience or perhaps struggling toward a deadline, with friends or family meeting them at the end. Others slowed down and became reflective, perhaps dreading the end of their adventure and wondering what post-trail life would hold for them. Wood Rat fell into the latter category: I saw him when he was less than 10 miles from that final mountain, and he was still at his campsite at 11 a.m. He thought it was such a beautiful place by the stream that he might just stay there all day. I had the feeling he just wasn't ready for his journey to end.

My ascent up Mt. Katahdin included every element that had made my journey such a growing experience. It even combined my on-trail adventure with its off-trail rewards.

The video production company had begun its work on a documentary about my adventure on the Appalachian Trail. Their cameraman climbed Mt. Katahdin with me to film the last day of my journey. Two men came along to help carry camera equipment up the mountain.

The four of us began our ascent at 7:15 a.m. on September 26, a rainy, misty, chilly day. I was carrying a light day pack with food, water, and extra clothes for warmth. The men were loaded down with equipment. I was grateful to be, for once, the one without a heavy backpack.

Vertically, Mt. Katahdin is exactly one mile high, but the trail covers 5.2 miles from base to summit as it winds its way up through the forest before breaking out above treeline. The grade gradually becomes steeper, the vegetation more scrub-like, and the rocks more challenging.

All at once, when rounding a bend halfway up the mountain, we came upon the beginning of a one-mile-long rock climb, with an intimidating route shooting straight up through huge boulders the size of semi-trucks and houses. I had heard about the boulder climb, but had never seen anything like it before. I was awestruck by the sight of sheer rock face jutting up into the sky.

Our group had already been on the trail nearly three hours and the camera crew was feeling the effects of their pack weight. Although the earlier rain had slowed to a drizzle and then stopped, the cloud cover was getting more dense. At times visibility was less than 50 feet, giving the boulders an ethereal feel—as if they comprised the entire world, with a drop-off into nothingness just beyond.

We each struggled through in our own way, stopping often to rest and do more filming. When the boulders finally released us from their clutches, the tablelands began—a fairly flat, rock-laden stretch covering the last 1.5 miles of the AT. And finally, the trail smiled upon us. The cloud cover started to dissipate and we were able to see sun and magnificent views of nearby mountains and valleys. The taskmaster offered that final reward for all the days, weeks, and months of labor: "Here, my dear. You've earned it."

It was relatively easy terrain the rest of the way, and suddenly I felt like running. I wanted to skip and run and do cartwheels the whole way to the end. The top was like a huge magnet pulling me more strongly every minute and yanking my emotions so forcefully that I thought they would arrive at the top before I did. "Isn't this beautiful? Look how gorgeous it is!"

The camera crew struggled to keep up. I didn't realize until they told me that I was, literally, running. They asked me to please slow down.

A mile from the top was a spring named for Henry David Thoreau, who hiked Mt. Katahdin in the 1830s. The sign there said *Baxter Peak: 1 mile.* One mile to the end of the journey. One mile left after a hike of 2,154. Unbelievable.

By the time I reached the large wooden sign at the summit, there was no way to contain the emotions that burst forth. Twenty-one hundred miles of rain, heat, cold, rocks, roots, mice, and bugs. Twenty-one hundred miles of pain, exhaustion, sweating, itching, aching, and grime. Twenty-one hundred miles of trees, flowers, streams, mountaintops, meadows, wildlife, waterfalls, and stunning views. Twenty-one hundred miles of people sharing, bonding, supporting, understanding, and caring. Twenty-one hundred miles surviving the risks, meeting the challenges, feeling the satisfaction, and reaping the rewards. A tear shed for every step taken. Five million steps. I had reached my goal.

What's next? It doesn't matter. Life will be good. In ways I'm just beginning to comprehend, it will include this journey, this quest, and its completion.

Afterword

During the many months I spent on its pathway, I came to think of the Appalachian Trail as a person, a teacher. The AT was sometimes benevolent and kind, offering up a magnificent view or gently rolling terrain as a reward or encouragement for its hard-working students. But more frequently, its alter ego was on display: the difficult taskmaster who pushed, prodded, tested, and always asked for more than we thought we had inside of us. The stern disciplinarian who made us struggle for each lesson learned. The master who said, "*This* is life. If you are willing to pay the price, I promise the lessons you learn will serve you well for the rest of your days."

When asked who was most responsible for shaping our values and pointing us in the right direction in life, which teacher do we mention? Isn't it always the one who made us work the hardest, dig the deepest, and find the best inside ourselves?

Perhaps a few of you will decide that your adventure awaits on the Appalachian Trail. A resource for people interested in information about the AT is the national headquarters of the Appalachian Trail Conference, P.O. Box 807, Harpers Ferry, WV, 25425, (304) 535-6331. With unfailing enthusiasm, the staff provides information, publications, membership services, and encouragement to all who call or stop by. The ATC newsletter, available to members, includes a catalogue of resources.

In Chapter 23, I mentioned Bunny, a 100-year-young lady who sent me an angel to protect me on my journey. I met her in October 1994, after returning from the trail. It was the beginning of a wonderful friendship; Bunny was one of the many rewards of my time on the Appalachian Trail. She died 14 months later, just after we made a date to have lunch the following week. (I think that's the way to go—still putting things on your calendar one hour before you sit down for a rest and quietly slip over to the other side.) Her zest and marvelous insights, culled from a century of living every moment to its fullest, made her a role model for all who knew and loved her. She shared her motto often: "Life is meant to be lived—not just to exist!" When you live by Bunny's philosophy, every day of your life becomes an adventure.

Thru-hiker Class of '94

The friends I made on the Appalachian Trail have, to an unexpected degree, remained a part of my life. I have seen several, talked to many on the phone, and kept up with more through letters. If you became intrigued while reading about them, perhaps you'll want to know who they are and what they're doing today (current as of March 1996). I sent surveys to those for whom I had addresses. Mail has a hard time catching up with many of them, and there were a few I couldn't locate. In some cases, I was able to fill in with what I knew from earlier correspondence.

Trail names and gender are followed by age when they started the trail, and dates they began and finished hiking the AT. An asterisk indicates they have traversed the entire Appalachian Trail, in 1994 unless otherwise stated. (Geezer and Greene King are '95 thru-hikers.)

A Harmony of Spheres*, male, 21, 4/3–11/4. After completing the trail, Harmony graduated from college with a degree in wildlife biology. He reports that he, Brrr, Feather, Mowgli, and PB Max were the last of the northbound thru-hikers to finish the trail in 1994, with Maine "almost all to ourselves, with incredible weather." (They climbed Katahdin on October 5 and then finished the rest of Maine.) He appreciates the comforts of life more now, but misses things like a hard day's hike, sun, dirt, reaching the top of a mountain, sleeping in his tent in the rain, and carrying his life on his back.

Bad DNA*, male, 31, 4/5–10/7. DNA was a biochemist with Virginia Tech before hiking the AT, and has since been a beach bum/Macintosh computer consultant in North Carolina, living at a marina. Perhaps he'll sail 'round the world one day. He writes wonderful letters: "I don't think that peace [found on the trail] will elude me so long as I have a chance to sail, or escape to the mountains, or every so often, write friends." In describing Maine, "I walked alone nearly the entire state, save for the occasional company of our family." Our family. Those two words bring tears to my eyes in their simple description of the bond that develops between thru-hikers.

Bohemian*, male, 33, 3/25–10/10. Bohemian had gone on three expeditions with the National Outdoor Leadership School (NOLS) and had trekked in Nepal and Borneo before thru-hiking the AT. He's an electrical designer for a small engineering company in Cincinnati, and he now also works part-time for an outfitter. I visited him with a small group of fellow thru-hikers recently. He says thru-hiking the AT was the best thing he's ever done, and he's done some pretty neat things!

Boots*, male, 47, 4/17–9/25. Boots had bagged peaks in the Adirondacks and backpacked in New England, the Northwest, Alaska, and Canada before doing the trail. Since then, he has driven cross-country twice, reaching 34 of the 50 state high points. He worked in computers at Corning Glass Works in New York both before and after his AT trek. He says that as time goes on, he remembers the good times and forgets the bad. He's afraid his selective memory may tempt him to hike the whole trail again.

Brrr*, female, 25, 3/17–11/4. Brrr and her hiking partner, Feather, decided to attempt the AT together during weekend trips with a backpacking class in college. Brrr lives in Baltimore, where she was and still is an assistant manager at a movie theater. She's currently taking college courses and is considering enrolling as a full-time student.

CC & the Mule*, male, 20s, 4/1–10/1. CC wrote me from Canada shortly after he finished the trail. Since then, I haven't tracked him down, but I heard he went to California to be the chef in Tortoise and Hare's restaurant.

Charlie and **(Pit Stop) Sally,** married, both 54, 4/1–5/27 (Sally) 4/1–5/31 (Charlie). Sally left the trail at Mt. Rogers Ranger Station in Virginia with an infected toe. Charlie intended to go on, but missed her and went home three days later. They live in Ohio, where they volunteer, babysit with their grandson, hike, and travel. Both retired, she was a telephone operator; he a fire chief. Sally was back on the trail in August 1995, and Charlie will attempt a thru-hike in 1996.

Del Doc*, male, 69, 4/1–9/22. Del Doc's seven-page report to the ATC included weather reports: it rained 37.3 percent of the days; temperature ranges: 30 to 100 degrees; numbers of pairs of boots he wore: 4; his average mileage per day: 14.1; the exact time he reached the top of Mt. Katahdin: 11:40 a.m.; and complete information about where and with whom he spent each night, trail conditions, equipment he used, animals he saw, thru-hikers he met, and medical conditions he treated. He now teaches medical students, is a consultant, and is the medical editor of the ATC newsletter.

Denver Dan, male, 42, 3/28–7/9. Denver Dan spent four days at Mountain Moma's and 16 days near Hot Springs, doing physical therapy on his knee. A variety of adventures and mishaps led him to Rockfish Gap, Virginia, on July 9, when he left the trail to visit his parents and decided not to return. He had been an aerospace engineer before being laid off in June 1993. In October 1995, he moved to Minneapolis to take a job, but I still call him Denver Dan. He was the first to phone me when I returned home after climbing Katahdin.

Dreamcatcher*, female, 27, 4/4–10/4. Before hiking the AT, Dreamcatcher lived in Massachusetts, where she worked as an audiologist. In January 1995, she and Magoo took over management of the Bears Den Hostel on the Appalachian Trail in northern Virginia. She also works part-time as an audiologist in a nearby town. The big event of their weekend is listening to Garrison Keillor, which "beats Saturday nights on the trail, when the highlight was pouring a little extra squeeze margarine onto whatever we were eating." Dreamcatcher finds there's no freedom like that you find walking down a trail with everything you need to survive on your back.

Drifter*, male, 33, 3/30–10/4. Before his thru-hike, Drifter had increased his hiking from overnighters to journeys of more than 300 miles. In 1993, he had section-hiked 1,000 miles of the AT. Since his trek, he has guided whitewater trips in Kentucky and done canoe trips in Florida, where he lives and works at TGI Friday's. He says his time on the AT showed him that we live in a totally materialistic world, and that he can be very content without many things he thought he needed.

Earth Frog*, male, 27, 4/7–10/2. Earth Frog has been on the move since completing the AT: He spent a month hitchhiking home from Maine to Virginia Beach, where he worked briefly in an environmental testing lab while playing guitar at a local coffeehouse. Since then he has been a commercial diver and kayak guide in Baja, Mexico; a NOLS instructor in Wyoming; and a climbing gym instructor, guitar player and surfer in San Diego. He says he found the rest of the world managed to continue on just fine without his participation while he was on the trail.

Feather*, female, 24, 3/17–11/4. After completing the AT, Feather worked with kindergartners while waiting for her Peace Corps application to be processed. On July 1, 1995, she arrived in Morocco, North Africa, to begin her training. She is in Ait Tambil, a village in the high Atlas Mountains where the living is primitive, with no electricity or running water. Feather says the people are even dirtier than thru-hikers! Her priority is hygiene education. She's learning two languages and meets with people in schools, at the health center, and in their homes. Although the cold winter has been difficult, "something happens every day that makes me want to stay—kind of like the trail."

Flare*, female, 24, 3/24–10/10. With no backpacking experience, Flare beat the odds and finished the whole trail. She was a college graduate working in a restaurant; now she is a manager at an outfitter store in Cincinnati (the same place Bohemian works part-time). She would love to move to North Carolina or Tennessee. Flare feels she has better balance in her life since her thru-hike. Her wedding is scheduled for June '96.

Geezer*, male, 52, 4/10–9/25, 1995. Since Geezer had hiked from Springer Mountain to Fontana Dam several times, he started his thru-hike at Fontana. He had taken an early-retirement offer from Southern Bell Telephone Company in 1992 and began working at his father-in-law's campground, 15 miles from the trail. Geezer celebrated his 53rd birthday on the trail in Virginia. (And he bought me a birthday card on *my* 53rd birthday in Maine!)

Goatherders, male, range in age from 22 to 27, 3/30–10/7. **Frenchy***, **Phishstick***, and **Pigeon** had gone to high school together in Atlanta; they met **Ox** in college. Frenchy graduated from Georgia Tech and the rest from North Georgia Military College. Ox and Pigeon left the trail in Virginia. Frenchy and Phishstick, along with the goat, finished the AT together. Today, Phishstick is a wilderness counselor at a private high school in Georgia, and the other three Goatherders work in the Occupational Therapy Program for the state, using wilderness experiences to counsel kids with behavioral problems. Phishstick

may join them soon. Their motto: Goatherders Forever!

Gophermagne* (Go-for-Maine), male, 22, 3/26–10/13. Gophermagne left the University of Georgia in spring of 1993 to earn money for his thru-hike. He will graduate in 1996. He says he misses the trail every day and laments, "I've fallen back into that brainwashed delirium that we were all in before Springer: nature through a window." He's planning a hike in the Grand Canyon over spring break in '96.

Gourmet John, male, 22, 6/26–10/2. Gourmet John began his trek at Harper's Ferry, West Virginia, and hiked to Katahdin. He had graduated from college with a degree in mathematics. He says hiking the AT was far and away the most challenging thing he's ever done—mentally or physically. He and Dr. Becky were married in August 1995; he is a graduate student in mechanical engineering at Vanderbilt and she is in medical school.

Greene King*, male, 67, 3/23–9/25, 1995. Greene King (named for an English beer) is a retired administrator, teacher, writer, management consultant. Since his thru-hike, he's been transcribing his 100,000-word trail journal for a possible book and radio scripts and planning for a 1996 hike in the Alps. He says he discovered on the AT that "I can be a sulky, miserable, angry old pig, but then anyone could have told me that before I started." For an angry old pig, he's a real sweetheart.

Howdy*, male, 52, 3/13–10/17. Howdy's outdoor experience includes nine years as a Scoutmaster with annual backpacking trips. He retired in 1994 as a Special Agent for the FBI and lives in Mississippi. He hiked more than 1,900 miles of the Pacific Crest Trail from May to October, 1995. He's a travelin' man, and I've seen him twice since the AT. He is looking into part-time work with the FBI. Howdy says his thru-hike made him much more emotional and spiritual. An emotional, spiritual FBI agent?

Jabberwocky and **White Rabbit**, married, 26 and 31, 4/1–5/15 (Jabberwocky) 4/1–6/15 (White Rabbit). After Jabberwocky left the trail, White Rabbit hiked another month before joining her for her first OB visit. He decided not to return to the AT, and they left for a one-month trip to Thailand. They are currently living in New York, where he is an ER physician and she is pursuing her master's degree in Secondary Science Education. Their baby, Ian Joseph, a.k.a. Little AT, travels on their hiking and cross-country skiing adventures in his child carrier on White Rabbit's back.

Larry, male, 52, 4/1–5/2. This was Larry's first backpacking/camping experience. He left the AT near Bland, Virginia, with a severe case of hypothermia. He had retired from a position as a machine operator in July 1993, and continues to keep fit with extensive bicycling and babysitting with his three grandchildren.

Magoo*, male, 24, 4/15–10/4. Magoo, a graduate of the University of Georgia, had backpacking and camping experience in the Southeast, mostly in the Smoky Mountains. He completed his thru-hike of the AT in the fall of 1995 by going south from Fontana Dam to Springer Mountain. He has been taking graduate courses and is helping manage the Bears Den Hostel (see Dreamcatcher).

Memphis*, male, 36, 3/20–10/12. Memphis had hiked 1,000 miles over a five-year period prior to this journey. He lives in Memphis, Tennessee, where he builds custom furniture and does cabinetry. He left home a married man but walked the trail with marital problems and returned home to later divorce. He and his wife agreed to separate during a phone call from Bascom Lodge on Mt. Greylock, the highest point in Massachusetts.

Methuselah, male, 75, 3/24–6/8. After leaving the trail to have surgery on his knee, Methuselah returned three weeks later to head north again with Choo Choo. They hiked another 55 miles before knee pain forced Methuselah to give up his plan to complete the trail. He lives in Georgia, where he writes, hikes, and helped to establish a local hospice. He is staying in shape in case the opportunity arises for another AT trek.

Model-T*, male, 58, 4/4–9/29. After retiring from the Marines, Model-T became a farmer and businessman before retiring a second time. He now enjoys gardening, fishing, and hiking in Tennessee. He says his 1994 hike was harder mentally than his 1990 thru-hike because he had blocked out all the really rough times and "it all came back, often, with a big WHAM!" He's considering future hikes, perhaps the AT again in '99. In the meantime, he's growing 12 kinds of lettuce in a greenhouse he built, and remembers that he would have killed for fresh salads on the trail.

Moses*, male, 65, 3/24/94–9/18/95. After six months on the trail in 1994, Moses decided to wait until 1995 to finish the AT. He returned in July and finished two months later. Moses has had quite a life, including a bike trip from Ohio to San Francisco, five months of biking and camping from Portugal to Austria, snow skiing, scuba diving, a field study trip to Andros in the Bahamas, and 18 years as an instructor at a YMCA. He and his wife live on a boat on St. John in the U.S. Virgin Islands. They are currently making repairs and recovering from the hurricane that struck three days before he finished his thru-hike of the AT.

Otter*, male, 37, 4/3–10/3. Before hiking the trail, Otter was a programmer analyst in Raleigh, North Carolina, and is now an information systems consultant there. Otter climbed Mt. Katahdin in "white-out" conditions (wind, snow, and ice) and reports that it was the most intense and awe-inspiring thing he's ever experienced in the outdoors. He says that thru-hiking the trail allowed him to follow nature's rhythms and cycles, something most people today have lost touch with.

Papillon Duo*, married, 49 and 50, 3/31–10/3. Prior to their hike, she was human-resources chief at Fort Monroe, Virginia; he is an Army retiree. After the AT, Papillon Duo took their Catalina 30 sailboat for a cruise down the Intracoastal Waterway and to the Bahamas, with a narrow escape from hurricane Erin. They've since purchased a larger sailboat, christened it *Katahdin*, and plan more extended sailing trips in the Caribbean and beyond. They will hike the Colorado Trail in the summer of 1996 with Sole Power and Colorado Slo-Goes.

Phineas*, male, 31, 4/22—8/31. Phineas had backpacked in the Green and White mountains and hiked extensively in Bolivia, where he lived before his thru-hike. Since his trek he has been teaching at a high school in upstate New York. He said the Appalachian Trail was an excellent reintroduction to the United States, but mentioned the "glaring lack of racial diversity" on the trail, something that was a puzzle to me, too: I met one Asian-American, and no African-American thru-hikers.

Pink Panthers*, married, 64 and 66, 3/30–10/9. The Pink Panthers (who wore hot-pink hiking shirts) are the ultimate backpackers: They've done New England's 100 highest peaks; all the 14,000-foot peaks in the "lower 48"; the high points in all 50 states; and have hiked in Mexico, Nepal, Austria, Switzerland, and New Zealand. They headed up Mt. Katahdin on Oct. 2, but severe weather kept them from reaching the top. Their second attempt, on Oct. 9, was successful.

Poet*, male, 72, 3/29/94–9/20/95. In 1994, Poet left the trail in Massachusetts, 650 miles short of Mt. Katahdin. The hike had become, for him, an ordeal. He returned to the trail on July 18, 1995, and completed his journey, leaving several messages for me in shelter registers in Maine. Poet had served in World War II and worked for 41 years at Westinghouse Electric until his retirement in 1982. Before hiking the trail, he had been despondent following the death of his wife of 50 years. His AT hike helped him refocus on the life he has ahead of him and to consider his grief as part of life and not the end of it.

Scrap Iron*, male, 49, 4/3–8/25. On May 22, his 50th birthday, Scrap Iron hiked 50 miles on the AT. He said it was the worst birthday present he ever gave himself: "It almost killed me!" Although his main hobby is running, he began doing one- and two-week hikes in 1989. Scrap Iron had worked 30 years at Navistar before retiring in 1993. Now he keeps busy being a cook, housekeeper, maintenance man, mechanic, gardener, landscaper, runner, hiker, and biker in Ohio, where he and his fiancée live.

Sher Bear* and **JettButt***, both 23, 4/5–10/4. Sher Bear and JettButt visited me in the spring of 1995. Following their May wedding in New York (attended by DNA, Big John, Dreamcatcher, and Magoo), they moved to Philadelphia. JettButt is in a master's program in physical therapy, and Sher Bear works in human services. JettButt says that hiking the AT with his future life partner was extremely challenging, but equally rewarding. Sher Bear often thought, "I'm not a tough outdoors woman. What am I doing here?" But she gradually discovered she could overcome any challenge if she were patient, focused, and really motivated. She realized she was stronger than she knew. Me too.

Slacker*, male, 22, 3/28–10/15. Slacker captured the weather variations he experienced on the trail in a recent letter: from tornadoes to snow, thunderstorms, 100+ degree temperatures, 80+ mile-per-hour winds, rain, more snow, and a string of sub-freezing nights. Since his thru-hike, he has graduated from college and worked on an organic farm in Maine. He teaches at a private high school, is assistant editor of *Maine Running and Fitness* magazine, and is involved in political activism with the Maine Green Party.

Sole Power*, married, 47 and 56, 3/31–10/3. With homes in California and Colorado and frequent motor-home trips to Canada and other parts of the United States, Sole Power have much to fill their time. They have connected with many of their thru-hiker friends. She had successful surgery on her knee following her AT trek, and they will join Papillon Duo and Colorado SloGoes to hike the Colorado Trail in 1996.

Sourball*, male, 46, 3/20–9/19. An avid backpacker, Sourball averages 200 to 300 miles per year. Since he had hiked all of Maine in previous years, he ended his thru-hike in Andover, Maine. He is a trail maintainer for a section of the AT in Maine. His post-trail life includes "working a day job" and writing a book. He has shared parts of it with me; he is a talented writer with a style that is unique and quite wonderful.

Steady Eddie*, male, 23, 7/93–6/94. Steady Eddie southbounded from Mt. Katahdin to Rusty's at Rockfish Gap in 1993 and finished the trail in 1994, hiking north to Rusty's. He had lived in Connecticut before hiking the trail; afterward he married Chaka Kahn, a southbounder whom he met at Rusty's in 1994, and they moved to El Paso. (Frenchy and the Yeti attended the wedding.) He works at a small publishing house, where he gets to see his wife and their baby daughter all day "so I won't miss a minute of her growing up."

Steve, the British guy*, male, 20s. Steve wrote me a wonderful condolence letter after I broke my leg, including the following passage: "[A broken bone] was the very thing that most of us dreaded as we began to realize that Katahdin was within reach if only the fates would be kind. Well, Atropos certainly did you no favours as she unraveled this particular thread of your destiny..." As I said, he is a classy guy. I haven't connected with him since he returned to England.

Suds* and **Canjo***, married, 62 and 60,

3/2–10/29. (They "flip-flopped"—hiked north to Pennsylvania and then jumped to Katahdin where they hiked back south to end their thru-hike near their home). Since their thru-hike, they have traveled extensively (except during tax season, when Canjo does taxes), seeing a number of thru-hiker friends, including Moses in the Virgin Islands. They have a cabin in Colorado, where they enjoy hiking, fishing, and rafting.

Swan Song*, female, 47, 3/28–9/20. Swan Song, who lived in Vermont before her hike, has since divorced, "which was bound to occur, although the AT speeded up the process." She was the caretaker at the Blackburn Center on the Appalachian Trail in Virginia during the spring and summer of 1995 before moving back to Vermont.

Tortoise*, female, 24, and **Hare***, male, 22, 3/27–10/5. Since their journey, Tortoise and Hare have become parents to Katahdin, born nine months after they reached the summit. Their birth announcement includes a picture of them at the top of Katahdin in the snow, along with one of baby "Kai." They both miss the simple life on the trail, but knew their decision to have a baby brought responsibilities, so they have purchased a café in California. Hare manages it and Tortoise helps out when she can.

Yeti*, male, 24, 3/28–10/7. The Yeti was a reporter in North Carolina before his hike, and has since moved back to Connecticut, where he grew up, to work on his master's degree in education and do a teaching internship. In writing me about his hike, he said, "Jean, you know the burn that forces you to abandon your friends and family, take to the trail, and wreck your body, so you know there's really no way to explain it to anyone who needs to ask. Maybe when I do find the words I'll start my own church." Didn't I tell you these young people are wonderful?

Order Form

There are Mountains to Climb

Telephone orders: 1-800-996-5627 or 317-573-0234
                     (VISA, MasterCard, or DiscoverCard)
FAX orders: 317-573-0239
Mail orders: Silverwood Press, 1508 East 86th Street, #105, Indianapolis, IN 46240

Ship to:

Name_____

Address_____

City_____ State_____ZIP_____

Telephone (_____)_____

Please send:

_____books at $12.95 $_____

Sales tax *(Indiana residents add $.65 per book)* $_____

Shipping and handling *(Add $3.00 for first book, $.75 per additional book)* $_____

TOTAL $_____

Quantity discounts available. Call for information.

Method of payment:

☐ check   ☐ VISA   ☐ MasterCard   ☐ DiscoverCard

Acct. number_____ Exp. date_____

Name on credit card_____

Signature_____

Jean continues to make speeches about her journey on the Appalachian Trail and the life lessons she learned along the way. For an information packet or to inquire about scheduling a speech, call 317-844-1690.

Silverwood Press
1508 East 86th Street, #105, Indianapolis, IN 46240
317-844-1690